EARLY ITALIAN WRITING-BOOKS

RENAISSANCE TO BAROQUE

by

Stanley Morison

Edited by Nicolas Barker

PRINTED FOR THE MEMBERS OF «HOC VOLO»
David R. Godine, Publisher, Boston

First U.S. edition printed in 1990 for the
members of «HOC VOLO»
David R. Godine Publisher, Inc.
Horticultural Hall, 300 Massachusetts Avenue
Boston, Massachusetts 02115

Library of Congress Catalog Card Number 90-85181
ISBN 0-87923-880-1

© 1990 by Literary Executors of Stanley Morison
and Edizioni Valdonega, Verona.

TO

CARLA MARZOLI

AN INSPIRATION AND STIMULUS

TO AUTHOR AND EDITOR

WHOSE PATIENCE,

ENTHUSIASM AND ENCOURAGEMENT

HAVE FINALLY BROUGHT

THIS WORK OUT

CONTENTS

9

INTRODUCTION

The appearance of a book some seventy years after its first conception requires an explanation. It was in 1899 that Edward Johnston began to teach at the London County Council School of Arts and Crafts, a date which can be taken as the beginning of the revival of interest in early handwriting for practical purposes in England. By 1913, the date of Morison's earliest surviving letter, addressed to Edward Johnston, his handwriting already had some 'italic' traits, perhaps acquired from M.M. Bridges' *A new handwriting for teachers* (1898) rather than Johnston's *Writing, illuminating and lettering* (1906). After the war he decided to reform his own hand, and his first letter to D. B. Updike, written on Christmas Eve 1919, shows how thoroughly he had done so: his fine hand was to captivate its first readers from now on.

What first put the notion of writing an account of Italian writing-books into Morison's mind was his visit to Berlin in the autumn of 1922. Peter Jessen, the director of the Kunstgewerbe Museum, proved an absorbing guide to the history of printing and modern fine printing, but also a mentor on the history of writing. He introduced Morison to the little writing there was on the subject, Manzoni's *Studi di bibliografia analitica*, of which he was quick to acquire a copy (later rescued from the blitzed ruins of his flat and now at the University Library, Cambridge), and the great 1789 folio of Servidori's *Reflexiones sobre la verdadera arte de escribir*. Although he wrote in Spanish, Servidori was Italian, and last heir to a direct line that went back to the sixteenth century. Morison's head was still full of his German discoveries when he wrote to Updike that Christmas.

It was Updike, too, that he first broached his plans for the present work, writing on 14 January 1923:

I have engaged myself to do a monograph upon 16th century Italian handwriting. For this Edward Johnston has agreed to write some twelve panels to be reproduced by collotype. This I shall publish at the Fleuron.

Updike replied, 'I hope you will put me down for your book on Sixteenth Century Italian Handwriting', but this was to reckon with out Johnston's special and irresistibly engaging gift for procrastination. Despite threats – 'that if the plates be not delivered by the right time you be boiled in oil until your ligatures melt & you suffer the loss of your majuscules' – Johnston continued elusive. Morison's energy and interest in the subject were channelled into *The Fleuron*, and into acquiring writing books and books printed by Arrighi for himself.

At Christmas 1924 a new and important influence came into Morison's life. He met Hans (later Giovanni) Mardersteig for the first time. They spent most of Christmas talking, Morison about the newly discovered Moyllus manuscript, Mardersteig about Feliciano. This conversation was to bear fruit over many years of friendship, from *A newly discovered treatise on classic letter design printed at Parma by Damianus Moyllus circa 1480*, printed by Mardersteig with an introduction by Morison and published in 1927, to *Felice Feliciano Veronese: Alphabetum Romanum*, edited and printed by Mardersteig in 1960. Immediately, however, it led to Morison's partnership with Frederic Warde and the printing, again by Mardersteig, and publication of *The calligraphic models of Ludovico degli Arrighi surnamed Vicentino* (1926).

In this, the first sketch of the present work saw print for the first time. Morison's fascination with the workings of the papal chancery and with the origins of humanistic script, which he saw as the ancestor of 'italic', is revealed in the introduction. Besides Arrighi, Tagliente and Ugo da Carpi, he mentions Fanti, Celebrino, Palatino, Amphiareo, and – rather surprisingly – Ruano, a copy of whose book he had found in the collection of his Milanese friend, the printer Raffaello Bertieri, in the summer of 1924. There is a good deal about Arrighi's printing (with references to 'my copy' of *Coryciana* and – a long favourite, both for matter and appearance – Zacharias Ferrerius *Hymni novi ecclesiastici*): printing and calligraphy were and remained indissoluble in Morison's mind, especially so in the case of Arrighi, whose typography had so great a posthumuous influence.

The book itself is a handsome piece of work in the new 'Arrighi' italic type that Morison and Frederic Warde devised together. The copy of *La operina* with *Il modo* used for the facsimile is not identified, but the British Museum copy was used, the photographs being carefully retouched by Mardersteig. The title-page is a cancel, for reasons that can be guessed (see *Stanley Morison*, 1972, pp. 207-9). From now on, Morison's calligraphic researches, still printed by Mardersteig, on *Damianus Moyllus* (1927), *Eustachio Celebrino da Udene* (1929) and *Andres Brun, Calligrapher of Saragossa* (1929) were published by the Pegasus Press: John Holroyd-Reece had allied himself first with Warde at Paris and then, when Warde returned to America, with Mardersteig as Morison's publisher. A. F. Johnson's 'Bibliography of Italian Writing-Books' was intended for publication in this series, but was adjourned, in this case until 1950, in *Signature*.

Morison himself had undertaken to peddle *The Calligraphic Models of Ludovico degli Arrighi* in London. In doing so, in September 1926, seeing a light late one evening, he knocked on the door of the booksellers, Birrell and Garnett, recently moved to 30 Gerrard Street in Soho. He was greeted there by Graham Pollard, inaugurating a long friendship, in which Italian writing books and the present work ran as a constant thread, woven with the history of printing and of the newspaper, the forgeries of T. J. Wise, the progress of communism, and much else. Morison's desperate financial straits immediately led to business: Pollard bought all Morison's writing books for £90. He was already planning the famous Birrell and Garnett *Catalogue* of typefounders' specimens and books on printing, which Morison had printed for him at the Cambridge University Press in 1928. It was to have been succeeded by a similar catalogue of writing-books, based on Morison's collection, which was actually advertised in the last *Fleuron*. This was never issued because Pollard sold the bulk of it (including Morison's books) to W. M. Ivins for the Metropolitan Museum of Art, New York.

The Fleuron concluded, Morison's energies were absorbed by *The Times*, but not to the exclusion of calligraphy. With some difficulty he found time to write his long introductory essay for Sir Ambrose Heal's *The English Writing-masters and their Copy-books*, printed under his eye at the Cambridge University Press and published in 1931. It was entitled 'The Development of Hand-writing: an Outline', and it includes a substantial piece about the Italian masters and their influence on English writing, his main subject. The book on Italian writing books was not forgotten, and the text, originally written in 1923-4 and much revised since, was set up in type and proofed by the Cambridge University Press in 193–. Characteristically, Morison set to work to revise it again. *The Times*, the Monotype Corporation, the Spanish Civil War, and then the outbreak of world war, all diverted Morison's attention, but not very far. Pollard, winding up Birrell and Garnett in the summer of 1939, sent him a present of writing books from time to time, among them Francisco Lucas *Arte de escrevir* 1580, which moved Morison to exclaim, 'For years I have longed sicut cervus desiderat ad fontes aquarum for any sort of copy of Lucas . . . and now this superb copy has come'. Miraculously, it survived the bombing of 10 Cambridge Gate, Morison's flat, on the night of 10-11 May 1941. Much did not, including all the material for Morison's collected papers, projected for publication by the Harvard University Press, and, it may be presumed, the revised galleys of the text on Italian writing books. Parts of what was lost were salvaged in '*Black Letter*' *Text* (1942) and *Notes on the Development of Latin Script* (1949, corrected to *c* 1962).

Immediately after the war, business for *The Times* took Morison to Chicago. There he met another Stanley, Pargellis, librarian of the Newberry Library, the American Mecca for all interested in the history of printing and writing. Together, Pargellis and Philip Hofer saw Morison's printing of *Luminario*, A. F. Johnson's translation of Verini's *Libro terzo*, in 1947. The same year, the Curator of the Wing Foundation at the Newberry Library, Ernst Detterer, died and Morison wrote Pargellis a long letter on the qualifications for his successor. He went to Chicago, and the link grew closer with what E. A. Lowe called 'Babylon-by-Lake-Michigan'. At Pargellis's instance, Morison interviewed a promising candidate for Detterer's job, James M. Wells, who was duly appointed on Morison's strong recommendation.

The history of the history of Italian writing books took a new direction now. In the first place, James Wardrop, whom Morison had first thought of for the Newberry, published a series of articles on the sixteenth century Italian masters in *Signature*, which Oliver Simon revived after the war. There, too, A. F. Johnson's long awaited 'Catalogue of Italian writing-book of the Sixteenth century' appeared in 1950. Morison was stimulated once more, and, yet again, the text of his book was set up in type, this time at *The Times* Private Printing Office, in April-May 1953, a modest by-product of Morison's herculean labours on the last volume of the *History of The Times*. Soon this too was covered with emendations, and 'pressure of business' again forced Morison to put it, not aside, but into the capable hands of James Wells.

By now Morison's eye-sight, strained by years of abuse, was beginning to give way. Wells retyped the proofs, much corrected not only by Morison but himself, and this draft was further corrected by Morison with, successively, pen, pencil and, his new-found toy, the biro. On the first page he wrote (in pen and ink) 'corrected 29 June 1960'. But correction continued. Carla Marzoli came and added substantially to his knowledge (and also to the task before him) with a learned catalogue of a remarkable collection of writing books, mostly Italian, to which Morison, drawn by a copy of Horfei's *Varie Inscrittioni*, wrote an enthusiastic introduction, fascinated by a new aspect of the Rome of one of his favourite popes, Sixtus V. He went on discussing these matters with Graham Pollard, who made them the subject of his Presidential Address to the Bibliographical Society in 1962.

By 1959 I had myself come, last and least, to join the band of those who were united by the task of helping Morison: helping with research, drafting, above all in trying to persuade him that *enough* had been done, that what he – or you – had already written was, if not sufficient, at least good enough to publish. It never was – or, at least, Morison could never be persuaded that it was. It was paradoxical that, as he grew older and more conscious that time would not be given him to do all he had 'in hand' even now, so he became more obstinately conscious that the real answer, the truth if it could be had, still lay round the corner.

By 1963, I had finished *The Likeness of Thomas More*, and was available (and ready and willing) to undertake the Italian writing books. I spent many happy hours in the British Museum and the Victoria and Albert Museum, in Paris and in Italy, retracing Morison's steps, covering the ground that he had already been over, teaching myself to see, a little, what he had already seen. The typescript grew yet more, as leaves of new writing on English quarto sprouted between Jim Wells's American onion-skin. I became fascinated by the complex problem of the chronology of the earliest books, and, since it threatened to take up more space than was appropriate in Morison's text, wrote a separate paper on it, which now appears as an appendix here. In the winter of 1965-6, however, Morison, troubled by his double debt to the Oxford University Press, the ancient debt of John Fell and the new debt of his 1957 Lyell lectures, took me off the Italian writing books, to try and put in order the already complex papers of the latter of these two.

The great letter-press pages of *John Fell* pursued their majestic path to the press. Morison's hand, once also majestic, shrivelled to a trickle of barely legible lines, with great white spaces between – a pattern dictated by his failing sight and fear of crossing over what he had already written. I wrote, and came to Whitehall Court, to read aloud what I had written and (increasingly) other things that needed to be read, and to meet others of the band, familiar by name from past reading, familiar now in friendship as Morison's gradually worsening condition stirred the realization that death was not far off.

It came on 11 October 1967. *John Fell* was just out, those other life-long preoccupations still to be finished. This task became, for me, a double one: the writing of Morison's life blended with the writing of the words that would finish an intellectual pilgrimage begun sixty years earlier. *Stanley Morison* and *Politics and script: aspects of authority and freedom in the development of Graeco-Roman script from the sixth century BC to the twentieth century AD* both appeared in 1972. I was now free, in theory, to go back to the Italian writing-books of the sixteenth century, and to redeem the promise that Morison had made Carla Marzoli and Giovanni Mardersteig, that they should have the printing and publishing of his book.

I did not find this task easy, the more so as I knew, from experience with the Lyell lectures, how hard it was to complete a half-finished phrase or reference, still more a thought left incomplete. Matters were still further complicated by the appearance of A. S. Osley's *Luminario*, also in 1972. This admirable work did so much that Morison had set himself to do as to make me wonder whether there was still a need for Morison's text. Other occupations came and filled the void left by this uncertainty. A decade passed before a visit to Milan and Verona renewed the vision. Alas, Morison's old friend and – I am proud to recall – mine, Giovanni Mardersteig, had died in the interval, but Carla Marzoli and Martino Mardersteig persuaded me to go back to the papers (which by now filled a carton). The text was, they said, a classic and should be treated as such; let there be no more delay in the interests of never-to-be-achieved perfection; the work as Morison left it should now be published as a tribute to his memory.

Even this was easier said than done. The script was a virtual palimpsest, written over and over again. As much as half of it I had myself re-written, and perhaps half of that was my own work (notably the passage on Francesco Alunno, a discovery shared with Mardersteig). I could not treat my own work as classic, in any sense. Worst of all, the footnotes were missing. But, as best I can, I have supplied the deficiencies, and the text is something near what Morison would have wished. I have taken advantage of some, but not all, more recent research. Casamassima's *Trattati di scrittura del cinquecento italiano* was too close to my own work to be ignored, but to borrow from Osley's *Luminario* would seem to anticipate reactions from Morison which I could not reasonably infer.

One complaint I must forestall. Why are there not more illustrations, especially since those in *Luminario*, though copious, were poorly reproduced? I can only say that this – Morison's book – is not the right vehicle for what is needed, a generous and well-informed set of reproductions of the main examples of the works of the Italian writing-masters. That would need a different book, and a different text, written and interlocking with the illustrations. The reader must judge, but I hope with some sympathy for the belief that illustrations *post hoc* would not have been possible on a larger scale than those printed here.

It only remains to offer thanks to those whose labours have all served to make this publication possible. The part of Updike, Mardersteig, Pollard (there are still some pages of notes in his characteristic hand among Morison's papers), James Wardrop and A. F. Johnson has been mentioned. All these, alas, will not see the final result of what they, as well as Morison, gave so much thought and time. No more will Henry Steinberg, the partner of Morison's investigation of medieval scribal specimens, the antecedent of our books, with which Morison and he comforted themselves in the bleak war years, nor will John

Carter, Morison's constant friend. Alfred Fairbank is dead, and only this last year two other old friends and fellow-workers in the vineyard, Arthur Osley and Emanuele Casamassima, have been taken untimely from us.

All these had a part, direct or indirect, in the completion of this work. Happily, there are others left to greet its final appearance. Chief of these are James Wells and Carla Marzoli, who worked for Morison, stimulated his dwindling energy and undiminished passion for the subject, and will find words that they wrote or suggested in the ensuing pages. There are others, too, who shared Morison's interests, and have been my familiar friends, the companions and sharers in the problems and discoveries that my own long pursuit of the subject has involved. Chief among these are James Mosley, André Jammes and Berthold Wolpe. I owe a great debt, too, to the many libraries where I have worked: I remember, in particular, the Biblioteca Nazionale Centrale in Florence during Casamassima's directorship, Joyce Irene Whalley at the Victoria and Albert Museum, the Newberry Library at Chicago, where Jim Wells, Bob Hunter Middleton and many others made me welcome, the Metropolitan Museum in New York, the Biblioteca Ambrosiana in Milan and its prefect Monsignor Paredi, the Humanities Research Center at the University of Texas, where the Marzoli collection now rests, and, as always, the British Museum, now the British Library.

Finally, there are two, whose names must be mentioned, whose part I know but cannot compute. First, Mabel Morison was the sharer in all her husband's early researches. She translated Ruano for him, made notes of Vatican manuscripts, shared the cold of Berlin and the friendship of Peter Jessen. Her part in *Damianus Moyllus* is recorded in two letters in the last paragraph of the introduction. Secondly, Olive Abbott devoted many years of work to research for Morison in continental libraries, notably in Paris; she, I think, began the translation of Servidori that Morison used and of which fragments still survive.

To all these, past and present, I offer my thanks. I also record the generous support and permission to publish the work accorded by Morison's literary executors, Brooke Crutchley and Arthur Crook. David McKitterick, librarian of Trinity College, Cambridge, and Brian Jenkins, custodian of Morison's papers and books at the University Library, Cambridge, have also been unstinting in their help and kindness. I am deeply indebted to Patricia Cooper and Juliet Walke, who provided a legible typescript from a final draft so often corrected as to be barely legible. Final thanks, not just mine, but of all those to whom this final work of Stanley Morison will come, are due to Martino Mardersteig for publishing it in his Edizioni Valdonega, and Carla Marzoli for encouraging the publisher and myself to realise this edition.

NICOLAS BARKER

PART ONE

Chapter 1
THE HISTORY OF WRITING

Little is known of the early history of teaching to write. Roman practice here, as in so many things, was copied from the Greeks. Quintilian (A.D. 39-95), describing the late classical period, states that learning the Latin ABC began at home; he was, however, formulating an ideal educational system for an aristocratic youth rather than describing common usage.[1] In all probability the less well-to-do did not learn to read or write until they began to attend primary school, at about seven years. The children possessed toy alphabets, no doubt of formal capitals, cut on ivory or wood; of these none has survived. The clever among them might receive as a reward little cakes shaped like the various letters. They learned to write by following, with stilus or pen, letters cut into a board or impressed from stamped patterns on a wax-covered tablet. After the child had acquired facility he was taught to use his stilus upon a wax slate or his pen upon papyrus.

The earliest surviving Latin alphabets (A B C D E F G H I K L M N O P Q R S T V X) date before A.D. 79 and were discovered on the systematic excavation of Pompeii begun in 1763.[2] A number of alphabets, or portions, survive on tombstones engraved during the early Christian period.[3] In 1877 Fiorelli reported the discovery of a sixth-century stone bearing a capital *abecedarium*.[4] In 1880 de Rossi announced the finding of moulds

1. *Institutio Oratoria*, Bk. I. H. I. Marrou, *A History of Education in Antiquity* (London, 1956) gives a good account of educational methods in Greece and Rome; Aubrey Gwinn, *Roman Education from Cicero to Quintilian* (Oxford, 1926) is still useful.
2. *C.I.L.*, IV, 164 ff.
3. G. B. de Rossi, 'Dell'alfabeto nei monumenti cristiani', *Bulletino di Archeologia Cristiana*, Ser. III, An. 6 (1881), p. 128 ff., discusses these, a number of which are shown in the plates of the 1880 volume.
4. *Notizie di Scavi* (1877), p. 80; reproduced by de Rossi, in 1881. Cf. *Atti della Reale Academia di Archeologia, Lettere e Belle Arti* VIII (1877), Appendice, p. 25.

of the capital alphabet cut deeply enough into marble so that
they might have been used for casting letters in soft metal; these
are believed to have orginated in the fourth century.[1] In 1934
the Egypt Exploration Society drew attention to two fourth-
century papyri fragments from Antinoë with Latin alphabets:
one a minuscule (a b c d e f g h i k l m n o p q r s t u) and the
other rustic capital (A B C D E F G H I K L M N O P Q R S T
V X Y Z). The significance of the additional symbols TH; CH/
CH; I; S; AE; E is unknown. The editor conjectures, from the
context, that the fragments may have been part of the introduction to some form of Roman shorthand system.[2]

A long blank then occurs before other alphabetical designs
have been recovered. Versified instructions on the letters of the
alphabet (similar to various mnemonic formulae used by the
Greeks and Romans) survive from the ninth century. One was
described by L. Müller in 1865[3] and another by H. Omont in
1881.[4] An ABC inserted in an unexpected place – the XIth century Winchester Troper (Cambridge, Corpus Christi College
MS 473) – is noted, though not reproduced, in W. H. Frere's
edition published by the Henry Bradshaw Society.[5] Well-formed though this alphabet is, in *textus prescissus*, it has no liturgical
significance and is obviously a *proba pennae*. The rubrics of the
Roman Pontifical for the dedication of a church prescribe the
diagonal tracing, by the bishop, of the Greek and Latin alphabets
to form a cross on the full length of the floor about to be con-

1. De Rossi, loc. cit.
2. H. J. Milne, *Greek Shorthand Manuals*, (London, 1934), p. 70, Pl. IX. The
whole subject is conveniently summarized in B. L. Ullman, 'Abecedaria and
their purpose', *Transactions of the Cambridge Bibliographical Society* III (1961),
pp. 181-6.
3. L. Müller, 'Versus Scoti cuiusdam de alphabeto', *Rheinisches Museum für Phi-
lologie*, N.F., xx (1865), pp. 364, 640.
4. H. Omont, 'Poème Anonyme sur les Lettres de l'Alphabet', *Bibliothèque de
l'École des Chartes*, XLII (1881).
5. W. H. Frere, *The Winchester Troper* (Cambridge, Henry Bradshaw Society
VIII, 1894). Also M. R. James, *A Descriptive Catalogue of the Manuscripts of Corpus
Christi College, Cambridge*, (Cambridge, 1912), Vol. II, pp. 473-74.

secrated. These 'liturgical' alphabets are set out in some of the mss. None is anterior to the XIth century.

The listing of the few Latin alphabets surving from the classical and early medieval periods is a task that awaits an editor. The later medieval alphabets that have descended to us are more numerous. From the same period we have several manuals of instruction in the art of writing.[1] The authors of the *Nouveau Traité* (1760-65) drew attention to an anonymous alphabetical codex of the XVth century, now at Montpelier (MS 512), described by L. Delisle in 1899.[2] In 1871 W. Wattenbach made a substantial contribution to the subject by reporting the discover of two late-medieval pedagogical specimens of calligraphy written out by Johann Brune of Erfurt and Johann von Haghen of Bodenwerder-on-the-Weser.[3] In 1896 C. Douais noted the specimen of Robertus de Turribus (1435-64)[4] and in 1899 Delisle commented upon it with other French specimen alphabets written by writing-masters, either for educational use or publicity purposes.[5] In 1909 the Augsburg historian A. Schroeder described Leonhard Wagner's *Proba scripturarum una manu exaratarum* written between 1507 (?) and 1517, when Wagner was Prior of SS. Ulrich and Afra.[6] His alphabet had been discussed earlier by the

1. C. Wehmer, 'Die Schreibmeisterblätter des späten Mittelalters', *Miscellanea Giovanni Mercati*, vol. vi, *Studi e Testi* CXXVI, (1946), pp. 147-61. There is an excellent list in S. H. Steinberg, 'Medieval Writing Masters', *The Library*, 4th ser., XXII, pp. 1-24, as well as a discussion. The Appendix to S. Morison, *The Typographic Arts* (London, 1949) contains considerable information on these, as well as a list which incorporates Steinberg's. See below, notes 23-4.
2. L. Delisle, 'Initiales Artistiques Extraites des Chartes du Maine', *Journal des Savants*, 3ᵉ ser., LXIV (1899), pp. 60-61; and 'Les maitres d'écriture au XVᵉ siècle', *L'Ecriture*, nos. 39-40 (1899) pp. 729-32, 745-50.
3. W. Wattenbach, *Das Schriftwesen im Mittelalter*, Leipzig, 1871; 3rd ed., 1896, pp. 488-91.
4. C. Douais, 'Une épreuve d'un maître d'école du 15ᵉ siècle', *Mélanges sur St. Sernin de Toulouse*, fasc. II, 1896, pp. 49-53.
5. Delisle, loc. cit. supra.
6. A. Schroeder, *Archiv für die Geschichte des Hochstifts Augsburg*, I. (1909-11), pp. 372 ff. The MS. is No. 85a in the Ordinariatsbibliothek, Augsburg. Other descriptions are listed in Morison, *op. cit.*, pp. 88-90, together with a discussion of Wagner's possible connection with Maximilian and the relationship between

antiquarian Bernhard Pez of Melk Abbey, a follower of Mabillon, who dissertated upon calligraphy in 1721 and mentioned a number of German alphabets and specimens.[1] In 1927 A. Hessel of Göttingen reproduced Johann von Haghen's specimen-sheet, reported by Wattenbach in 1889, and made upon it far-reaching observations that have been the starting-point of recent research which may now be briefly chronicled.[2]

In 1932 C. Wehmer, in a thorough investigation of the gothic scripts, gave a new turn to the discussion of Wagner's calligraphic specimen-book and dissertated upon other alphabetical specimens produced by itinerant writing-masters.[3] In 1935 B. Kruitwagen described hitherto unrecorded specimens by Herman Strepel of Münster, dated 1447, in the Nijhoff Collection at the Hague.[4]

In 1937 a list of all known medieval specimens, i.e. those produced in the years immediately preceding or contemporary with the invention of printing, was attempted by S. Morison.[5] In 1937 a XVth century *Modus* was discovered by E. Ph. Goldschmidt at the Benedictine Abbey of Melk, on the Danube; in 1940 it was reproduced in facsimile with an introduction by B. Bischoff, S. H. Steinberg, and S. Morison.[6] In 1941 S. H. Steinberg read before the Bibliographical Society a paper on 'The *Forma Scribendi* of Hugo Spechtshart' (1285-1360) of Reutlingen in Swabia, author of the first known systematic pedagogical manual of the art of writing, two copies of which survive, at Krem-

certain of his scripts and early fraktur types. See, now, Carl Wehmer, *Leonhard Wagners Proba centum scripturarum* (Leipzig, 1963).

1. B. Pez, *Thesaurus anecdotorum novissimus* (Augsburg, 1721), I. xxxiv-v.
2. A. Hessel, 'Neue Forschungsprobleme der Paläographie', *Archiv für Urkundenforschung* IX (Berlin, 1926), pp. 161-7.
3. C. Wehmer, *Die Namen der gotischen Buchschriften* (Berlin Phil. Diss., 1932), pp. 27, 29; *Zentralblatt für Buchwesen*, 49, 1-5 Hft.
4. B. Kruitwagen, 'De Munstersche Schrijfmeester Herman Strepel en de Schriftsoorten van de Broeders van het Gemeene Leven', *Het Boek* XXII (1935), 3 and 4.
5. S. Morison, *The art of printing* (London, 1938), pp. 26-7.
6. *A fifteenth-century modus scribendi from the abbey of Melk* (Cambridge, 1940).

smünster and Basle.[1] Of these the older, dating from 1370, bears the full title of *Tractatus orthographie magistri Hugonis de summa scribendi*. S. Morison's list of the works of the medieval writing-masters was amplified in 1943 by S. H. Steinberg in his 'Handlist of Specimens of Medieval Writing Masters', which he divided into (1) manuscript manuals of calligraphy; (2) manuscript specimens of writing-masters; (3) printed specimens of writing-masters; (4) antiquarian alphabets.[2] In 1949 S. Morison printed a revised list based upon S. H. Steinberg's scheme.[3] This is the present state of bibliographical knowledge of the specimens produced by the medieval masters. The specimens listed by S. H. Steinberg ended with that of Robert Jones (*fl* 1542-67) described by J. Wardrop in 1937.[4] S. A. Van Dijk described in 1958 his discovery at the Bodleian Library fragments of an English (? Oxford) master's specimen sheet (XIIIth century?);[5] the translation and expansion of B. Kruitwagen's articles in *Het Boek* is in hand with S. A. Van Dijk and S. Morison.[6]

In point of matter the correct bibliographical classification of this subject seems to be, as it seemed to Quintilian, with that sub-branch of educational apparatus that considers orthography. Medieval authors were in agreement that the author of any *tractatus in omnem modum scribendi* should teach the shapes of the letters as well as the meanings of the words. The drafting of the several letters and their combinations into words, being thus

---

1. S. H. Steinberg, 'The *Forma Scribendi* of Hugo Spechtshart', *The Library*, 4th ser. XXI (1941), pp. 264-78.
2. S. H. Steinberg, 'Medieval Writing Masters' and 'A Hand-list of Specimens of Medieval Writing Masters', *The Library*, 4th ser. XXII (1941), pp. 1-24, and XXIII (1943), pp. 191-3.
3. S. Morison, *Notes on the development of Latin script from early to modern times* (Cambridge, 1949).
4. *Victoria and Albert Museum Review of the Principal Acquisitions during the Year 1937* (1938), pp. 37-9 and pl. 18; J. I. Whalley, *English Handwriting 1540-1853*, London, 1969, pls. 1-4.
5. S. A. van Dijk, 'An Advertisement Sheet of an Early Fourteenth-Century Writing Master at Oxford', *Scriptorium* X (1956), pp. 47-64.
6. This task remained, and remains, unfulfilled.

treated in such *modi scribendi*, their authors (at least in Germany) became known as 'modisten'.[1]

When printed books succeeded the manuscript books in the XVIth century, the term 'Modus' was superseded by the vernacular 'Schreibbuch' and the 'Modisten' became 'Schreibmeister' – equivalent to the English 'writing-master', the French 'maître d'écriture', the Italian 'scrittore' or 'calligrafo' and the Spanish 'caligrafo'. The printed works of writing-masters of any period or school are not easily listed. Notwithstanding their significance in artistic quality and publishing quantity, the existing critical and bibliographical literature on the subject is comparatively small. The best studies of any national school of calligraphy are Spanish. Mabillon apart, the native dissertations on the old Spanish literary and diplomatic scripts have not been surpassed. P. Merino bequeathed the methodical example of his digest of the antique scripts[2] to D. M. Servidori, whose account of modern, i.e. post XVIth-century, hands of the Italian, Spanish, and English masters, coupled with his superb collection of plates, is still the best in any language.[3] His close follower, T. Torio de la Riva,[4] supplies a markedly inferior collection of plates and his text is incomplete by the side of D. M. Servidori's, but it still remains of value, a tribute to the compulsion of P. Merino's method. E. Cotarelo y Mori's monumental bio-bibliographical dictionary of the Spanish calligraphers is still the best work of its kind;[5] it contains, in addition to its studies of the national masters, useful notes on the Italians – L. Arrighi, G. A. Tagliente,

1. W. Doede, *Bibliographie deutscher Schreibmeisterbücher von Neudörffer bis 1800*, Hamburg, 1958, p. 7; P. Jessen, *Meister der Schreibkunst aus drei Jahrhunderten*, Stuttgart, 1923, pp. 6-7.
2. A. Merino, *Escuela de leer letras cursivas antiguas y modernas, desde la entrada de los godos en Espana, hasta nuestros tiempos* (Madrid, 1780).
3. D. Servidori, *Reflexiones sobre la verdadera arte de escribir* (Madrid, 1789).
4. T. Torio de la Riva, *Arte de escribir por reglas y con muestras, segun la doctrina de los mejores autores antiguos y modernos, extranjeros y nacionales* (Madrid, 1798).
5. E. Cotarelo y Mori, *Dicionario biografico y bibliografico de caligrafos espanoles* (Madrid, 1916).

G. B. Palatino – who influenced A. Brun, J. de Yciar, and F. Lucas.

The early Italian writing-books have been listed and described by A. F. Johnson, who has also provided where possible biographical notices of their authors.[1] The list of Paris writing-masters in the appendices to J. Grand-Carteret's book on old French papers[2] is very partial, and makes no attempt to link them with their Roman and Venetian sources. For the English masters, A. Heal's bibliography, with full biographical notes, supersedes in thoroughness and completeness all other works on the subject, from W. Massey's XVIIIth-century attempt on.[3] In the introduction to A. Heal, S. Morison attempted a sketch of the history of English handwriting and to link it with its Italian, Dutch, and French sources. R. Nash has published a bibliography, with historical introduction, of the early American writing-books, which he plans to extend in a second volume.[4] W. Doede has published a similiar work on the German school.[5] H. de Campos Ferreira Lima has published a brief biobibliography of Portuguese masters.[6] Works on the French and Netherlandish schools are necessary before any serious study of modern Western handwriting can be completed.

The *Katalog der Ornamentstich-Sammlung der Staatlichen Kunstbibliothek Berlin* (1936), the considerably revised and enlarged version of the catalogue first made under P. Jessen's supervision in 1894, contains descriptions of one of the richest collections

1. A. F. Johnson, 'A Catalogue of Italian Writing Books in the Sixteenth Century', *Signature*, new ser., x (1950), pp. 24-48, hereafter 'Johnson'.
2. J. Grand-Carteret, *Papeterie et papetiers de l'ancien temps* (Paris, 1913).
3. W. Massey, *The Origin and Progress of Letters*, London, 1763; Ambrose Heal, *The English Writing-masters and their Copy-books, 1570-1830*, Cambridge, 1931.
4. R. Nash, *American Writing Masters and Copybooks: History and Bibliography through Colonial Times*, Boston, 1959, and *American Penmanship 1800-1850*, Worcester, 1969.
5. W. Doede, *Bibliographie deutscher Schreibmusterbücher von Neudörffer bis 1800* (Hamburg, 1958).
6. H. de Campos Ferreira Lima, *Subsidios para um dicionario bio-bibliografico dos caligrafos portugueses* (Lisbon, 1923).

of writing-books described in print, now, after the alarms and excursions of the war and the ensuing years, again available to the scholar. It was the intention of the late C. Bonacini to prepare a complete bibliography of western calligraphy.[1] This ambitious project was someway short of completion when the compiler died, and the text as it stood (largely based on printed sources) was published *faute de mieux*; some curious specimens of Bonacini's imitations of sixteenth century calligraphy are illustrated. It remains that the most pressing need is a consecutive account of the first and most influential of a writing schools – the Italian, practising from the XVIth to the mid-XVIIth centuries.

The surviving manuscript specimens (in the sense of formal demonstrations) of renaissance calligraphy since the invention of printing remain unlisted for the most part, with the exception of works dealing with the classical roman capitals made geometrically.[2] It is to be hoped that the growing interest in the subject, stimulated by Wardrop's discovery of Palatino's two manuscript specimens at Oxford and Berlin and the work of Fairbank and Casamassima on Arrighi, will with the assistance of the printed *exempla* at the V. & A., Harvard, Texas and the Newberry Library (the two last based on the admirable collections of Signora Carla Marzoli, and of John L. Wing and C. L. Ricketts, respectively), be directed towards the listing of the manuscript specimens of the period. Such a list of manuscripts may turn out to be of doubtful stylistic importance as compared with the printed works, but in any event it is necessary to know to what extent, if any, the forms in the manuscript specimens anticipate those in the printed books (both relief and intaglio) and to know whether they illustrate or motivate

---

1. C. Bonacini, *Bibliographia delle arti scrittorie e della calligrafia* (Florence, 1953).
2. G. Mardersteig, *Leon Battista Alberti e la rinascita del carattere lapidario romano* (Padua, 1959); G. B. Verini, *Luminario*, trans. A. F. Johnson (Cambridge and Chicago, 1947); E. Casamassima, *Trattati di scrittura del cinquecento italiano* (Milan, 1966), pp. 17-36, hereafter 'Casamassima'.

the calligraphic variation. Even when they are of inferior quality, one must remember that bad writing may be as interesting to the scientific student as good. The press, by its mere power to multiply, stimulated calligraphical development, since the availability of printed treatises necessarily expanded the profession; the professionals, in turn, supported their claims with specimens, both written and printed. If only to study this process a list of manuscript specimens is desirable before any satisfactory account of the development of calligraphy in the late Renaissance can be written.

Chapter 2
ITALIAN SCRIPT BEFORE 1500

An attempt at the present time merely to outline, on the basis of the known Italian manuals, the development of writing from the date of the invention of printing to the rise of the French, Spanish, and Dutch schools must be incomplete, and possibly misleading. The resources of the Italian libraries have still not been surveyed, and editions of the printed Italian manuals existing in the libraries even of Rome, Venice and Florence remain unlisted. Until that has been done an attempt, such as the present, to criticize Italian handwriting, so far as it is illustrated in printed examples, can only be tentative.

The study of Italian printed manuals of writing was first defined by G. Manzoni 'con metodo razionale'.[1] By 'razionale' the bibliographer means a competent ordination of selected specimens of writing, having their respective alphabets methodically arranged in accordance with the conventions governing the several sorts of scribal work: artistic, legal, liturgical, ceremonial, domestic, or commercial. The models used in most late medieval writing in Italy for literary, commercial, legal, or domestic purposes were inherited from the XIIth century when, in the Italian chanceries, a cursive was employed for the mass of writing.[2] This was an upright, ligatured hand with varying length of ascender and varying fullness of loop. This looped cursive hand held a favoured position for two centuries, when it began to suffer competition from a slightly slanted, less ligatured, unlooped script that had been made fashionable for Latin

1. G. Manzoni, *Studii di bibliografia analitica* 1 (Bologna, 1882), p. 81.
2. The various hands used in the Italian chanceries, and their development, can be traced in V. Federici's *La Scrittura delle Cancellerie Italiane dal Secolo XII al XVII* (Rome, 1934). See also S. Morison, *Politics and Script* (Oxford, 1972), pp. 228-9, 242.

literature by a group of Florentine intellectuals and artists.[1] To a lesser degree, the formal hands used in the chanceries of the Holy See and of the city-states in the peninsula either for the initial sentences (or occasionally for the whole text) of papal, imperial, ducal, or other diplomatic instruments also felt the competition.[2]

The competition was gradual, since it did not issue from an act of state, as had been the case with the archetype of the new script seven centuries before, the so-called Carolingian minuscule. The new fashion was a piece of private enterprise, the hobby of an intellectual club concerning itself with the criteria of knowledge and necessarily involving a scrutiny of sources, primarily literary, and first of all Latin; it was not adopted officially – in the Papal chancery – until it had already won wide acceptance privately, among the Humanists. The leaders of the movement were Coluccio Salutati (1331-1406), Niccolo Niccoli (1363-1437) and Poggio Bracciolini (1380-1459), and it is through their evangelism that the new script was promulgated. The work of evangelization was to some extent accidental, the product of Coluccio's generosity in giving and lending both copies and books. Twenty years after his death Poggio, writing to Leonardo Bruni, reminded him how Coluccio's books were as much the property of all learned men as his own. It has been well said that his library was 'in an informed sense, the forerunner of the first modern public library',[3] and so indeed it came to be in a formal sense. After Coluccio's death in 1406, his heirs

1. For discussion, facsimiles, and further bibliography, see S. Morison, 'Early Humanistic Script and the First Roman Type', *The Library*, 4th ser. XXIV (1943), pp. 1-29. See also B. L. Ullman, *The Origin and Development of Humanistic Script* (Rome, 1960); J. Wardrop *The Script of Humanism* (Oxford, 1963), p. 3 ff; and A. C. de la Mare, *The Handwriting of Italian Humanists* I (Oxford, 1973).
2. The papal briefs and other documents may be studied in J. Battelli, *Actus Pontificum*, Fasc. III of *Exempla Scripturarum* (Vatican, 1933). See also B. L. Ullman, *The Humanism of Coluccio Salutati* (Medioevo e Umanesimo 4, Padua, 1963).
3. B. L. Ullman, *The Humanism of Coluccio Salutati* (Medioevo e Umanesimo 4, Padua, 1963), p. 136.

sold his books, the main part to Niccoli. Niccoli himself considered the establishment of a public library in the monastery of S. Maria degli Angeli, but when he died in 1437, Coluccio's heirs were still not paid in full, and his purpose remained unfulfilled.[1] It was left to Cosimo de' Medici to pay off Niccoli's debts and to present his books, for public use, to the new monastery of San Marco in 1441.

The main object of the Humanists was to discover new classical texts, to improve known texts, and to disseminate their discoveries. Cicero was re-read and, in order to be understood, was edited and transcribed. To the leaders of the movement, Coluccio Salutati, Niccolo de' Niccoli and G. Poggio, it was a logical editorial amenity to revive the ancient Latin script with ancient text. The 'littera antica', as the new movement called it, was, in their sight, not only an older and more contemporary, but a simpler and more beautiful form than the 'lettera moderna' in current use, which, they also discovered, counted a calligraphical lineage of but five or six generations.

The oldest available codices for new editions of the classics, including Cicero, were written in characters then thought to be very ancient; though, in fact, they usually dated only from the XIth and XIIth centuries, although occasionally earlier. An example of the model used by Niccoli in refashioning his personal book-script is the Cicero, now Marcianus 257,[2] in the Laurenziana, endorsed 'De hereditate Nicolai Nicoli, viri doctissimi et Florentini'.

In the Carolingian period good writing fell into the usual two classes, very formal and less formal. When the Florentines began collecting they naturally accepted indifferent pieces of writing as well as the good. They certainly knew bad 'ancient' writing when they saw it, and valued the inspiration of the more formal

1. B. L. Ullman & P. A. Stadter, *The Public Library of Renaissance Florence: Niccolo Niccoli, Cosimo de' Medici and the Library of San Marco* (Padua, 1972), p. 225 (no. 862).
2. E. Chatelain, *Paléographie des Classiques Latins* (Paris, 1884-92), pl. XXXVII.

calligraphical models for adaptation in the contemporary first class editions they ordered to be transcribed by trained scribes. Being practical people, they saw the point of a regular, disciplined, cursive hand, as exemplified in the Cicero just mentioned (Marcianus 257) as well as of the upright cursive to be seen in another Cicero (Laurentianus 45) reproduced by Chatelain as plate XLII. In printers' language, Niccoli used an 'italic' bookhand as well as a 'roman'. The italic in the hands of a professional scribe, which Niccoli never was, could be raised to the rank of a good second class book-script.

In general Poggio's and Niccoli's calligraphy looked back to manuscripts of the later Carolingian period. A number, probably most, came from Alamannic centres, principally St. Gall and the houses stylistically dependent thereupon. Here a sort of cursive 'sloped roman' had been accepted by mid-IXth century and acquired a position it never attained at, say, Tours. Chatelain dates Marcianus 257 from the IXth century: Eberling makes it XIth century, which seems more likely. In any event, the 'sloped roman', as we may even (and sensibly) call it, or 'italic' minuscule was regularly employed by good writers in the late Carolingian period of active transcription of classic texts. It was natural for the Florentines, independently, to adopt an 'italic'. In any case, for the early humanists, the calligraphic style of one 'antique' manuscript was virtually as 'antique' as that of any other: hence a second-class copy of a late – or for that matter early – Carolingian Cicero possessed complete literary appropriateness provided it had calligraphical style (that is, its form was consistent). From the first, therefore, the Florentine theory of the classical revival embraced, in point of calligraphy, both the 'italic' and the 'roman' hands. The humanist 'italic' in its Florentine form, was, like that of St. Gall, slightly slanted. The St. Gall example exercised a notable calligraphical influence, since the tradition in Italy of writing a vertical hand, whether formal or informal, for books – and even for business – was old and tenacious. If Poggio and Niccoli had collected only earlier Carolingian manuscripts, or those from Tours, where verticality was the governing rule for books until XIIth century, the history of italic might be different. Even as it was, Poggio never deserted the upright gothic notarial cursive. It is from Niccoli that the slanted cursive Carolingian derives although it may not be demonstrable that his 'italic' is a derivative of an early St. Gall example (that would be very difficult to prove). If it had not been for Niccoli, 'italic' might well not have been revived almost simultaneously with 'roman' or at any rate might not later have been used for the transcription of fine books; it might even have never been revived at all. On the other hand, Latin humanistic books written out in 'italic' appear early and soon may even be found richly illuminated. Niccoli's own example is significant enough; the Lucretius that he wrote out between 1425 and 1435 is in 'italic'; so to is the Lucretius which may have been used and worked upon by Angelo Poliziano. It may be taken to be the fact that just as the early humanistic calligraphical canon included seriffed projectors in the minuscule, *ct* ligature, straight *d* and double-bodied *g*, so it evolved to embrace 'italic' as well as 'roman'.

The choice of these two forms of the same script, both considered equally appropriate for classical texts, depended upon the circumstances in which the scribe was placed. The early humanists were just as aware as their St. Gall forerunners that the 'italic' hand, while more rapidly made and more economic of space, looked less majestic. The clients of Vespasiano da Bisticci and other eminent booksellers who served the Florentine movement with finely written books in the 'lettera antica' style did not share Federigo of Urbino's indifference to cost. Niccoli died in 1437, some ten years after the completion of his Lucretius (of all writers), in the 'italic' hand he had cultivated since at least 1410. Flavio Biondo's 'italic' Cicero *Brutus* is dated 1422.[1]

1. Flavio Biondo's 'fast cursive', while undoubtedly humanistic, is only slightly and irregularly sloped; see Chatelain, pl. xxa. For other reproductions, and

The trade followed these illustrious examples. 'Italic' economised the vellum or paper of the stationer and the time of the scribe; it could be speedy and yet not look hurried. These were the factors that gave this satisfactory second-class book-script a future not envisaged by the founders of the Movement: a use in diplomacy. Finally, it obtained a dominating position in private correspondence in Italian and other vernaculars and, in its sixteenth century form, may be seen practised in America two hundred years later. The first state of this evolution, i.e. as a diplomatic hand, may briefly be noted.

A humanistic 'roman', i.e. a version of the upright 'lettera antica', was adopted by Martin V not later than 1423 in substitution for the Gothic cursive in use in the Roman Chancery since 1390 for the engrossing of a minor class of document, the brief.[1] This represented not the mere substitution of one cursive for another, but of a full cursive for a design less so. The humanistic 'roman' used by Martin V was not a pure humanistic script, for its constituent letters were regularly run together and ligatured: also flourishes were permitted to the initial words of sentences. No doubt Poggio, who became Secretary to the Chancery in 1423, was responsible for the suppression of Gothic cursive and the adoption of this new 'roman'. He had not yet mastered the canon, for the *ct* is missing. Martin V's successor was Eugenius IV (1431-47) who continued the same hand for the writing of briefs; significantly the Pope himself wrote a good 'italic'.

details of the circumstances in which Biondo copied the *Brutus*, see B. Nogara, *Scritti inediti e rari di Biondo Flavio: Studi e Testi* XLVIII (1972), pp. xxxvi-vii and pl. III.

1. For the origin and development of the brief, see K. A. Fink, 'Untersuchungen über die päpstlichen Breven des 15. Jhdts.', in *Römische Quartalschrift*, XLIII (1943), pp. 56-86, with facsimiles, and the same author's 'Die ältesten Breven und Brevenregister', in *Quellen und Forschungen aus italienischen Archiven und Bibliotheken* XXV (1933/4), pp. 292-307. The papal secretaries are listed and identified in W. von Hofmann, *Forschungen zur Geschichte der Kurialen Behörden*, (Rome, 1914). See also Wardrop, *The Script of Humanism*, pp. 40-2.

Not later than 1462, and perhaps earlier, i.e. under Calixtus III (1455-58) or possibly Pius II (1458-64), 'italic' superseded 'roman' in the Papal Chancery. In 1462, the Secretary for Briefs was Jacopo Piccolomini-Ammanati (1422-79). He had been appointed by Calixtus III in 1450; he was well known as a humanist and prospered under his relative Pius II, who made him a Cardinal. Piccolomini's 'italic' is so neatly, though not elegantly, written that, with its well-formed serifs to the ascenders, it is almost a sloped roman. It had a double-bodied *a*; *ct*; straight *d*; and *g* with a closed lower bowl, often flourished. This remains the earliest known Chancery use of the 'italic' hand. The original brief, signed 'G. d[e] Piccolomin[ibus]' is addressed to the magistrates of Basel (where it is still preserved in the State archives) and concerns the removal of interdicts upon certain persons.[1] It may well be that the discovery of other briefs of the reign of Calixtus III will reveal an earlier date than 1462 for the adoption and reservation of 'italic' as a standard of the papal chancery for this class of document. It is difficult to account otherwise for the use for the vernacular in the chancery of Modena, also in 1462, of an upright humanistic hand, which is uncanonical and, having round *a* and *d*, is impure; a *bastarda*, in fact. In Ferrara ten years later an upright humanistic of canonical rank, complete with *ct*, may be found in use for civil correspondence. Before the end of the century the cursive form of humanistic, i.e. 'italic', was firmly established in the chanceries of the Italian city-states, though often bastardised with the old notarial script, i.e. gothic secretary, for legal documents and records. This process may be followed in the plates collected by Federici.[2] An example is Pl. XCIV, a minute-book of the

1. The gothic cursive used in the earliest briefs is shown by Fink, 'Untersuchungen . . .', with briefs of Boniface IX dating from 1390 and 1392. Martin V's 1423 brief is facsimiled in W. F. Arndt & M. Tangl, *Schrifttafeln zur Erlernung der Lateinischen Palaeographie*, (1929), Pl. 99. Pl. 24 of Arndt-Tangl shows a brief of Eugenius IV. dated 1446. The 1462 brief of Pius II written by Piccolomini is reproduced by A. Brackmann, *Papsturkunden* (Leipzig, 1914), pl. XII.
2. See above, p. 32, n. 2.

Council of Florence (1478) written in a script using *l* and *h* with looped ascenders. Thus the diplomatic use of 'italic' in varying degrees of purity was firmly set by the time printing was introduced into Italy. So too was its use as a book-script, as detailed earlier. While the great scribes of the period, Antonio di Mario, Gherardo di Giovanni de Ciriagio, Antonio Sinibaldi and others, used only the most formal upright of romans, there is no lack of fine illuminated manuscripts of Cicero, Vergil and other texts, written in italic between 1465-1500, as J. Wardrop showed in his study of Pierantonio Sallando.[1] The use of italic for plain, as distinct from illuminated manuscripts, persisted long after printing was established in the principal Italian cities. Its compactness, coupled with the extreme difficulty of engraving a script of the kind, gave it a life well protracted into the age of typography.

The delay in the typographical appearance of italic at first excites surprise. Italic type made its first appearance on the title-page of Aldus' beautiful edition of the letters of St. Catherine of Siena (Venice, 1500),[2] and was first used for a complete book in his Virgil of the next year. During the thirty-five years since the introduction of the art into Italy at Subiaco there had been little extension of typographical resources. Most notable had been Aldus' previous improvement upon the romans of Sweynheim and Pannartz (Rome) and those of Johann and Wendelin Speyer and Nicolas Jenson (Venice) with the type cut for him by the most talented engraver of the time, Francesco Griffo da Bologna and used for Bembo's *De Aetna* (1495). The same engraver was responsible for the first italic of 1500, as well as for the second italic (showing considerable improvement in design) cut for G. Soncino of Fano in 1503 and also the Soncino Hebrew of 1509.

1. J. Wardrop, 'Pierantonio Sallando', *Signature*, new ser. II (1946).
2. A. A. Renouard, *Annales de l'imprimerie des Alde*, 3rd ed. (Paris, 1834), pp. 23-4.

Despite Griffo's supreme craftsmanship, his first italic was not beautiful and suggests no fine model; it must be allowed, however, that it was a work of cutting and casting of the utmost difficulty, a *tour-de-force* of the engraver and typefounder. The motives for cutting an italic were doubtless not aesthetic, but economic: to satisfy a market accustomed to reading books in such letters.[1] In the half century since Niccoli wrote out his Lucretius in cursive humanistic, ordinary men had been accustomed to reading the classics in the same compact script. Moreover, Aldus had been reproached by scholarly friends for printing books whose lavish handsomeness made them unduly expensive.[2]

In Italy printing had been introduced at a period when rich and luxurious, frequently highly illuminated, folio manuscripts were usual. The productions of the first generation of bookprinters were often decorated sumptuously by illuminators. The Italian proto-typographers have to their credit a great number of magnificently illustrated and illuminated folios and quartos. Only when the market was saturated with such costly editions, and printers forced to cut prices to move their wares, was the full economic benefit of the invention extended to the wide literary public, such as it was. In the second stage of the invention booksellers no longer emblazoned the owner's shield on the front page of the printed volume; the broad margins originally left for illumination – and more often than not unused – were cut down. The economic trend by now discouraged the folio, and even the large quarto, in favour of a smaller format. There remained a considerable market still untouched: that for cheap editions at a low price, currently met by books written at speed in italic, sometimes by the scholar himself, often by professional scribes. Long after 1465 it remained profitable for a book-

1. L. Febvre and H. J. Martin, *L'Apparition du Livre* (Paris, 1958), Ch. IV, has interesting statistics on the comparative costs of paper, presswork, etc., in the sixteenth century.
2. A. Firmin-Didot, *Alde Manuce et l'Hellenisme à Venise* (Paris, 1875), p. 123.

seller to commission and sell a small Virgil written in a small italic.

The Princeton University Library has such a small Virgil, exhibited at the Walters Art Gallery in its 1949 exhibition of illuminated manuscripts (Number 196 in the catalogue of that exhibition), written apparently about 1500, approximately the same time that Aldus was printing his pocket Virgil, which closely resembles the latter in size (5×3 inches), format, and script. Whether either is a copy of the other is of slight importance; that it was still economically sound to write such a book as late as 1500 is of considerable interest. Aldus sought a new market, the comparatively poor scholar, with his cheap octavos composed in what he called his 'cancellaresco italico' which cut down the cost of the paper, generally the most expensive component of the book.[1] Three years earlier a friend, Urceus Codrus, had complained that his folio Aristotle, with its lavish margins, was too magnificent for students; its five volumes cost as much as ten fine manuscripts.[2] It remains odd that typefounders and punchcutters in the age of Cellini should not earlier have achieved an aesthetically successful design in small size. But one of Cellini's circle succeeded in the effort to create a fine italic. Lautizio of Perugia's engraving of Arrighi's small chancery hand (1527) must be ranked as a splendid achievement. The scale, however, is larger than Arrighi's and is anything but economic. An italic, however fine, cut in the equivalent of a 16 or 18 point body could have no extensive present, and no future at all. True, the first types, whether gothic or roman, had been comparatively large. Fust and Schoeffer's Durandus (Mainz 1459) had made use of a large 14-point 'gotico-antiqua'; the *Catholicon* of the next year, attributed to Gutenberg, was successfully composed in an informal 'gothic' which, although

1. It was the small type and format, not the italic letter itself, that provided the economy.
2. Letter printed by L. Dorez, 'Alde Manuce et Ange Politien', *Revue des Bibliothèques* VI (1896), pp. 310-26.

raggedly cut, represents no small feat of engraving and casting and is approximately 12 point. Adolf Rusch's type (Strassburg 1467) is cut as near as may be on a pica body.

The first roman types cut in Italy, approximately the same year were cast, so to say, on an 18-point body. The uniquely elegant formal humanistic script used by Poggio from 1425 had an x-height more or less equivalent to pica, yet no pica roman was cut in Italy until 1507, when Soncino of Fano used it for his *Decachordum Christianum*: this was some years after Aldus's pica 'cancelleresco italico' was cut and cast. Undoubtedly the small size was the basis of its success. Apparently the skill of the best Italian engravers was not at first attracted into the service of the printing and punch-cutting trades. This is certainly one reason for the late appearance of printed specimens of the new calligraphy. As late as 1514 it was apparently impossible to find an engraver in wood or metal skilful enough to reproduce handwriting in normal scale. When (as we shall see) in 1514, Sigismondo Fanti required such reproduction for his *Theorica*, he was forced to leave blanks to be filled in by a scribe. This probably explains the fact that not for two generations after the bringing of the press into Italy did any pedagogic manuals of the art of writing appear in print. Handwriting, in the sizes normally used for domestic and commercial purposes, was far smaller in scale than the letters used in bookwork. It was nearly another generation after the publication of the first writing books before Robert Granjon could execute (*c.* 1546) his masterpiece of roman and italic on a nonpareil body (i.e. 6 point). Before Aldus's time the application of engraving to typography in terms of economy of space had scarcely begun. The few types engraved for casting on a very small body were faithful copies of the smallest gothic formal hands developed over the centuries for bibles and works of canon law. Thus Froben's pocket bibles of the 1490s, set in a small gothic type on an almost 6 point body, merely repeat a scribal economy which had been achieved two hundred years earlier. A knowledge of the economic production of texts was still almost limited to scribes, not a few of whom could write out in italic quicker and cheaper than Jenson could print in roman. Printing in Italy in the fifteenth century was still largely romantic.

Chapter 3

THE PIONEER: SIGISMONDO FANTI

We have considered in some detail the early development of the cursive hand, which, amplified and refined in many varieties and forms, was to be one of the two main staples of the writing masters of the sixteenth century. But owing to the practical difficulties of reproducing this script, it was the other staple that was first disseminated by the printing press, the antique Roman capitals. It is important to remember that these were, throughout the sixteenth century, considered an integral part of the equipment of a writing master. This coalescence of two – to our eye – different forms is hard to imagine now after centuries in which the writing hand and the inscriptional capital have taken such different paths. But to Giovanfrancesco Cresci, the greatest exponent of either form in the sixteenth century, the roman capitals were 'the origin and foundation of perfect writing'. 'The antique latin letter' he goes on, 'which is to be seen in Rome excellently engraved in several inscriptions and antique marbles, is the principle, whence latin letters derive; since the basis of the beautiful forms of the "antica tonda" [thus he names the upright humanistic minuscule, as written by Poggio, which preceded the sloped cursive of Niccoli], with their curves and the contrasted thickening and thinning of their strokes, all comes from and depends upon a mastery of the forms of the antique Roman capital.'[1] This fusion of a lapidary and a written form took place in the fifteenth century, and by the end of the century it was virtually complete, as may be seen in the Aldine italic type.

The process, however, had been a long one. The revival of the roman capital proceeded *pari passu* with the written minuscule, but the serious consideration of its forms had been the

1. G. F. Cresci, *L'Idea, con le circonstanze naturali, che a quella si ricercano, per voler legittimamente posseder l'Arte maggiore, e minore dello scrivere* (Milan, 1622), p. 13.

prerogative of the architect and metal worker. Their opinion of it is summed up in the directions of Lorenzo Ghiberti – to whom is due the prime credit for the revival – for the inscription on the arch of Saint Zenobius in the Duomo, that it is in 'lettere antiche in honore del sancto'. So it came about that towards the end of the fifteenth century, the only engraved alphabet to be produced consisted of antique roman capitals, intended for the use rather of architects, sculptors, painters and craftsmen, aware that these letters owed their proportions to the use of geometrical instruments.[1] No doubt Poggio's capitals, as used in his displayed colophons, were inspired by inscriptional precedents. But he did not measure the capitals or interest himself in any mathematical basis that they might have. Enthusiastic collectors of inscriptions, such as Ciriaco d'Ancona and Fra Giovanni Giocondo, were interested first in the literary aspects, the meaning and style, of what they found. Their aesthetic interest was limited to the layout of the inscription, although they paid tribute to the beauty of the incised letters by attempting equally fine scribal forms. (The manuscripts of Giocondo's *Sylloge* attributable to Bartolomeo di Sanvito are perhaps the finest.) The geometrical construction of letters was a branch of the renaissance preoccupation with the revival of the classical canons, such as Alberti found in Vitruvius; as such its theory might engage the dilettante as well as its practice the craftsman. The obvious places to find traces of such speculation might be Rome or Florence – Rome where Brunelleschi and Donatello found so much to measure and admire in 1402-5, Florence where both, with Ghiberti and Alberti, spent so much of their working lives. Yet is was not at Florence, but Padua, that the first pure classical roman lettering is found, in Mantegna's painting; the first manuscript and printed treatises follow in the same area, namely at Verona and Parma. It is tempting to see the impetus of this unexpected flowering in the Po valley in the

1. A number of the geometric alphabets are discussed, with facsimiles, in M. Meiss, *Andrea Mantegna as Illuminator* (N. Y., 1957).

visit of Donatello to Padua from 1443 to 1453, but Donatello's lettering, although classical in feeling, does not have the qualities which Mantegna's derives from the direct copying of classical examples. Indeed, Florentine inscriptions, although they could be very close to the classical tradition (as in the Bilietto tombstone in Santa Croce), reveal a different tradition, characterised by Casamassima as an example of the persistence of the gothic tradition both in rhythm and in its tall, thin and compressed proportions.[1] Its persistence delayed the impact of the new classical lapidary style in Florence until the end of the century. But it is no coincidence that the earliest set of geometrical diagrams of roman capitals, made in 1463 by the eccentric Veronese antiquary, Felice Feliciano, comes from the immediate circle of Mantegna.[2] The first printed book, printed from woodblocks $6\frac{1}{2} \times 6\frac{1}{2}$ cm in dimension, followed some twenty years later from the press of Damiano da Moille, a scribe and illuminator turned printer. The unique surviving copy, discovered by Leo Olschki, was reproduced in facsimile, with an introduction by S. Morison, in 1927.[3] There are numerous extant manuscripts as well as printed books of this kind produced before the first appearance in print of any pedagogic manual of handwriting, humanistic or other; they are surveyed briefly in the introduction to the translation by A. F. Johnson of Chapter III of Verini's *Luminario* (1527).[4]

Note has already been taken of the survival of manuscript specimens of literary and legal hands as taught by itinerant calligraphers in the fifteenth century. As to the writing-master's specimen in print, it would be reasonable to expect that Germany, as the European centre of the metal trade and the cradle of the printing industry, would have been the first to produce

1. Casamassima, p. 20.
2. Felice Feliciano, *Alphabetum romanum*, ed. G. Mardersteig (Verona, 1960).
3. *A newly discovered treatise on classic letter design printed at Parma by Damianus Moyllus*, intr. by S. Morison (Paris, 1927).
4. G. B. Verini, *Luminario or the third chapter of the Liber Elementorum Litterarum*, trans. A. F. Johnson, intr. S. Morison (Cambridge and Chicago, 1947).

it. In the absence of such German activity, it would not have been surprising if the first important printed writing-book, or 'specimen', had been produced in Venice, the centre of the Italian book trade. The great mathematical work of the period, Luca Pacioli's *Divina Proportione*, had come out in 1509 from a Venetian press, which it had been incubating for years. It naturally included a set of roman capitals geometrically made, but it did no more for calligraphy than that, and hence failed to develop the printed manual of lettering further than it had been taken by Moille.

But the letters used by the printer, Paganino of Toscolano, which he calls 'characteres elegantissimos', represent a notable step forward for Venetian craftsmanship. These 'most elegant' types are an italic of great interest for their size, smaller than Aldus's and form, which is upright. Paganino had been anticipated by the printer, Benedict Dulcebellum of Carpi in 1506, who well described himself as 'Impressor elegantissimus' and his letter as 'pulcherrimus'. The types are a fine, small, italic, only slightly inclined. Giovanni de Rubeo of Venice published in 1514 the mathematician Sigismondo Fanti's *Theorica et pratica . . . de modo scribendi fabricandique omnes litterarum species*. Here at last is the first printed pedagogic work claiming to deal not only with roman capitals but with all sorts of lettering ('omnes litterarum species') and illustrated with examples. These are all, however, still large scale diagrams for the geometrical construction of single letters. And that is really all, for Fanti's blockmaker could not, or did not, produce engraved replicas of actual handwriting actual size, since the spaces (in all the known copies) are left blank. Probably the intention was that they were to be filled in by hand by a master or pupil working under direction. An alternative possibility is that the spaces were for pasted-in slips from copperplates, like the engravings after Botticelli in the 1481 Dante. I have never seen a copy in which these blanks have been utilized by either pen or plate.

Fanti's book is a small quarto, dedicated to Alfonso d'Este,

47

and printed in roman type with ornamental woodcut borders to the introduction and to the initial page of each of the four books of the treatise which, despite the Latin title, is in Italian. The 'omnes species litterarum' amount to four, three of which are demonstrated geometrically. Fanti's *Liber Primus* discusses (*Considerationes I-XXXVI*) the suitability of various paper surfaces, smooth or otherwise, for different hands, and gives high praise to the papers of Fabriano. He also talks of inks, the right manner of cutting and holding the pen, proper posture, the use of the straight-edge, scissors, dividers and other instruments, and of course the utility of geometry and mathematics in the making of letters. He considers in detail the height and other proportions of the classical *A* (xxxvii) and of *B C D E F G H* (xlii), and, in due space, deals with the rest of the alphabet. It is in *Consideratio* xl that he makes the first mention of the Chancery hand, or '*littera cancellaria*', as he calls it:

> You will learn by heart this instruction, with those preceding and those still to come. The distance between the lines in the 'littera cancellaria' should be four times the face [X-height] of the letter, however large or small it is to be. The ascending and descending letters should all be equal and should be three-quarters of the distance between lines, or a little less, else there may be confusion. You must make sure that the faces are all equal. If the ascenders, descenders, and faces have a small serif to the left, naturally and quickly written, this makes for good design. It is impossible to cut such letters on wood so that they may be perfect. However, if you consider the reasoning together with the example you will be able to make graceful letters with the pen according to our precepts.

Liber Secundus is devoted to the 'littera fermata moderna', i.e. round gothic, made *ragione geometrica*, with cuts of the alphabet a-y. Fanti also provides varying sorts, such as the round *r*. *Liber Tertius* describes 'littera gallica', or pointed gothic, also geometrically constructed, with cuts. All are distorted, even when, as in certain cases (i.e. *d* and *p*) alternative designs are provided. The worst characters are *a*, *g*, *p*, *t*, *x*, *y*, *z*. *Liber Quartus* deals with 'littera antiqua', i.e. roman capitals, made geometrically, with cuts A-Z and with a sole variant, another A at the end.

Fanti's achievement consists first of his description of chancery letters for which, however, he did not provide diagrams; and secondly his application of the geometrical method already applied to the antique roman by Feliciano, *et. al.*, to the two main types of gothic script. These specimens were cut on wood and printed mainly for the benefit of engravers, cutters of inscriptions, and writers and decorators of antiphonaries and graduals – a class of manuscript book still written long after the beginning of printing. Fanti's 'lettera antiqua', the roman capitals set out in Book IV, derives from Pacioli. The blocks for all three sets are well engraved and his text as a whole is well considered. The book is, in fact, a secretary's manual, not a text-book for pupils intended to be taught individually or as a group by a master with the *Theorica* in his hand. The provision of other materials useful to artists and craftsmen, not uncommon in writing-books, pattern-books, and the like, helped to broaden the potential market. The competent secretary or scribe wished to know the arrangement of a book, the layout of a page or an epistle, the quality of paper surfaces as well as of pens and inks, and the method of holding pens cut appropriately for the several kinds of writing. Fanti tells him all this, and gives him instructions for varied layouts and arrangements of glosses, shoulder or footnotes, etc. The instructions regarding pens specify that they must be cut especially to suit the script, and that the scribe must therefore have several kinds: 'penna pertenente a la cancellarescha littera, a la formata moderna e a la minuscula antiqua'. It is unfortunate that Fanti could find no engraver skilled enough to cut small sizes of 'littera cancellaria'; it is unlikely that one so interested as he was in lettering should not make every effort to find a craftsman with the requisite talent; we are deprived as a consequence of the means for judging the celebrated mathematician's cursives – chancery or commercial. But it could only be a matter of time before an engraver would try his hand at the task.

Chapter 4

THE INVENTOR: ARRIGHI

Eight years after the publication of Fanti's *Theorica* there was invented the first book of printed cursive writing models. It was the by-product of the ecclesiastical bureaucracy centred in Rome. Its author had a special position; he was entitled to call himself a Writer in the Apostolic Chancery. His book stands first on the list of published, printed specimens of cursive calligraphy (I exclude Neudorffer's 1519 *Fundament*, since it was apparently printed for private circulation among the master's pupils and friends and was never regularly published).[1] It consists of sixteen leaves only, but it is a job of which the Roman press may well be proud. It was the printed book that, by example, as well as by precept, taught the hand that, in a modified form, was destined to spread all over Europe. The book, entitled *La Operina di Ludovico Vicentino, da imparare di scriuere littera Cancellarescha* was written for publication in Rome in 1522. Its author was Lodovico degli Arrighi of Vicenza, *latine* Ludovicus Henricus Vicentinus.[2]

Arrighi's first calligraphical publication sets out plainly, and with some parade of modesty, its purpose in its engraved title and half title: it was the *Operina*, the 'little work', of Ludovico Vicentino, 'Writer of Apostolic Briefs in Rome', designed to teach the Method and Rule of writing cursive or Chancery script. The book consists of 32 pages limited to the hand called 'lettera Cancellarescha' (already, as has been seen above, described in Latin as 'littera cancellaria' by Fanti in 1514) which the author, at the request of many friends, had laboured to produce in practical form. Since it was impossible for him, by his own hand, to make all the copies demanded, he made use of

1. Doede, op. cit., no. 1.
2. J. Wardrop, 'Arrighi Revived', *Signature* XII (1939), pp. 26-46; Johnson, pp. 24-6; Casamassima pp. 37-45, 85-6.

what he calls '*questa nuova inventione de lettere*', i.e. engraving and printing, despite his conviction that the press (*la stampa*) cannot in all points reproduce the living hand.

The engraving, in whole or part probably the handiwork of Ugo da Carpi, is a notable achievement. It alone made publication possible to an audience including, first, the trained secretaries who, in Fanti's opinion, could follow complicated instructions, and, secondly, the more ordinary and less highly skilled people who, required to write in a universally legible style by an economy rapidly expanding both in size and in geographic distribution, needed a handy manual. Without Ugo da Carpi's skill Arrighi could have made no advance on Fanti. The form of the new book admirably fits both audiences. No more simple, complete combination of the practical and the attractive has been produced. We do not know what arrangements Arrighi made with Ugo da Carpi, but it is obvious from Fanti's failure that Arrighi was indebted to an inventor who was responsible for the technical basis of his artistic and commercial success. It cannot be doubted that the inventor-engraver was well aware of the contribution he had made to the success of Arrighi' book. The degree of his responsibility may well have been the cause of the quarrel which led Arrighi to obliterate his name from the colophon in the earliest surviving issue of the *Operina*. We know that in 1525 Clement VII's privilege for the book was transferred to Ugo da Carpi, which argues that the latter had been able to make out a good case for his unique responsibility for the book's success.

All the thirty-two pages of Arrighi's text are engraved in relief for surface printing. If Ugo da Carpi cut the whole set of these blocks single-handed, he must have worked with a high degree of concentration over a considerable period. The text thus engraved provides analyses and instructions for the making of the strokes and of the component parts of the various letters, the organization of their proportions and parts, the arrangement of their variation and combination, and the manner of connecting them. Arrighi details the spacing of the small letters (*lettere piccole*), the words, and the lines of the script. Capitals (*maiuscule*), being less of a problem, are dealt with summarily. Thus the instructions for the small letters occupy sixteen pages, while those for the capitals are compressed into two. The rest of the book is filled with specimens of Chancery script, mainly aphorisms, written according to the rules laid down, and abbreviations for the forms of address, with flourished initial capitals. The *Operina* ends with a colophon embodying the claim that [the Book of] the Art of Writing Cursive or Chancery Script was printed in Rome '*per inventione di Ludovico Vicentino, scrittore*'. The word 'inventione' is obviously significant but of precisely what, it is difficult to say. In all probability it refers not to the engraving or the printing but to the concept, i.e. the idea of setting forth the instructions in the script intended to be seen, observed and copied by the owner of the book. The colophon is completed by a cartouche in which the words CUM GRATIA & PRIVILEGIO are engraved for printing in white letters on a solid ground, beneath which, in the Harvard copy, can be read the continuation '& Ugo da Carpi Intagliatore'. It may have been that its meaning was a bone of contention to the two inventors, and it is clear that Arrighi's high-handed action in obliterating his partner's name (as a stationer, he may have had sole charge of selling the printed copies) must have given great offence. The terms of the privilege transferred to Ugo da Carpi suggest that he had wished to join Arrighi in exploiting the market by printing more calligraphic books, and that Arrighi had rejected his proposal or obstructed him in a legal right to such a partnership. At all events, Arrighi's self-description as a scrivener (*scrittore*) recalls that in 1510 he was in business as printer and publisher (*stampatore*) and further that at the time the *Operina* was being drafted he was a writer of briefs (*scrittore de brevi*). Nowhere in the *Operina* does he repeat his claim to be 'stampatore' or 'stampatore e scrittore', though the conspicuous display given to the statement that the book was printed under privilege suggests that he must have believed that this was a just statement to make at the time the blocks were engraved. That the book was in any way clandestine is not to be imagined although its publication must have been clouded by the quarrel with Ugo da Carpi. Arrighi's official position would make a complete abuse of the privilege claimed on the colophon difficult; on the other hand, since Ugo was able to obtain its transference to himself three years later, it seems likely that he had some share in the original privilege.

We do not know the printer of the sheets which make up Arrighi's first book. *La Operina* contains no letterpress: the production of such a work without the use of type was Arrighi's invention, and he is entitled to the credit for it. But if he did not own a press of his own, he was probably engaged to provide himself with one. Whatever the exact circumstances of the actual printing of the blocks, *La Operina* was a successful invention, which was to have many imitators.

As to the hand taught by Arrighi, its basis lies (as he reiterates in the sixteen pages devoted to the small letters) in two initial strokes, one flat and thick, the other angular and thin: the first begins *a b c d f g h k l o q s x y z*; the second *e i m n p r t u*. Secondly, the letters are to be thought of as formed within a narrow upright oblong, not rectangular but sloping slightly to the right. It is important to observe that Arrighi does not, in these basic principles, lay down a complete formula for the construction of all letters. He is content to describe the beginning of each letter, and the shape common to all letters. The flexibility, in the formation and variation of letters, that Arrighi allows himself is the secret of the vitality of his script. Other writers who advocated a more rigid formula were less able to hold the balance between fluid grace and formal beauty. In the later *cancelleresca bastarda*, as it came to be called, Arrighi's flexible scheme, with its natural *ductus*, is extended and codified into a formula of extreme rigour. The free cursive of the earlier century is confined in just such a straitjacket as the late middle ages imposed on the old minuscule to produce the gothic letter, or as the humanists called it 'littera moderna'. It is to be remarked that, in the pure chancery hand as Arrighi wrote it, the heads of the ascenders *b d f h k l* and long *s* and the tails of the descenders *f p q* long *s x* and *y* continue the diagonal slope of the upright with a curve ending in a pear-shaped termination (only the second letter in the ligature *ff*, long *ss* ends with a horizontal footstroke): the slanted oblong is implied but not stated. In the later *bastarda*, the upper curve is replaced with the angular thin up-stroke and the lower by flat thick horizontal stroke: the addition of these 'serifs' is to convert the oblong from a pattern shape into an area within which the letters must be contained. These features are only incidental, not an integral part of the development which overtook the chancery hand. This, as will be seen, was more a question of condensation of form coupled with a more acutely angled pen. The development of the *bastarda* is however symptomatic.

Arrighi's second book, *Il modo di temperare le Penne Con le varie Sorti de lettere ordinato per Ludouico Vicentino* (The Way to Cut Pens), seems to have been due for publication in the following year, 1523. The preface apologizes for the omission from *La Operina* of any rules for cutting or holding the pen. These are supplied in the first six pages of the new work, in which the text is set in type. The rest of the book is taken up with the 'Various Sorts of letters' promised in the subtitle; *La Operina* had only dealt with one, the Chancery hand. Arrighi's interest in writing or in publishing books about writing had broadened; he had probably, like Fanti, seen the possibility of a wider market for alphabets for metal-workers, illuminators and other craftsmen. These are also the various scripts other than chancery required by the professional scrivener: mercantile, notarial, bollatic, ecclesiastical, and the letter for briefs with its seriffed descenders.

It is particularly frustrating that neither the date nor the place of publication of *Il Modo* can be established with any certainty, since it almost certainly marks a turning point in Arrighi's career. The writer of apostolic briefs in 1522 had by 1524 become printer and publisher to a gifted group of humanists and writers, to which Arrighi owed his introduction to Gian Giorgio Trissino, a fellow-citizen from Verona and his principal patron. It was a short career, of considerable activity, which, with the group itself and perhaps Arrighi's life, was extinguished in the sack of Rome in May-June 1527. No less than 36 publications are recorded in less than three years, by authors such as Aretino, Firenzuola, Tolomei, Vida and Trissino himself. Nor did Arrighi's connection with the papal chancery cease: he printed several documents issued under the name of Clement VII. All of these are printed in a number of original italic types cut for Arrighi by Lautizio Perugino, who, if Manzoni's attribution is correct, is to be equated with 'the great Lautizio', as Cellini calls him, Lautizio di Bartolommeo dei Rotelli, the goldsmith and seal-engraver. The skill of the punch-cutting bears out the equation. A bull dated 12 June 1524 is perhaps uncertain evidence, but the partnership must have been in existence by July 1524 when they printed the *Coryciana* of Blosio Palladio, one of the papal secretaries (evidence of Arrighi's continuing link with the chancery) who was later to sign the papal privilege for Palatino's first book. Another 8 publications came out before the end of the year; those with a month date include another in July, 2 in September, 4 in October and 4 in December. In 1525 they issued another 10 works, of which 6 are dated at fairly regular intervals from January to April, the last being C. Marcellus *In Psalmum Usque quo Domine oblivisceris mei* which carries the date 12 April 1525. 5 books are dated 1526, without month or day, and 3 publications have month dates in April, May and June 1527, the last, a papal brief, being perhaps posthumous.

It appears, then, that there is a gap of perhaps a year or more in Arrighi's publications, from the middle of 1525 onwards. The gap is underlined by two other circumstances: the change in Arrighi's types between 1524-5 and 1526-7, and the disappearance of Lautizio's name from the publications of the latter period. This is not the place to analyse Arrighi's italics, a task much complicated by the large number of alternative sorts he used, but a distinction can be made between the smaller x-height of the earlier types and the larger x-height of the later, although both are cast on the same body. In the former, rounded ascenders and descenders predominate, although the seriffed descenders of the *litera da brevi* are found. In the latter, ascenders and descenders are both seriffed: it is, in fact, a *bastarda*.

How is the publication of *Il Modo* to be fitted into the pattern of Arrighi's later career? The title page 'In Roma nel anno MDXXIII' ('con gratia e privilegio' appears below it, on a smaller cartouche then that in *La Operina*) seems to leave no room for doubt that the book was designed to be printed in the year following *La Operina*, and thus precedes Arrighi's work for Trissino and his circle. But the colophon 'Sta'pata in Venetia per Ludouico Vicentino & Eustachio Celebrino Intagliator' contradicts the title page in point of place, and the dated text pages throw doubt on the date as well. They are, in order of appearance, the second page of 'littera da Merchanti' (b1v) 'In Vinetia a xiij di Febraro M d xxv. Ludo. Vicentinus Scribebat Venetiis'; the page of 'Littera per Notari' (b3r), which is dated at Rome, Tuesday, 17 September 1523; and the 'littera da Brevi' page (b4v), which is also dated Rome 1523; (the second page of reversed interlaced initials is also signed Rome). The discrepancy between title and colophon is given a new and sharper point by these examples.

Now, errors and unusual circumstances excepted, there is no reason why a date in printer's type should long precede the publication of the book in which it appears. But if a date appears in a scrivener's specimen book, which had then to be laboriously engraved on wood blocks – a lengthy process, however skilled the engraver, the date of publication of the book may be rather longer after the date in the text. When, moreover, the text of the specimen so engraved is made up of fragments of documents (possibly real documents lying conveniently to hand as the specimen book is prepared), it is possible that a long interval may elapse between the date in the text and the appearance of the book. It is improbable, on the other hand, that dates in the text will be fictitious future dates; the information in Arrighi's pages is generally correct where it can be checked. It follows then that the earliest date for the publication of *Il Modo* must be after, and probably some time after, 14 February 1525.[1]

But Arrighi, we know, was very busy in the earlier part of 1525, and in Rome. The last dated book in 1525 is as late as 12 April, and it is possible that Arrighi was still in Rome as late as 18 July. It seems likely then that *Il Modo*, if printed in Venice, must have appeared late in 1525 or even early in 1526, and that Arrighi's visit to Venice therefore coincides with the interval in his printing career in Rome. The sequence of events from 1522 to 1526 may now be reconstructed. Sometime in 1522, not before August (the date on Div), Arrighi finished the specimens for *La Operina*. Sometime later, perhaps at the end of 1522 but possibly in 1523, Ugo da Carpi finished the blocks and *La Operina* was printed, perhaps by Arrighi himself, certainly by someone closer to him than to Ugo da Carpi, since, when the two quarrelled, it was Arrighi who had Ugo's name cancelled in the colophon, and not *vice versa*. This event presumably took place during or soon after printing, since no uncancelled copies survive. It is probable that most of the first impression was destroyed, since only one cancelled copy survives, and the second impression with Ugo's name erased from the block was then printed, again either by Arrighi or his nominee.[2] It is possible that it was now, when there is at least a year's gap in his life, that Arrighi went to Venice, and that most of the surviving

1. See below, pp. 181-91.
2. P. Hofer, 'Variant issues of the first edition of Ludovico Arrighi Vicentino's *Operina*', *Calligraphy and Palaeography: Essays presented to Alfred Fairbank*, ed. A. S. Osley, (London, 1965), pp. 95-106.

copies of his second book, and some at least of his first, were printed there.

It is not possible here to attempt an investigation into the details of Arrighi's business arrangements at the time. But it is important to note the transfer of his privilege to Ugo da Carpi in 1525. The possibility if it existed of friction among the *scrittori* within the Papal Court may have been one motive for Arrighi's leaving the Chancery. Important, too, is the fact that he took care in the colophon to this second venture to join with his own name that of his new engraver: Eustachio Celebrino. Moreover, Although Arrighi signs himself 'in Roma' his book was printed in Venice where Celebrino had been working, at least since the previous year. Celebrino was a first-class engraver and general worker in the publishing trade, who published in 1525 a little manual engraved from his own mercantile hand and who also worked for Arrighi's nearest rival on a competing book which came out a year after *Il Modo*. Arrighi, according to Servidori, had taught writing in Venice before moving to Rome: we do not know whether or not he returned to see his second book through the press. If so, his sojourn would have been a short one, since he was working in Rome as a publisher and printer the next year. As has been seen, Arrighi was certainly planning his edition of Trissino and Palladius at this time, since they appeared the next year in new italic types of his own design, probably again cut by his partner Lautizio Perugino. Printing seems to have been Arrighi's principal occupation after 1524, for he made no further attempt at popularizing handwriting. Was he discouraged by the loss of the privilege for *La Operina*? We cannot say. In any case, it would appear that without Celebrino, or another equally competent engraver (and there is no evidence that such competence was usual), he could not have produced a third copy-book. Celebrino himself was too occupied with work for Hieronymo Soncino of Cesena and Francesci Bindoni of Venice to come south. Celebrino may have had some premonition that the wrath of Charles V was to fall upon Clement VII in 1527. Also – and this is the point that concerns us – Celebrino's services, with those of his assistants, had been retained by Giovanantonio Tagliente for a book that that author doubtless hoped would surpass Arrighi's pioneer work.

But Arrighi was to prove difficult either to copy or to beat. The dangers involved in the imitation of his hand wheher by a decorative scribe (Tagliente) or a rational scribe (Palatino) will become clear. In the meantime, it is worth noting that the extreme vigour of the *ductus*, the means of writing reduced to two strokes, confined the free cursive of the earlier century in a straitjacket such as the late middle ages imposed on the old minuscule to produce the gothic letter, or as the humanists called it 'littera moderna'. Arrighi could afford to set himself such an inflexible model, since he could combine liberty and discretion with an absolute certainty which is to be found in all his work, written and printed. His followers did not find the task so easy.

Chapter 5

THE DEVELOPER: TAGLIENTE

The titles of the early editions of Tagliente vary almost as much as the contents. The title, as it became stabilised, was: *La vera arte delo Excellente scrivere de diverse varie sorti di Litere*, by G. A. Tagliente.[1] The first of many editions appeared in Venice in 1524. The *Vera arte* is an expansion of Fanti's *Theorica* which is designed to combine the features of both books of Arrighi. Tagliente claims to describe the principal different scripts, whether made geometrically or otherwise, and does so, though he does not give displayed headings, titles, or designations of the sort Arrighi often provides. Rather, he works the names of the respective scripts into the descriptive and instructive text. Tagliente (greatly assisted by Celebrino's skill as an engraver, perhaps) appears as a painstaking scribe whose greater ingenuity and love of pattern – he also published a lace-pattern book[2] – made him anxious to exhibit his superior skill by complicating what Arrighi had properly kept simple. Tagliente gives

1. The copy of Tagliente's writing-book I have used mainly in discussing his work is a 1524 edition in 44 leaves, with typographic title-page reading *Opera di Giovanne Antonio Taiente che insegna a scrivere di molte Qualita di lettere Intitulata Lucidario*. A full bibliography and a biographical note will be found in Johnson, pp. 26-30. Fuller biographical data is contained in J. Wardrop, 'A Note on Giovanantonio Tagliente', *Signature*, new ser. VIII (1949), p. 57 f., with facsimiles, including a document in Tagliente's hand; in V. Lazzarini, 'Un maestro di scrittura nella cancelleria veneziana', in his *Scritti di Paleografia e Diplomatica* (Venice, 1938), p. 62 f.; J. Wells, introduction to *Opera di Giovanniantonio Tagliente 1525* (Chicago, 1952), with a facsimile of the 1525 pocket-size edition; and Casamassima, pp. 45-9, 86.

Further comment on Arrighi's and Tagliente's types may be found in A. F. Johnson, *Type Designs* (London, 1934, 2nd ed., 1959); A. F. Johnson and S. Morison, 'The Chancery Types of Italy and France', *The Fleuron* 3 (1924), p. 23 f., with facsimiles; S. Morison, *A Tally of Types* (Cambridge, 1953), also dealing with their modern derivatives; Alfred Fairbank, 'Die Cancellaresca in Handschrift und Druck', *Imprimatur*, N. F. 1 (1957), p. 53 f. See also below, pp. 00-00.

2. *Essempio di recammi* (Venice, 1524); see E. Potter, *Splendour of Ornament* (London, 1968).

61

the standard chancery and mercantile hands, but indulges in much calligraphic sleight-of-hand. Thus there is a curious *cancelleresca pendente*, over-strongly inclined to the left; a much-flourished and barely legible *trattizata*, highly inflected with ligatures; *Bollatica* and *Imperiale*, both laid out to display their decorative qualities to highest advantage; a number of reverse plates (white on black); several exotic alphabets, among them Hebrew, Greek (from type), and Arabic; and several sets of capitals for the use of illuminators and other craftsmen.

The instructions are printed in a noteworthy italic type. We do not know its engraver nor its designer, but it is a reasonable assumption that Tagliente was concerned in its execution. I cannot find that it was used by anybody before him, or elsewhere than in his books. Like Tagliente's calligraphy itself, his italic is less simple than any of Arrighi's. Equally Tagliente's prose is more turgid and his style more verbose. Tagliente, unlike Arrighi, was a professional writing-master, who had taught in the school of the Venetian Chancery. Like his predecessor, he deals with cutting the pen, holding it, the stroking, choosing paper (like Fanti, he considers Fabriano paper the most praiseworthy; a somewhat firmer and stiffer paper is preferable for the *lettera mercadantescha*), the instruments (e.g. rule, compass, lead, square, etc), and ink. Of the many scripts he exhibits, the *lettera cancelleresca*, already used in the chanceries of all the cities of Italy, is extolled as the most important. He gives 15 pages of instructions concerning it, while dismissing the mercantile letter in a few paragraphs. Indeed, Tagliente dissertates at much greater length than his predecessor, a relatively inexpensive proceeding when type is used for the text instead of engraving. He begins by listing three essential pen movements (the addition to Arrighi's two is the vertical body-stroke), and he repeats Arrighi's diagram of the oblong form with four dots. The means for creating the straitjacket of later years are in this formula. Tagliente escapes it by the variety of the forms which he used and proudly lists: 'torte, dritte, tonde, et non tonde, trattizate, et senza tratti' and so forth. Among the details treated at length is the combining of characters, since Tagliente as a calligrapher was immensely proud of his ligaturing and as a professional writing-master was eager to display his craftsmanship in this and other respects. He carried into his type many more sorts than *ct* and *st*, as well as varieties of these two. Tagliente's punchcutter, while no mean engraver, does not compare with Arrighi's colleague Lautizio of Perugia.[1] For example, the latter's swash characters for Arrighi's 1524 edition of Palladio's *Coryciana* are managed vastly better than Tagliente's. Yet the latter's italic remains a remarkable feat, since the engraver had attempted a dozen complicated ligatures and special sorts over and above the ampersand and long 's' combinations. Many of these, as well as the engraved specimens of Tagliente's hand, show Byzantine and Arabic influence – not unnatural in Venice, a cultural and commercial entrepôt for Eastern ideas and merchandise.[2] Even so, it cannot be claimed that his italic achieved more than a moderate success – one reason, perhaps, being that it possessed too many of these special sorts to appeal to the printer no matter how they gladdened the calligrapher's eye. The fount is seen again in Tagliente's *Luminario di Arithmetica* (Venice 1525); for the text of the *Opera nuova che insegna a le donne a cusire, a racamare & a disegnar a ciascuno* ... (Venice, 1527), his fine lace-pattern book, the first in Italy and particularly notable for its arabesques, well engraved by Piron da Carpi but miserably worked off the brothers a Sabbio; and for his two books of model epistles, the *Opera amorosa*, etc (Venice 1533) and the *Formulario nuovo che insegna ditta lettere missive* (Venice, 1538).[3] Thereafter no use seems to have been made of the fount.

1. This remark refers to the design rather than the engraving of the type.
2. For information on Byzantine influence on humanistic handwriting see D. Fava, 'La scrittura libraria di Ciriaco d'Ancona' in *Scritti di Paleografia in e Diplomatica in Onore di Vincenzo Federici* (v Florence, 1945), p. 295 f., with numerous plates of Ciriaco's scripts; S. Morison, *Byzantine Elements in Humanistic Script* (Chicago, 1952), and *Venice and the Arabesque* (London, 1955).
3. The best list of Tagliente's output is that contained in P. Riccardi, *Biblioteca*

Doubtless its size, equivalent to 20pt., limited its usefulness; it gave way to a small roman in the editions of Tagliente's writing-book published after 1525. The punches of such a scriptorial italic must have been prone to fracture.

Tagliente's greatest calligraphical defect is that too much style was laid on. His mercantile hands are overloaded with flourish; his chancery hands are too clever and ornate. The geometric alphabets are limited to pointed and round gothic; there is no set of geometrically made roman capitals, as might have been expected from a penman evidently acquainted with Fanti's *Theorica*. The pointed gothic is a complete failure and his rounded gothic only less obviously so. These are simple enough, but there seems no real need, except for the author's vanity, for their inclusion. There is no evidence, even in the very largest antiphonaries, that the so-called 'moderna' or rounded gothic was in fact made geometrically. But Tagliente wanted to outdistance Arrighi and Fanti and, as an industrious compiler and merchant of educational material, prove his superior knowledge of every kind of writing. With Tagliente, professional calligraphy entered upon its 'tricky', showing off, stage. Tagliente, like Fanti, was one of the first 'professors' writing primarily for other professionals, while Arrighi, in addition, cultivated the general public. Tagliente was more typical of his class; he had a full share of that vanity which inspires professionals to demonstrate their virtuosity before their peers, a vanity which was to prove the bane of many a future writing-master.

One attraction possessed by Tagliente's writing-books is the excellence of their printing (at least in the early editions) and engraving. The blocks of the writing-books (or at least many of them) apparently came from the studio of Eustachio Celebrino, who may have also taken an interest in the printing.

In 1525 Eustachio Celebrino published a little (the average size of the blocks in 2½"×4") octavo exposition in eight pages:

Matematica, Pt. I, Vol. 2 (Modena, 1873-76), p. 432 f., and Potter, op. cit., pp. 32-9.

Il modo di imparare di scrivere lettera merchantescha, etc.[1] It is Celebrino's sole writing-book published under his own name as author and was printed in what must have been an active year for his studio: 1525 was the year in which Tagliente brought out the edition of his book *Intagliato per Eustachio Cellebrino da Udene*, many of the blocks cut independently of the 1524 edition. As the title of Celebrino's publication makes clear, he limited its pedagogic purpose to the '*lettera merchantescha*', to which are added the arts of making ink and choosing paper. But although Celebrino does not say so, his mercantile specimen displays not one but several varieties of the hand, the major one being that displayed by Arrighi in his second manual (*Il Modo*, dated two years earlier, for which Celebrino cut the blocks). There is also a set of '*Capi versi*' capitals, signed '*Cellebrin' foroiulianus*', similar to Arrighi's and Tagliente's; the page on choosing paper is written in a hand mixing looped with unlooped ascenders, similar to Tagliente's *Mercantesca Genovese*; the page entitled *Documento nel scrivere* is in a script with seriffed ascenders, unlooped except for *f* and long *s*. The colophon, *Instromenti del schriptore*, bears a well-cut reverse plate on a stippled ground of the scribal tools, and the signature 'EVS. CELLEBRINO MDXXV'.

Just as Arrighi's *La Operina* of 1522 was the first manual limited to the exposition of the *lettera cancellarescha*, Celebrino's is the first limited to the exposition of the *lettera merchantescha*. It may have been published in Rome or Venice (most probably the latter, since at the time its author was doing the major part of his work for Venetian publishers) three years after the date of

1. See S. Morison, *Eustachio Celebrino da Udene* (Paris, 1929), with facsimile of Celebrino's manual; Johnson, p. 31; Casamassima, pp. 49-50; L. Servolini, 'Eustachio Celebrino da Udene: Intagliatore, Calligrafo, Poligrafo ed Editore del Sec. XVI'. *Gutenberg-Jahrbuch 1944/1949* (Mainz, 1949), p. 179, gives facsimiles of Celebrino's engravings and a list of his illustrations and publications. This list and Morison's are amplified by G. Commelli, 'Ricettario di Bellezza di Eustachio Celebrino, Medico e Incisore del Cinquecento', in *Scritti Vari Dedicati a Marino Parenti* (Florence, 1960), p. 137 f.

La Operina. During that interval Tagliente's first edition had appeared in Venice and been printed several times, a couple of the editions bearing a splendid cartouche reading *Intagliato per Eustachio Celebrino da Vdene*; the Duc de Rivoli records a Roman edition with the device of Antonio Blado (cancelled Venetian sheets, perhaps), dated the same year as Celebrino's book. This was the year that visitors crowded Rome for the 'anno santo'. It is necessary to bear these dates in mind if Celebrino is to have the credit he deserves. He had cut the blocks for Arrighi's second publication; for Tagliente's 1524 and 1525 editions, both of which included engravings of *lettera merchantescha* from specimens written by Arrighi and Tagliente respectively. Celebrino's engravings after his own specimens are, irrespective of the superiority shown in their cutting, far finer. His book is important to the understanding of the success of the next generation of writing-masters, above all of G. F. Cresci.

The origins of the process by which the second stage of the chancery hand came to differ from the first, in which the angularity gave way to smoothness, are better seen in Celebrino's pages than in Arrighi's or Tagliente's. The latter do not provide, as Celebrino does, a set of specimens that enable us to mark the tendencies which would influence Amphiareo (Venice, 1548), who in turn influenced Cresci (Rome, 1560). We shall return to this point in due chronological order. Here it remains only to summarize Celebrino's book as providing specimens of the chief commercial hands written and engraved in first class, but practical and unadorned, style. Despite these virtues, it was apparently a commercial failure, since it was issued in a small edition (judging from its rarity) and any reprints called for have not descended to us and hence cannot have been numerous.

Almost two decades were to elapse between the publication of Tagliente's first edition (1524) and the emergence of a new and major talent. Political and social conditions in Italy may well have been largely responsible; the almost constant struggle between the French kings and the Hapsburgs, for which Italy was the major battleground (and especially the sack of Rome in 1527) must have inhibited both the writing and publication of new works. A few managed to appear. Ugo da Carpi's role in cutting blocks for Arrighi's first book has already been mentioned, as well as the transfer of its privilege to him in 1525. He was an engraver, well known for his chiaroscuro prints. His *Thesauro de' Scrittori* (Rome 1525), printed by Blado, is the first in a long and still flourishing line of anthologies of the writing-masters;[1] it includes, in its 46 leaves, material from Arrighi, Tagliente, and Fanti, as well as a *Ragione dabbaco* by Angelus Mutinensis. Book-keepers and merchants were likely customers, and the inclusion of a ready reckoner would prove an added attraction for them. The book was successful enough, at any rate, to be steadily reprinted until 1550. The hands demonstrated are standard ones: *lettera antiqua tonda; cancellaresca; merchantescha; bollatica*, and so forth. The type-set instructions, primarily taken from his predecessors, represent no advance. Ugo da Carpi may not have been an original calligrapher – or for that matter, a calligrapher at all – but at least he usually acknowledged the sources of his borrowings. Giovambaptista Verini is a different case, for he was both hack and plagiarist, freely stealing from others – especially Tagliente – and giving no credit to his betters. His *Luminario* (without place or printer, but undoubtedly printed by A. Paganini at Toscolano, about 1527) is notable neither for its engraving nor its press work.[2] It contains four books of 32 pages each: Book I, on 'Lettera Moderna' (round gothic, the style currently in use for writing graduals, antiphoners, and other large liturgical books); Book II, rules for making the same letters geometrically; Book III, on the geometrical construction of '*Litere Antiche*', i.e. Roman capitals: Book IV,

1. Facsimile, ed. E. Potter (London, 1968); Johnson, pp. 30-1; Casamassima, pp. 48-9.
2. S. Morison, 'Some new light on Verini', *Newberry Library Bulletin* III (1953), pp. 41-5; Casamassima, pp. 27-30.

divers commercial and correspondence hands, as well as an elaborately flourished ornamental alphabet. Each book contains its own title-page, and may have been sold separately. Books V and VI seem to have disappeared; of Book VII, two editions at Milan (printed by Pier Paolo Verini of Florence) in 1536 and one at Brescia in 1538 are known to survive. Verini also printed some indifferent verse. His later works are, for the most part, even more wretchedly produced than the Toscolano book, and emanate from a number of presses, mainly in the provinces. In all probability Verini was publishing primarily for his students and the circle immediately around him rather than for general sale in the important Rome-Venice markets. These later books are extremely haphazard in organization, usually being mere rearrangements of his badly worn blocks.

Verini's copying and borrowings are easier to excuse than those of Ugo da Carpi. He was no professional engraver trying to capitalize on artistic or literary property to which he had only doubtful claim or none at all; but a vulgariser, who hardly understood the sources he drew on but was anxious to make them available to a less professional audience. His sources are widely different and sometimes contradictory. Thus the first book looks back to the 'littera moderna' rejected by the humanists. It is a work of reaction, behind its times, a reflection of no known source but of the tradition of letter-forming built up in the later middle ages. It is valuable as a statement of the little-documented doctrines of this tradition, notably those on fusion and union, which Verini clearly illustrates. The principal source of the second and third books is clearly Fanti's *Theorica*, whom Verini imitates both in matter and form. His account of the roman capitals is enlivened by some rather naive adaptations and parallels from Vitruvius, and in his simple way Verini is livelier and more lucid than his model. The fourth book derives in part from the models of Arrighi and Tagliente (three of the plates of *mercantesca* are dated 1526). The ornamental capitals 'a *groppi*' probably come from the same source as the *moderna* of Book I; like it, they belong to the traditional equipment of the ecclesiastical book industry. Adapted for the headings of official documents they were to become a regular part of the writing masters' specimens, although less so in Italy than elsewhere. Book VII is a rather more direct plagiarism of Tagliente.

Verini's productions are a by-path from the main course taken by the manuals of the sixteenth century. Like most diversions, they illuminate the more important works by contrast. They are also important as a record of a tradition which died without any other serious exposition.

Chapter 6

THE THEORIST: PALATINO

The sack of Rome in 1527 which brought Arrighi's career to an end is one of the two main dividing lines in our period. It is no coincidence that fifteen years were to elapse before the emergence of a new talent, and when this occurred, the whole climate of the times had changed. Italy had become the major battleground in Europe, the scene of the perpetual strife between the Hapsburgs and the Valois. If the present was cold to the arts, there was also the future frost of the Counter-Reform in the air. All the arts retreated, fortifying themselves as best they could against this unfriendly atmosphere. Artists found refuge in mannerism, music in the vernacular frivolities which nearly led the Council of Trent to suppress polyphonic music, and writers and the literati in academies. Giovanbattista Palatino was the one calligrapher of his age. Before, the authors of Italian writing books had been of two classes: the civil servants, such as Arrighi or Tagliente, aiming their wares at young men aspiring to posts in bureaucracy or business; or alternatively hacks, like Verini, turning their hands to what promised to be a vendible line. Palatino found his way early to the kind of society Arrighi reached in his last years. He was a member of academies, a sonneteer, a man of scholarly interests, political sympathies and social connections. These aspects of his career have been sympathetically and minutely described by Wardrop, and need not detain us. He was not perhaps quite such a sympathetic character as Wardrop makes out; he was, as Casamassima truly says, 'piuttosto un dilettante, un orecchiante che huomo di vera cultura', and his fellow-academicians may not have taken him at his own valuation. Nevertheless, his combination of calligraphic skill and philosophico-literary pretensions had a lasting effect on the form of the writing book, and on the valuation given to it. Where Arrighi and Tagliente had concentrated on the functional and decorative aspects of writing. Palatino with his erudite descriptions and samples of hands which had no practical value made it clear that calligraphy was a matter to engage the intelligence of the scholarly and educated. Now that the printing press had taken over so many of the tasks that engaged the writer's skill, Palatino sought to give it a higher place and purpose.[1]

The justly named *Libro Nvovo d'Imparare a Scrivere Tutte Sorte Lettere* of 1540, Palatino's first printed work, was published opportunely when Rome had to a certain extent recovered from its brutal invasion, and the whole peninsula was comparatively calm. Paul III (1534-49), who recognized clearly the need for changes in the Church, was beginning the long work of reform by elevating to the college of cardinals eminent scholars and serious churchmen. In the literary and academic circles which Palatino frequented (often under the patronage of eminent clerics), the *Sdegnati*, of which he was secretary, acknowledged Cardinal Alessandro Farnese, grandson of the Pope and a lover of fine manuscripts, as its protector. It is possible, as we shall see, that the cardinal had a decisive influence on the development of writing in Italy. For the moment, it is enough to say that as among the earlier humanists, a fine hand was cultivated among the group which he patronised.

Palatino was not one to be overwhelmed by the company he kept. The *Libro Nvovo* opens with two features, which were to become standard in later writing-books, which show no tendency to self-deprecation. First, there is on the title page a fine large woodcut portrait of the author, an innovation that would

1. The best account of Palatino's life and works is that contained in J. Wardrop, 'Civis Romanus Sum: Giovanbattista Palatino and His Circle', *Signature*, new ser. XIV (1952), pp. 3-39, with facsimiles of his engraved books and manuscripts and a photograph of the inscription he cut for the *Porta del Popolo* in Rome. Johnson, pp. 31-3, contains a biographical note by Wardrop as well as a list of the various editions of Palatino. See also Casamassima, pp. 50-3, 88-9. The editions used mainly in the following discussion are those of 1540, 1548 and 1566, all from copies at the Newberry Library.

be followed as a precedent by many later masters. The likeness is of a proud-looking, well-dressed, young man. Secondly, there is a laudatory sonnet by his admiring friend, Thomasso Spica de li Spinteri, congratulating and praising him, 'Il cui Spirto immortal sacro, e divino Non cape un humil monte o un picciol piano'. A portrait of the author became a regular part of the later masters' attempts to assert their own personality in the hands that they taught. Such sonnets were also destined to become conventional; Palatino's works are the first of many to be peppered with the praise of friends, the names of important acquaintances, and dedications to men of consequence. But Palatino was more than a mere literary name-dropper, attempting to get on in the world through judicious application of his contacts. He was also a man of intelligence, capable of organizing his material logically, writing his directions clearly, and seeing that his engraver and printer[1] produced decent-looking books. He was also a considerable calligrapher, if over-addicted to conceits and fancies; like Arrighi, his gifts are not fully realised by his engraver, and his two manuscript specimen books, at Oxford and Berlin, testify to his skill.[2] His versatility also extended in all probability to inscriptions on stone: 'G. B. Palatino' is recorded in the accounts for the inscription on the outer face of the Porta del Popolo (1562-5) in Rome.[3]

Palatino's book is deliberately named: he intended to surpass all his predecessors. The *Libro Nvovo* is an amalgamation of the forms of his two leading predecessors: it is a combined manual of the chancery hand, and an encyclopaedia of all the other hands. Palatino's instructions on the chancery hand are 'displayed' as in Arrighi; i.e. they are engraved (admirably) by an anonymous craftsman, while those for the other hands are set in type, as in Tagliente, though in roman rather than italic.

1. Baldassare Cartolari had come to Rome recently from Perugia. F. Ascarelli, *La tipografia cinquecentina italiana* (Florence, 1953), pp. 68, 98, 148.
2. J. Wardrop, *The Script of Humanism* (Oxford, 1963), pp. 46-7.
3. See above, p. 71; J. Mosley, 'Trajan Revived', *Alphabet* (1964), pp. 17-48.

After the prelims, which include a 4-page dedication to the Cardinal Robert de Lenoncourt, full of complimentary references to the French, and a notice of the invention of printing by Gutenberg in Mainz in 1453, the book begins with ten pages of general instructions on the right way to hold the right kind of pen in the right order to make the right strokes in the right proportions. These pages of wisdom correspond with the first four pages of Arrighi's *La Operina*, and are excellently printed from engraved blocks, protected with thick and thin rule borders, making an average text size of 4"×6", roughly the same size blocks as Arrighi's if the borders are disregarded. Tagliente's blocks, it has been seen, are fuller on the page. All Palatino's hands are signalled with titles, engraved in cartouches or otherwise displayed. The contents, while various, are systematically arranged; he goes on to give eight pages of *Regole particolari* (title in white on black cartouche) which provide detailed instructions for constructing the characters of the minuscule alphabet, somewhat less well cut than the preliminary instructions. *Regole generali* (also in reverse on a different but likewise decorative cartouche) provide the principles of correctly spacing letters, words, and lines of Chancery script. (Cf. Arrighi's *La Operina*, pp. 4-21.)

Following these general instructions, Palatino gives various plates of models: *Maiuscole Cancellaresche*, chancery capitals both plain and flourished; *Essempio per fermar la Mano*, an alphabet of chancery minuscule with verse example; a page of flourished Chancery abbreviations. All these are similar to Arrighi and Tagliente. Palatino, as a post-Arrighi practitioner, was inevitably dependent upon his predecessor, but he has as sure a sense of layout as Arrighi. He also resembles him in being scrupulous, as a rule, about signing and dating his pieces. He was not indisposed to using Arrighi's italics for his instructions.

Palatino follows his Chancery section with an assortment of mercantile scripts: Milanese, Roman, Venetian, Florentine, Sienese, and Genoese, followed by a page of mercantile capitals.

These are commercial texts, several of them variously signed and dated in 1539: they show a steadily increasing interest in the mercantile scripts. Palatino, who frequented literary and humanistic circles, found it wise and profitable to show the widest range to date of mercantiles. Arrighi had provided only one such script, untitled, in the special circumstances of his visit to Venice: it corresponds fairly closely to the Venetian patterns exemplified in the books of Tagliente and Celebrino. Arrighi, it must be remembered, was, professionally, a diplomatic scribe as one may see in his briefs which have been identified. Tagliente, working in a city whose interests were far more commercial than Rome's, had supplied a number of mercantile and diplomatic scripts, and had labelled the more popular ones: two Florentine scripts, notarial or commercial (*fiorentina naturale* and *bastarda*); *venetiana*; *genovese*.

Celebrino, the first to issue an all-mercantile manual had also provided a range of scripts, but identified none. The majority are close to the hand identified by Palatino as 'Venetiana': the title-page, the *Proemio*, and the text on *la Penna*; the text on *L'Inchiostro* resembles the *Romana*; that on *la Carta*, *Genovese*. All the books provide a set of similar mercantile capitals. Celebrino also provided at least one hand, for the page headed '*Documento nel Scrivere*' which is unrepresented in the other manuals: with its seriffed ascenders, coupled with restraint in looping and ligaturing, and the looped long *s*, it is a hand intermediate between Tagliente's *fiorentina bastarda* and *naturale*; it was a hand destined to be carried considerably further by Amphiareo. In his later editions (starting with 1545), Palatino added other mercantiles: *Bergamasca*; *Anticha*; apparently he had gauged his market shrewdly.

The mercantile section in the 1540 edition is followed by another designed immediately for a Vatican Chancery audience: a page of *Lettera de Bolle Apostoliche*, similar to that provided by Arrighi and Tagliente: also *Lettera di Brevi*, a diplomatic text (dated 1540) garnished with the name of François I King of the Gauls, a *cancellaresca romana* with rounded ascenders, a thicker, more sharply angled, version of Arrighi's letter of the same name. There follow two pages of directions on *cancellaresca formata*, in Blado's roman type, and a full-page engraved specimen with alphabet of the formal italic book hand of the period, here described and illustrated in print for the first time.

Palatino proceeds with a selection of non-mercantile vernacular hands: *Napolitana; Francese; Spagnola; Longobarda; Tedesca*. *Napolitana*, an upright *antica* characterized by tall slightly clubbed ascenders and descenders and gothic *r*, was occasionally used as a book hand; *Francese*, *Spagnola* and *Tedesca* use gothic secretary hands, the latter including showings of Schwabacher and small gothic text; *Longobarda* is a semi-formal bastard Beneventan with slightly clubbed ascenders and descenders, perhaps a version of an imperfectly understood Visigothic.[1] A second *Lettera Francese*, followed by a reverse plate with alphabet, is a decorated pointed text, like Tagliente's. *Lettera Mancina* is a 'trick' script, a mirror-written chancery; *Lettera Trattizata* displays highly flourished *cancellaresca* capitals. A double page spread which follows, Palatino's alphabet of inscriptional roman capitals in an *entrelac* border, is again in the Arrighi-Tagliente tradition. It is a first-rate piece of lettering and engraving, suffering, as is usual, from the printer's incapacity to ink and print well large surfaces of black.

Another Palatino innovation is a long section on cipher writing. It contains twelve pages of instructions in roman type, followed by two engraved specimens of artificial cipher alphabets, signed (in cipher) 'Palatinus Scribebat'. In his instructions, Palatino shows himself a highly conscientious author: he cites earlier authorities, expresses profuse thanks to numerous contemporaries, and gives several examples of use. This, in an age noted for secret diplomacy and in a city whose major industry was international relations, was of obvious utility.

1. See E. Casamassima, 'Litterae Gothicae', *La Bibliofilia* LXII (1960), p. 126 and figs. 1 and 2.

The next two pages of ingenious interlaced alphabetical ciphers, while perhaps of no great practical value, are highly competent and decorative. They are placed against a white-on-black arabesque ground. These are followed by a *Sonetto Figurato*, i.e. a four-page rebus, the text of which is perhaps a sonnet of Palatino's own writing; one assumes that this conceit appealed more to the members of the Sdegnati than to modern taste. The 'Alphabetum Latinorum' is a set of Latin inscriptional capitals which are typographic in quality, its hierarchic rank indicated by the crown above its title. Next is a collection of exotics: *Graecum; Hebraicum, Hebraicum ante Esdram*; alphabet and syllabary *Chaldearum; Caldiacum Antiquum; Arabum; Egiptiorum; Indicum; Siriorum; Iliricum Sclavorum; Saracenorum*. These are all displayed on elaborate jagged scrolls (Wardrop well calls them 'mannerist'). The appeal is again to the academic and the antiquary rather than to the practicing craftsman. The page of *Lettera Formata*, however, would even in the mid-sixteenth century have had practical application. It is round Gothic, majuscule and minuscule alphabets with liturgical texts, a hand still used for writing large service books well into the next century.

Palatino's full-page cut of the scribal instruments is closely modelled on that of Tagliente. Neither is as straightforwardly didactic as Arrighi's cut of quill-cutting.[1] Palatino's instructions, in seven pages of roman type, deal with the inkpot, ink, quills, penknife, thimble, pounce, ruler, square, stylus, and other instruments of the trade, as well as the cutting of pens. He goes on to recommend the '*modo tocca da Quintiliano*', i.e. tracing of the letters with a stylus from an engraved pattern. The first edition, like most of the subsequent ones, ends with Palatino's emblematic device, a moth and a lighted candle, encircled with

1. Translated, with the engraving reproduced, by the Rev. H. K. Pierce, *The Instruments of Writing* (Newport, R. I., 1948, repr. 1953). The pamphlet also includes technical notes by John Howard Benson and a translation of Arrighi's directions for pen-cutting by E. A. O. Taylor, with reproductions of Arrighi's illustrations. All three can be conveniently compared in O. Ogg, *Three Classics of Italian Calligraphy* (New York, 1953), pp. 42, 107 and 234.

the motto "Et so ben ch'io vo dietro a Quel che m'arde", taken from a sonnet by Petrarch.

The additions in Palatino's later editions are generally dismissed as a decline from the standard of 1540. But two of the new plates in the 1545 edition, the 'Cancelleresca Romana' and the 'Cancelleresca Romana Bastarda', if poorly cut, are of great importance as evidence of the development of the Italian hand. The rest are indeed mainly insignificant hands: two more mercantiles, *Bergamasca* and *Anticha*; such fanciful scripts as *Rognosa*, a jagged wavy minuscule, possibly of use in embroidery (its title, Italian for 'itchy' or 'scabby', suggests its quality) and *Tagliata*, an upright semi-bollatica uniformly bisected with a horizontal white line; *Pretesca*, a fanciful runic alphabet, and *Notaresca*, another secretary hand. Several of the new plates were of use to metal workers, *Fiammenga*, an outline Flemish pointed Gothic of the sort used locally for brasses, and *Moderna*, an outline version of the round Gothic used in Italy for liturgical books. Palatino illustrates this also in his manuscripts, evidently proud of the evenness of his parallel lines. There is also a new two-page set of entrelac Gothic capitals, comparable to Arrighi's, and several new exotics.

It was more than twenty years before Palatino altered his text again. He had, knowingly or unknowingly, diverged from the path taken by Arrighi and Tagliente in a direction in which further progress was impossible. He realised that he had gone beyond them, in the length and detail of his instructions, and in the variety of hands shown. But his debt to them is considerable, and ungenerously repaid. From Arrighi he took the form of his book, the emphasis on and (in part) the execution of the chancery hand; from Tagliente, he borrowed the idea of variety of scripts, and the essential three movements, which he renamed *testa* (horizontal – Tagliente calls it *corpo*), *taglio* (vertical) and *traverso* (diagonal). Arrighi he implicitly criticises in rejecting the instructions given by his predecessors (criticism of one's predecessors, like the portrait and the admiring sonnets, became a regular part of the preliminaries of a writing book). From Tagliente he borrows without acknowledgement. But Palatino's achievement wholly transcends his predecessors in one respect – the extreme logicality of his approach. Arrighi and Tagliente showed a variety of hands: Palatino increased the number shown, and organised the material into a rational order of mercantile, vernacular, foreign and antique scripts. Arrighi and Tagliente, again, sketched a framework for the chancery letter which they treated freely and irrationally. It was left to Palatino to develop their precepts into a formula as rigid as a demonstration in Euclid. His clear-cut, sharply angled and contrasted, uniform style, and his advocacy of the pen 'cut slightly lame', i.e. with one corner shorter than the other, crystallised and petrified the free script of Arrighi and Tagliente. As with the other arts, so in writing, a reaction set in against too much licence. In troubled times, the natural instinct is to create a stronghold. Palatino's artifical formula was the creature of its time.[1]

It is possible that, as with other species that have ceased to evolve, the chancery hand might have thus become extinct, if the rigid formula devised by Palatino had not been exploded by Cresci, the greatest of all the writing masters and fully capable of rebutting the logician in his own terms. The full story of their dispute, which is central to the present theme, will be dealt with later. One word from Cresci explains the dangers involved in Palatino's theories: *gotica*. It was, as Wardrop says, 'the old black-letter formula over again',[2] the preference for logic and pattern over clarity, speed and grace which Petrarch and Coluccio had objected to 150 years earlier.

Yet it was Palatino's logic which earned him his reputation, especially with the amateur and the scholar. It is perhaps too much to claim for him the popularisation of the Italian hand all over Europe, but his example is acknowledged by Yciar in Spain (where Palatino's black-letter propensities were character-

1. It is significant that he dropped the geometrical construction of the letters.
2. Wardrop, 'Civis Romanus Sum', p. 19.

istically developed), and 'the sweet Roman hand' may be partly due to the most Roman of all the sixteenth century writing masters.[1] The number of editions of the three recensions of the *Nvovo Modo* is exceeded only by those of Tagliente, and figures may be misleading in judging the impact of the two. The most interesting testimony to the permanence of Palatino's reputation is that he is the only sixteenth century Italian scribe mentioned by Mabillon (1707) or Astle (1803).[2] However that may be, Palatino was abundantly justified in feeling proud of his *Libro Nvovo* of 1540, upon which he and his engravers must have worked long and hard. Handsomely printed by the leading Roman printer of the day, Antonio Blado, it remains indispensable to anyone desirous of tracing the development of the chancery hand, identifying the main types, or of studying the theory of letters as it appeared to an intelligent and thoughtful writer in the middle of the sixteenth century.

1. Wardrop, opp. citt.; A. Fairbank and B. Wolpe, *Renaissance Handwriting: an Anthology of Italic Scripts* (London, 1960), p. 25.
2. Cf. Wardrop, 'Civis Romanus Sum', p. 3.

Chapter 7

A REFLECTION: ALUNNO

The printed books just described, i.e. those of Arrighi (1522-23) to Tagliente (1524) to Palatino in 1540 comprise, so far as format and primary intention are concerned, a single group. It has been said that Arrighi's is addressed to a general literate public, Tagliente's to the professional secretary, and Palatino's to an amalgam of the two. What Tagliente began with his varying entries, Palatino expanded into an encyclopaedia. The major calligraphic factor common to the books of these twenty years is the Chancery cursive which, after Palatino in 1540, assumes even greater importance. It will be seen in the books published after the middle of the sixteenth century that what had begun as a simple, expeditious, legible, angular, and, on occasion, beautiful hand was elaborated by the efficiency of scribes and the suppleness of their quills into a more involved, less legible, smooth and more frequently a deliberately elegant performance. That tendency may be traced to the writing of the old gothic cursive habitual to the scriveners of the papal chancery for the dignifying of documents of higher importance than the brief. The script of the papal bull was essentially decorative. It is customary to describe the deliberate elegance of the mid-century chancery hand as 'baroque' and this is not an inaccurate description, even if it anticipates the conventional term of the style in art and architecture. But the tendency is observable in gothic cursive and it is not impossible that its appearance in chancery cursive is due as much to the old, as to the new, habit of decoration. In any case, it is impossible to suppress decoration in any cursive. Arrighi only succeeded in restraining it.

There were other influences at work as well. The papal chancery was one of the most influential vehicles of the Italian hand in the sixteenth century. The adoption of the humanistic cursive, attributed by de Mas Latrie to the papacy of the Venetian Eugenius IV, seems in fact to have taken place under Pius II (1458-64),[1] but the finished form, the chancery cursive demonstrated by Arrighi, was not established until the beginning of the sixteenth century. The requirements of the papal brief entailed a different development of the humanistic cursive from that demanded by the other main influence, the printing press. Both were alike in demanding economy, but, where the punch-cutter demanded economy in the shape of the individual letter and reduction in the number of ligatures, the influence of the papal brief was dictated by the material on which it was written. Even in the relatively stable times of Leo X (1513-21), vellum was scarce and expensive: the wars which preceded and succeeded the sack of Rome can only have made it more so. The size of the papal brief was dictated by the number of pieces of vellum that could be cut out of a skin, and the dimensions which became standard were 5 by 18 inches – the full width of the short side of the skin, cut five or six times across. It was from these limitations 'that papal scriptors caught the habit of over-compression and angularity in their writing.'[2]

In the writing of the briefs of Leo X, ascenders and descenders are always curved, but perhaps under Clement VII, a further economy suggested itself. The original cursive of Niccoli, who followed his 'antique' exemplars, had seriffed ascenders and descenders. This form was regular until the end of the fifteenth century, and was adopted, for obvious reasons of convenience, by Griffo for his first italic type. The realisation of the decorative possibilities of curved ascenders and descenders came late; its progress can be traced in the manuscripts of, for example, Antonio Sinibaldi, from 1460 to 1490, although he never abandoned the serif for his formal book hand.[3] It is possible that

1. Wardrop, *The Script of Humanism*, pp. 41-2; Morison, *Politics and Script*, p. 282; above, pp. 37-8.
2. Wardrop, op. cit., p. 43.
3. B. L. Ullman, *The Origin and Development of Humanistic Script*, pp. 118-23, 126-8.

curved ascenders became increasingly popular with scribes to differentiate their work from print; at any rate, they became standard in the papal chancery.

It is interesting, then, to find in Arrighi's second book of the 'Littera da Brevi' differentiated from the chancery cursive of *La Operina*, notably in the seriffed forms of *p* and *q*. It suggests that the distinction was breaking down under economic pressure, and that the scribe was now cutting short his ascenders and descenders with a serif for the same reason as the printer, namely to save vertical space. Thus, the division which had grown up between chancery and book hand was in danger of disappearing, and it is interesting to see that when Palatino illustrates the *cancelleresca formata* in 1540, he considers it, alone of the many hands he illustrates, to need two pages of description and distinction. The importance of this passage has been underlined by Wardrop, and his summary of it deserves repetition.[1] Palatino's views are not very clearly expressed, but he points out that *cancellaresca formata* is really a misnomer, since it is round and not oblong, as a chancery hand should be. It is more a *mercantile* script in its proportions. It differs again in having serifs, like the *francese formata*, and for this reason is only suitable for small books (where the economy of space would be valuable). It is moreover too slow, most of the letters needing two strokes which in *cancelleresca* are written with one. Palatino, in effect, summarises the reasons why the *formata*, as it came to be called (it is significant that the *cancelleresca* was dropped), although respected by the writing-masters, did not find a large or important part in their specimen books.

In 1545, Palatino added two plates to his collection which added two further forms of *cancelleresca*, called *Romana* and *Romana Bastarda*. There is no explanation to differentiate them from the standard *cancelleresca* and the *formata*. The former has curved

1. J. Wardrop, 'The Vatican scriptors: documents for Ruano and Cresci', *Signature*, new ser. v (2948), p. 6.

ascenders, but differs from the standard in its extreme condensation; the *bastarda* resembles it in this respect, but the ascenders and descenders have sharp and angled serifs. The *Romana* represents very clearly the variation in the earlier papal chancery hand observed by Wardrop. The *bastarda* is rather harder to define. The term was not, as we shall see, applied to a particular hand, but to any synthesis of hands, chancery and literary, chancery and mercantile, free and formal, even the mixture of two national styles. At any time it might be applied to a different hand, and some caution must be used in judging which mixture is meant by the description *bastarda*. Palatino does not elaborate these distinctions, but one of his contemporaries did.

Francesco del Bailo, better known as Francesco Alunno or Alumnus, was by his own account (and that of others) one of the foremost scribes of his time, and an author and poet of some repute. Born in Ferrara about 1485, he spent most of his life in Lombardy. Most of the details of his life are derived from his published works, into which they are inserted by main force. From *Le Ricchezze della Lingua Volgare* first published in 1543, we learn that he was scribe to the northern town of Udine, of which Celebrino was a citizen. Later he moved to Venice, where he became 'scrittore unico e abbachista rarissimo' to the Signoria. The second edition of the *Ricchezze*, enlarged and corrected, was dedicated to Palatino's patron. Cardinal Alessandro Farnese, *La Fabrica del Mondo*, an encyclopaedia based on the works of Dante, Petrarch and Boccaccio, first published in 1546 and many times reprinted, was Alunno's largest and most popular work. In it he refers to the generosity of the Republic, 'sola refugio de virtuosi', which provided him with a pension; like Tagliente, he was 'provisionato'. He died at Venice on 11 November 1556.

Alunno might be better known as a calligrapher if he had had more respect for the printing press. In describing the beauty of his specimens, however, he says that all his compositions were newly written by himself, and not the printed things which many people use: the implication is obvious. His work seems to have survived only (in public collections, at least) in an unique document, a sort of combined notebook and scrap-book, in the British Museum.[1] It is just the sort of collection Palatino might have made: it contains examples of Alunno's skill in every kind of letter, from the cursive to the *antica tonda*, greek, hebrew and even more exotic hands, any number of decorated initials, and geometric constructions for roman capitals; it also contains pages taken from books, mainly in greek or cyrillic, but including some from a copy of Tagliente, and engraved letters from various sources. This volume, however, is an informal specimen for the writer's own use. It is regrettable that Alunno's pieces for public display, which he describes in such detail, seem to have disappeared. One magnificent example was in the collection of Baron Adolphe de Rothschild. This consisted of 89 'cartoni', preserved in their original box in the form of a book bound in red morocco, gilt and with gilt clasps, dated variously between 1549 and 1551. The specimens included chancery and other 'cursive' hands, gothic and fantastic, hebrew, greek and cyrillic, and letters from Pietro Aretino, Nicolò Franco, Marco Antonio Magno, Antonio Ghisolino (Alunno's pupil and successor at Udine), Amphiareo (who like Alunno came from Ferrara) and Girolamo Argenta. It is clear from Arrigoni's facsimiles that Alunno's gifts both as an artist and scribe were of a very high order, and it is to be hoped that this example of his skill will be once more retrieved.

Alunno was, then, an experienced and capable scribe and author, if given to self-praise; this description of the craft, although not allied to a printed specimen, would be invaluable. In *La Fabbrica del Mondo*, in the section on the heavens, under the

---

1. B. L. Add. MS. 27869: but there are other MSS; see now, G. Mardersteig, 'Francesco Alunno da Ferrara: noto grammatico, ma calligrafo sconosciuto', *Un augurio a Raffaele Mattioli* (Florence [Verona], 1970), pp. 1-28, with colour plates of the *cartoni*, now at the university library at Genoa (MS. G. VI. 18); a similar collection is at Vienna (ÖNB, Cod. Ser. nov. 2631).

sub-section Mercury, is the article 'Scrittore', which provides this description. Scribes are, he says of different kinds:

Some occupy themselves with the method, measure and art of writing those sorts of letters which we call *cursive, formate, maiuscole*, and *minori*. Others devote their skill to exotic letters, Chaldee, Arabic, Turkish, Saracen, Assyrian, Indian, Hebrew, Greek and Armenian, Serbian, Asian, Jacobite, Coptic, Phoenician, Gothic, Cyrillic, Tuscan, Slavonic, and an infinite number of others. These can be seen in their specimen sheets. Others do not trouble with these variations, but concentrate on perfecting their letters, so that they are well finished, equal in size, and properly spaced and aligned, in three styles only. The first is *Cancelleresca*, which must be large, full, tall, continuous (*ben legata*) and tilted slightly from the left; the second, called *mercantesca*, is quite different, being small, thin, round and tilted slightly to the right; the third, Bastarda, combines the two. Again, there are some who practice the *antica minuta*, broad and rounded in all its parts, and graduated according to its size . . . There are also those who want to go further and practise engraving the ancient Roman capitals using the correct compass method for the curves, and the nine-to-one proportion of height to stroke, with the proper relation of thick and thin strokes and their spacing. And there are those who have left to posterity a thousand beautiful alphabets of *lettere Longobarde* or *Capitonse*, engraved within a circle divided into three which gives them their oval shape; and also *lettere moderne*, with a proportion of four to one. Finally there is no lack of scribes who have written in a white *corsiva minuta* or greek on a black ground, engraving them on the actual paper, a rare thing, and also *corsiva* in gold or other colours; with letters for briefs, with boughs or foliage, knotted (*a groppi*), illuminated, and so executed with the pen that neither eye nor brain can conceive better. For example, one can write the *In Principio* and the *Ave Maria* with very few abbreviations

85

in a circle made with a small coin, such as the Venetian *soldo*. Whoever can show in his examples and specimen sheets that he can write and use his pen in all these effects is an accomplished and experienced writer.[1]

Alunno may have been thinking mainly of himself when he summarised all the activities of a scribe, but he has contrived to list as well all the different achievements of all the writers so far considered. His three main divisions are especially valuable since they distinguish three separate *métiers*. If the description of the *antica minuta*, which seems something of an afterthought, is transferred to the first group, we can identify the three groups as book scribes, learned scribes and commercial or professional scribes. Arrighi and Tagliente can be seen to belong almost exclusively to the last group, and Palatino to all three, the second predominating. Among the special letters which follow the three main groups, Alunno anticipates the custom of the later writing masters in emphasizing the importance of the 'ancient' Roman capitals. His interest in *lettere Longobarde* parallels Palatino. The description of 'engraving' white letters on black on the paper itself throws new light on the means by which the originals of Tagliente's delicate cartouche blocks were prepared.

Alunno is mentioned by only one of the later writing masters, fifty years after his death, but there seems little ground to doubt his exposition as an authoritative statement of the professional activities of scribes in the middle of the sixteenth century. Although he treats his groups as separate, the increased professionalism (and the decline in book work) in the latter half of the century drew them together, as the forms of the letters were also assimilated. It is perhaps significant that when the pupils of the greatest of all the later masters, Giovanfrancesco Cresci, looked back to their predecessors, it was not to Arrighi or yet Palatino, though both must have been known to them, but to

1. *La Fabbrica del Mondo* (Venice, 1560), f. 108.

the little-known Francesco da Monterchi, 'the first of our time to give grace to the art of writing'. Vasari records his masterpiece, the Farnese Hours (like Palatino and Alunno, Monterchi enjoyed the patronage of the great Cardinal Alessandro), illuminated by Giulio Clovio and written in an exquisite *formata*: the book was finished in 1546, the year in which *La Fabbrica del Mondo* appeared, and is now in the Pierpont Morgan Library (MS. M. 69). B. L. Harley MS. 3541, the 'Paraphrase on the Psalms' of Marcantonio Flaminio, is in the same hand. Other manuscripts in a hand of equal beauty and precision may be by him, but enough evidence does not exist to distinguish them with certainty from the work of similarly gifted contemporaries such as Ruano. It is hardly possible then to discover what were the characteristics which so distinguished him in the eyes of his successors.

There is, however, a passage in a famous letter of Aretino which may help to explain the position. Palatino complained that his *cancelleresca formata* was too slow. The later scribes, who had other means of writing fast, would consider this irrelevant: if regularity and beauty were required, the speed with which they were achieved was unimportant. The standard was set by the printing press, a high standard in point of regularity if easier to surpass in beauty. Thus Aretino, writing to Gianfrancesco Pocopanno in 1537 and surveying the state of science and the arts, points to the high standard of writing current, of which

The style of *messer* Francesco Alunno bears witness, whose skill and diligence is such that one can believe what is printed to be written by hand, and what is written with a pen to be the product of the press.[1]

Palatino, perhaps without knowing it, certainly reluctantly, is showing the way to a new concept of the art of writing, a more self-conscious, self-regarding, and in some ways defensive at-

1. The full text of Aretino's letter is given by Mardersteig, pp. 26-7.

87

titude. Where the early manuals provide simple technical instructions for a craft like any other, the later writers offer two qualities, speed and beauty, which demanded special treatment quite apart from the requirements of the text. For the first, there was the *cancelleresca testeggiata*, which developed into the standard round hand, and for the second, the *formata*; the old chancery cursive, the original 'Roman hand', was no longer an essential part of the scribes repertoire. Whether Monterchi was in any sense the inventor or perfector of the new style we cannot say, but this development can be seen at work in the next two books to be considered, although both are, in a sense, backwaters in the main stream of the development of writing in Italy. The clash between the old style and the new was to come twenty years after Palatino's first edition indicated that change was on the way.

Chapter 8

AMPHIAREO AND RUANO

The first copy-book in oblong format appeared in 1548. Its
original edition is one of the very rarest issues of the period,
although the 1554 and succeeding editions are numerous.[1] Between 1548 and 1620 upwards of a score of impressions of this
book came from Venice. It was the work of a Franciscan Friar,
Fr Vespasiano Amphiareo, born probably about 1490 (some
authorities cite 1501 as his birthdate, 1563 as the date of his death)
into the noble family of the Albertazzi in Lendinara, near Ferrara, and christened Alfonso. A fellow townsman was Sigismondo Fanti, who may have inspired his career. Amphiareo early
gained a reputation as a calligrapher and teacher of writing in
Florence and, by 1518 had moved to Venice where he taught a
hand which he termed '*bastarda del Frate*' and for whose invention
he claimed credit.

Amphiareo's *Vn Novo Modo d'Insegnar a Scrivere et Formar
Lettere di Piv Sorti* (Venice, 1548) is handsomely engraved and
well printed by Curtio Troiano d'i Navo. While the hands
shown are, as the Friar says, 'of every kind', they do not repeat
Tagliente's worst excesses, though the Friar's dependence upon
his predecessor is obvious. Amphiareo's thirty years of teaching,
alluded to in his preface, spanned the period of the greatest
popularity of Tagliente; he had been reprinted in at least twenty-
five, mainly Venetian, but progressively deteriorating editions,
before the Friar got out his *Novo Modo*. Whether for reasons of
copyright or of market, Palatino had no Venetian editions before 1578, according to Johnson, although he had had eight
Roman printings between 1540 and 1548.

Amphiareo's hands, like Palatino's, are no mere copies of Tagliente's, although they reflect his influence. The Friar was so

1. *Das Schreibbuch des Vespasiano Amphiareo*, facsimile and introduction by Jan
Tschichold (Stuttgart, 1975).

proud of his new method or invention that he changed the title of his second edition to make explicit reference to it: '*Et massime una lettera bastarda da lui novamente con sua industria ritrovata, la quel serve al Cancellaresco et mercantesco.*' That was the real point of his book, the *bastarda* that was a cross between the new chancery and the old mercantile, between humanistic and gothic cursive, made to serve the purpose of the prince and the merchant. Amphiareo gives the lion's share of his twelve plates of *bastarda* and mercantiles to the script of his own devising, labelled as such on three of them; he also shows chancery minuscules and majuscules, and a number of gothic hands: *bollatica, francesca, rognosa*, etc., all in appropriate texts; a number of alphabets: ornate roman capitals signed in interlaced ciphers of the sort expounded by Palatino, followed by a debased set of decorated roman capitals made up of twisted boughs or logs; a handsome set of gothic entrelac initials, two to the page, decorated with *putti*, heads, and the like; a decorated gothic set, also two to the page;[1] a set of simplified geometrically constructed minuscules, round gothic, based on Fanti's; and roman inscriptional outline capitals, against horizontally ruled squares.

The Friar's text is very brief; besides a typographic titlepage with one of the printer's two marks (the other is used on the verso), there is a brief dedication to Principe Francesco Donato, followed by 3½ pages of terse instructions, set in roman and italic types; the plates are followed by directions on pen-cutting (a mere nine lines), a six-line table of contents doubling as binder's register, a recipe for making ink, and a list of errata. In the table of contents he explains that he has given only one mercantile example, since he commends the use of his *bastarda* instead. Obviously, unlike Tagliente and Palatino, he believed example better than precept, putting his emphasis upon his *exempla*. His anonymous blockmaker served him well; in fact, if one may judge from the two manuscripts in his hand which

---

1. A second set appeared for the first time in 1572; see Tschichold, p. 12.

have been located, he improved and regularized the Friar's hand somewhat.[1]

The one book Amphiareo published held its position for an appreciable time and never deteriorated in point of production as Tagliente's did. Nor, on the other hand, did he or any agent of his attempt revisions of substantial supplements; later editions show exactly the same blocks as the first, and only minor additions to the text: a letter to the reader explaining his purpose, brief directions for writing in gold colours. The popularity of the book is remarkable. He died in 1563; a new edition came out in 1564. The most convincing proof of the Friar's practicality is that an edition is recorded as having appeared in 1620. His contribution is a distinct one. He deserves full credit, such as it is, for seeing that to the unprofessional eye the old round, upright, very current mercantile (Palatino's *Milanese*, *Romana* or *Venetiana*, for instance), familiar to all, was not so dissimilar to the new chancery hand that the two could not be satisfactorily mixed. By doing so there would result a less slanting, less narrow-bodied hand than either Arrighi's or Palatino's, written more rapidly because of its loops and frequent ligatures. The effect, therefore, of the Friar's invention is to produce an upright, ligatured, italic hand, with an angular lower-case similar to the type of G. A. Castiglione, produced in Milan some years before, in 1541.[2] There can be no doubt judging from the impressive number of editions chronicled by Johnson, that Amphiareo's manual must have met a need in certain circles, although it is to be doubted if his *bastarda* achieved the universal currency in chanceries and counting houses that he had hoped for.

Amphiareo's choice of format – adopted by his chief successor, G. F. Cresci, of whom we shall treat later – was also a significant change. The books of his predecessors, from 1514 until

---

1. J. Wardrop, 'Six Italian Manuscripts in the Department of Graphic Arts', *Harvard Library Bulletin* VII (1953), p. 224 and pl. iv.
2. S. Morison and A. F. Johnson, 'The Chancery Types of Italy and France', *Fleuron* III (1924), pp. 23-51.

his own, had all been vertical octavos, apart from Tagliente's one (perhaps abortive) experiment in this format in 1525. Their layouts were modelled on book practice. Amphiareo's format showed off to best advantage his layouts, inspired not by book pages but by epistolary practice. The letter of his day was generally written on a wide, short sheet of paper or vellum, folded after writing to produce an envelope – somewhat on the order of today's airletter form turned sideways. Amphiareo's pages suggest this shape quite successfully.

To preserve chronological order it is necessary to record at this point a book that was as ephemeral as it was sumptuous: Ferdinando Ruano's *Sette Alphabeti di Varie Lettere* (Rome, 1554).[1] It is a small folio dedicated, in a page that backs the title, to Cardinal Marcello Cervini; the latter's arms are displayed in a handsome woodcut on the title-page. Early in the Dedicatory Epistle, Ruano, a Spaniard who was one of the scribes in the Vatican Library, confesses his interest in the application of geometry to lettering, and how he arrived at it. 'I have taken rules and measurements from the ancient letters to be seen in most places in Rome, as I promised your Serene Reverence when you asked me if I knew the measure of a capital letter that I had in my hand.' It can only be a matter of speculation what it was that Ruano held in his hand when Cervini spoke to him. Wardrop thought it might have been a fragment of a classical inscription. But if Ruano's duties as a Vatican scriptor extended in the same direction as those of Horfei a generation later, and he was regularly employed in preparing the final drawings for the mason to follow in engraving inscriptions as well as in writing codices, it might have been the outline of a single large inscriptional letter that he held, either of his own drawing or stencilled or traced from a standard model. Such letters in stencil form and in various sizes are still used by the Lavoratorio Marmi

1. Facsimile, Miland (Nieuwkoop, 1971); Johnson, pp. 36-7; Casamassima, pp. 63-4, 90-1.

in the Vatican City today, some preserving the form of letter spread all over Rome by the works of Sixtus V.[1]

To satisfy friends who made the convenient request that he should tackle geometrically some of the other letters in use, he had applied himself to that task as well. However, his *Sette Alphabeti* begins with the inscriptional capitals, and comprise not only the antique letters from the monuments but the fourth century Vergilius Vaticanus called 'Aureus', written in *capitalis quadrata*, whose adjective he considers equally applicable to the antique minuscules. Ruano gives the rules for making the square and then proceeds seriatim with the majuscules A-Z, two to a page. The second section deals with the geometric making of the *antica minuscula*, whose form he says, without going into detail, originates in the foregoing. It was, Ruano says, used in all the antique codices, and is now adapted by contemporary printers; but the *minuscula* is not used for inscriptions like the capitals. In his alphabet a-z, likewise printed two to a page, he provides the geometrical construction of each letter. His 'e' had a diagonal cross-bar; 'h' is in the quasi-uncial form b, not deliberately but because it is part of his constructivist rule that the 'h' must conform to the 'b', its circular body being terminated with a slight horizontal foot. His third section, *lettera moderna*, so called he explains, because in recent years it had been used for the larger codex in which the *antica* had come to be employed. The *lettera moderna* is a round gothic minuscule, again geometrically demonstrated two to a page, with both round and straight 'd', as well as variant 'r'. Section four, 'lettera majuscola moderna', displays A-Z in roman capitals, made geometrically but without the accompanying printed instructions provided for the earlier sets. So far Ruano had attempted only what was to be found in Fanti, forty years earlier. But his next section is a novelty, nothing less than the application of geometry to cursive.

1. Mosley, 'Trajan Revived', p. 29 and n. 31.

Ruano's prefatory remarks 'della *lettera cancellaresca formata*' disclaim any credit for the hand itself, now very much in vogue and already described and taught by many excellent writers. Although he disclaims any originality, his application of the compass and rule to the making of the chancery letters was a pioneer (and misguided) effort. He gives a detailed letter by letter instruction, again two to a page, for a formal chancery minuscule of the sort used as a book hand. His ascenders have the orthodox bent-over heads, inclined to the right; 'h' is again for like 'b'. Ruano's *formata* has very little slope, ascenders and descenders being almost vertical; his letters are distinctively narrow and have quite short ascenders and descenders since spatial of economy is demanded of a book script.

In section six, *lettera maiuscola bollatica*, Ruano dispenses with detailed instructions and geometrical regulations. It may be because of the limited appeal of the letter since, he explains in his preface, it is used only at the Roman Curia, there primarily for one class of document only, the Apostolic Bull. These are highly ornamented letters, with foliage, knotwork, exaggerated swellings; since they were to be done freehand, and the blocks were not very well cut, much is left to the discretion of the scribe, who is enjoined to improve on the models. The seventh alphabet, *lettera maiuscola thedesca*, likewise dispensed with geometric construction and detailed discussion. These Ruano tells us, are used by illuminators in music codices and notarial books, in colours or even outlined in gold. There are two main sorts, knotted and unknotted; once the basic outline letter has been mastered, the scribe can work out decoration. These are simpler than Amphiareo's *tedescha*, and not so well cut.

Arrighi too had been attached to the Vatican staff, but to the Chancery; his interests were mainly in the rapid, efficient cursive hands. Ruano, while also a member of the papal entourage was, as Wardrop remarked, not a *scriptor brevium* but a *scriptor latinus*, exclusively and permanently assigned to the Library. Hence his interests lay not so much in correspondence hands as in book hands, less in rapid and efficient methodology than in theory. Sumptuous as his book was, and supported as it must have been by his influential friends, it still must have early been recognized as a failure – few of the writing books could not boast a second edition. Ruano died in 1560, the year that witnessed the appearance of one of the most influential writing-books of the century.

Chapter 9

A WIND OF CHANGE: CRESCI

Like Ruano, Gianfrancesco Cresci was also a scribe in the service of the Papal Court. Brought up in Milan, where his father had been agent and procurator for Cardinals Salviati and Cibò, Cresci moved to Rome in 1552. Four years later, possibly helped by his excellent connections but well qualified by his own talents, he received an appointment as Scriptor in the Vatican Library; in 1560 his evident capacity earned him a dual appointment as writer to the Sistine Chapel. In the same year, his first book, *Essemplare di Piu Sorti Lettere* was printed for him by Antonio Blado.[1] Despite his experience as a scribe in writing out books (and his Cassiodorus, Cod. Vat. Lat. 569, shown by Wardrop, attests to his skill), Cresci's main interest was in perfecting a practical, speedy hand for correspondence. Writing twelve years after Amphiareo's first edition, he also saw the point of mixing the chancery with the legal gothic, and likewise developed a distinctive *bastarda*, although he did not call it by that name. Disregarding Ruano's example, he saw the virtues of Amphiareo's horizontal, epistolary-inspired format. But more vital than the similarities between the two are their differences. With Cresci's first book we mark the first printed specimen of a 'baroque' development of the typical renaissance chancery hand,[2] as well as the grafting upon it of new qualities which made it an influential and long-lived commercial and especially correspondence hand: increased roundness, easier ligaturing, and increased slope, all qualities that promote increased speed.

The first edition of Cresci's book is extremely rare – the Newberry copy is both made up and defective, being completed

1. Facsimiles of *Essemplare di piu sorti lettere* (London, 1968) and *Il perfetto scrittore* (Nieuwkoop, 1972); Wardrop, 'Vatican scriptors', *Signature*, new ser. v (1948), pp. 3-28; Johnson, 37-40; Casamassima, 14-79, 91-3.
2. See above, p. 80.

with photostats from an unidentified copy. The copy in the Bibliothèque Nationale is also defective, and the Victoria and Albert Museum has only recently been able to acquire a perfect copy. The vellum dedication copy mentioned in Wardrop's *Signature* article is still tantalizingly unavailable (according to the records of L'Art Ancien, it was sold to a Prague collector before the war). The book would be well worth issuing in facsimile. The chancery hand, made according to Cresci's method, was destined to win the favour of the educated classes of Italy, France, the Netherlands, and England, and may even be found exercising its distant and attenuated influence upon English and American handwriting of the eighteenth century.[1] The hand's increased slope and marked sinuosity, arising from the consistent joining of the characters, increased the speed rapidly in the hands of a competent scrivener, despite the ornamentation and flourishing. A conspicuous decorative feature, or at least such was the intention, is the heavily weighted head (which earned the hand its name, '*testeggiato*') to the ascenders *b*, *d*, *h*, *l*; the ascenders are curved to the right and bear such heavily dotted terminals that the resulting concentration of ink on the paper of the period has frequently corroded it. Cresci's capitals are heavily embellished as a matter of course, and the '*P*' and '*V*' are frequently flourished.

Cresci, following a dedication to Cardinal Borromeo, in which he boasts of his qualifications, announces his way in a statement that was both confident and prophetic. Dissatisfied with the work of previous authors, he had sought, he says in an Epistle to the Reader, to learn and to teach a genuine method of writing cursive chancery script. He had arrived, after many years of toil, at a 'vero modo di scrivere Cancelleresco Corsivo', based upon modern, beautiful and well-based proportions. His models are both more free (*piu correnti*) and more expeditious

---

1. S. Morison, introduction to A. Heal, *The English Writing-masters and their Copy-books* (Cambridge, 1931), p. xxxi.

97

(*piu spediti*) than those handed down by earlier writers. He did not doubt that those who had already tried out his '*moderno modo di formar caratteri*' (and he instanced all the 'noble scribes of Rome' who have already put it into use) would appreciate his efforts. Those who have not done so, and initially resist the claim, will have to admit in the long run that Cresci's is the true chancery cursive script. This is our author's point: it is the business of the chancery cursive to be truly cursive, and this is the best, the only real cursive. A clerk of the Court must be quick at joining one letter to another, yet he must write cleanly and neatly; at the same time he must adorn his script with flourishes (*con alcuni tratti*) as he has shown in his specimen. The chancery script has won its place because of its added beauty and grace, as well as because of the handicaps of the older letters: the latter are slow and deliberate, and do not give the least impression of beauty or rapidity. His charge of slowness is not without substance, yet his judgment of the best writing of his predecessors is somewhat harsh.

Cresci says (and rightly) that the 'old' model, *il bastarda antico*, (the model, that is, of Arrighi, Tagliente, and Palatino) was a 'thing of points and angles'. It follows, too, that by reason of the principle of angular construction, it is none too easy to link any one letter to its neighbour. Cresci makes the technical point that slowness in writing resulted from holding the pen at too oblique an angle; in his own examples, ligatures are easily made because the letters are more rounded, the slope better adjusted, the pen point somewhat closer and rounder cut than in the past. Moreover, the flourishes are comely and yet the hand can be written quickly because of the deftness of the stroke used.

Cresci goes on to denounce artificial variations in letter form (he was thinking of *rognosa*, *tagliata*, and the like), as well as majuscules adorned with grotesques or made of ribbons or twisted boughs: 'I, and all men of good sense, consider them useless and of no importance. I do not wish to show these, which delight the immature and the frivolous, because they are a mere digression and a waste of time.'[1] Cresci evidently had in mind Palatino, whose twenty-year old *Libro Nuovo* still held the field in Rome, and Amphiareo, whose works abound with decorated capitals and held a comparable position in Venice. Moreover, Palatino was still vigorously in practice in Rome. It was necessary to free cursive from the artificial difficulties imposed by the angular school and propagate a simpler method. To write good chancery cursive was not as difficult as it was made out to be. 'In fact, one can easily learn to write the hand if the cares to write it slowly and use his common sense.'

There was much in this that was revolutionary in 1560, and more that was calculated to provoke established calligraphers of the old school such as Palatino. Palatino's retaliation did not come out until 1566, when he published the third and last revision of the *Libro nuovo* under the title *Compendio del gran volume*. Here the pages demonstrating the chancery cursive have been entirely recut in a hand similar in style to Cresci's *testeggiata*, although not so sloped. But any appearance of conversion was belied by the instructions which remain unaltered as in 1540; and, according to Cresci himself (and it is plausible enough), the new examples were not by Palatino himself at all, who, having tried and failed to write the new *tondetta*, called in Cesare Moreggio to write them for him.[2] How far this is true is hard to say; certainly no later than 1575, the date of the relevant page in the Berlin volume, Palatino was writing the *testeggiata* himself, if in a slightly shaky hand. Certainly Moreggio's name is singled out in the preface, as one who Palatino hopes will be the *exemplar* for another book he proposes. Moreggio enjoyed a high reputation among his contemporaries, although he seems to have published nothing. He is mentioned by Conretto da

1. Cresci's text, with translation by A. S. Osley, in *Essemplare* (London, 1968), p. 31.
2. *L'Idea con le circonstanze naturali che a quella si ricercano, per voler legittimamente posseder l'Arte maggiore, e minore dello scrivere* (Milan, 1622), p. 25.

Monte Regale, Gagliardelli and Luca Orfei; Gagliardelli praises him in much the same terms as he reserves for Monterchi.

It is clear however from the new 'address to the reader' that Palatino was concerned to repel an attack. He regrets that he is unable to publish in its entirety his great specimen book (the *gran volume* of the title page, a book like the Berlin and Bodleian manuscripts, presumably, but adapted to Palatino's own use like the Alunno manuscript in the British Museum). But at least, he says, the specimens that he has been able to publish show him the master of every variety of hand: he is a scribe, not a copyist with only one or two hands at his disposal. He refers obliquely to the 'modern' style, which, although called cursive is in fact a common round bastard (*bastarda ronda commune*): the trick of joining letters in it was nothing new, but as old as the type of Aldus Manutius. Finally, in a passage that must be a direct attack on Cresci, Palatino sneers at those who are incapable of designing capital letters but must borrow them from ancient inscriptions, an easy task in Rome, where there are more examples of ancient lettering than fools who vaunt one style of lettering as more important than the rest.

It is worth noting that both Cresci and Palatino refer to their opponent's chancery cursive as a 'bastarda', a circumstance that makes it no easier to define the meaning of that elusive term. It is probable that both were using the term to convey a mixture of chancery cursive and printer's italic. Cresci's complaint was one of slowness and rigidity, two difficulties implicit in Palatino's hand and theories. Palatino perhaps saw the danger in the smooth uniformity of the new cursive, his idea of even the *formata* being more fluid than that of Cresci.[1] This apart, Cresci had little difficulty in countering Palatino's objections. He reiterates the necessity of following the eye, rather than instruments, in designing capitals. Also, the relatively small number of hands is due to his anxiety to help others like himself,

1. Wardrop, *The Script of Humanism*, pp. 46-7.

with ambitions of getting on in the world. His preface to the 1570 *Il Perfetto Scrittore* is outspoken: Those who boast of their ability to write hundreds of sorts of scripts, when they try to imitate this system, will realize its value to those who wish to get on in this profession, and will understand how much they deceive themselves in wasting time on other scripts which are both foolish and futile. Many who have tried to copy these latter (i.e., *rognosa*, *tagliata*, et al.) have done so only to win a reputation as a great master, especially of those scripts without utility or beauty. Such showing off is indeed vain. First and last, writing is a practical task. Those who wish to learn to write well can, if they follow Cresci's advice, understand the methods and counsel which he as a conscientious master expounds, and can achieve that steadiness of hand necessary for writing the finest cursive. Cresci refutes the calumnies alleged by his detractors, some of whom are alleged to have stated that when he taught he never let the pupil see more than one character a day. This, he says, was a practice they followed themselves. The essential thing for the beginner is to learn the more important rules and wrinkles first. He then warms to the attack: his opponents have the defects in writing they attribute to him, holding their pens so clumsily and so pitifully that all they can turn out is a straggly, irregular, shaky letter, with lines so crooked as to be useless to their pupils. They are merely envious, talking rubbish, poorly equipped in the art of writing, not realizing that artistry and judgment – the qualities his pupils were taught – help the hand towards ability to draw any letter, 'be it Greek, Hebrew, Chaldean, or what you will'.

To return to the 1560 *Essemplare*; the prelims, besides the 'Dedication and the Epistle to the Reader', include ten pages of instructions set in Blado's small chancery italic. It is an oblong of fourteen leaves, typeset, followed by 55 numbered plates (woodcuts engraved for surface printing) and a final unnumbered arabesque cartouche. The pages are surrounded by ornamental borders in two styles: (a) baroque, decorated with *putti*, architectural motifs, etc. engraved on wood used for the prelims; (b) arabesque, engraved, apparently, on metal. The plates are prefaced with a note on their printing, in which Cresci defends the pale (*quasi smorto*) inking of the backgrounds of his inscriptional capitals, since heavier inking would have distorted the outlines of the letters themselves. He gives credit for the cutting of all the blocks to 'M. Gio. Francesco Aureri da Crema, intagliator in Roma', of whom nothing, only his work for Cresci, seems to be known.

The blocks which comprise the illustrative part of the book begin with their own title, *La vera maniera del scriver corsivo cancelleresco*; the first two quires and the first page of the third have the baroque border (thereafter the arabesque is used). The first sixteen blocks demonstrate specimens and alphabets of the chancery cursive in the expeditious form that Cresci sought to make graceful, in varying sizes; the signatures, which vary in form, attest to Cresci's Milanese origin, his residence in Rome, and his employment at the Vatican. Next come two pages of minuscule alphabets and ligatures, with variant forms of some letters: 'h' is written with four degrees of closure to its bowl, 'p' may have either a flourish or a serif to its descender, 'r' may be either ɾ or ɀ. A plate of chancery capitals (xx) gives letters with varying degrees of flourish including some (F, I, L, N, H, with an outline main stroke). There is the customary showing of abbreviations and forms of address, followed by four sample layouts of letters addressed to Princes of the Church: the Cardinals of Naples, de Medici, Boromeo [sic], and de Nobili. The next six plates, the first two entitled *Cancellaresca Formata*, show the chancery cursive with the old style ascenders in varying sizes. An untitled plate shows *Lettere de Bolle* and is dated 1559, one of the few so marked. There are several plates of mercantiles, including one of majuscules, followed by three pages of *Testeggiate* (i.e. club-head) minuscules analyzed by stroke sequence.

The section of white on black plates, even though they suffer from the under-inking required to keep the lines of the block from filling in, are exceptionally handsome. After a text in 36-point minuscules and an alphabet of formal roman titling capitals about 20 point, Cresci provides an alphabet of antique roman capitals, two to a page, each letter fifteen picas high. Cresci's capitals, he tells us in his introduction, are not made by recourse to geometry or rule, but by observation and study of the finest antique models, in which Rome abounds; he is especially fond of the inscriptional letters on the Trajan column and 'a small antique epitaph called Ossa Neronis', since disappeared.[1] Here he makes a point of importance. As a practical scribe he detaches himself from the superstitions of the earlier treatises (e.g. by Pacioli, Fanti, Moille) which overelaborated the geometrical basis of the formation of inscriptional letters.

At least seven editions of the *Essemplare* were published in Rome and Venice between 1560 and 1600. A decade after its first publication Cresci was ready with another, more ambitious work: *Il Perfetto Scrittore* (Rome, 1570) was privately printed 'In Roma in casa del proprio autore & intagliato per l'Eccellente intagliator M. Francesco Aureri da Crema', who had also been the engraver of the earlier publication. It appeared in two parts, the first of which bears a splendidly rich baroque copper-plate title-page with a portrait of the author, its text printed typographically. The new plates in this first section are all framed in deep baroque borders of which there are four varieties cut on wood; the calligraphical blocks are engraved and printed separately. It may be inferred from the otherwise inexplicable blanks in the make-up that originally the book was printed for sale in part-form and, when complete, bound up with title, privilege, dedication, epistle to the reader, and instruction, all of which are unpaged.[2] The title and privilege, which are conjugate, are on thicker paper than the rest of the prelims, which extend to

1. Once on the Porta Flaminia (C.I.L., VI. 887+31193).
2. No copies with blanks have been observed by N. B., but sheets with the borders only may have been sold as exercise sheets, like the Gagliardelli manuscript in the Victoria and Albert Museum.

8 pages. The bulk of Part I, consisting of 46 leaves, is on thinner paper, printed letterpress. The several hands are each preceded by a page or more of description and instruction.

The first of these is the *Lettera Cancellaresca chiamata formatella*, i.e., a chancery hand not fully formal, appropriate for letters and books, with 7 pages of specimens. It is a plain version of Cresci's characteristic *testeggiata*, with ligatures generally made by convenience rather than rule. These conclude with minuscule and majuscule alphabets. *Lettera Cancellaresca alquanto corrente*, which follows, is given 5 specimens, including alphabets; it is a curious, highly flourished version of the preceding having the alternative ſ form of *h*, gothic *e* as well as chancery *e*, and a flattened final *i*. *Cancellaresca corrente*, for those who have mastered 1 and 2, is a more strongly sloped cursive, with ſ form of *h* with flourished ascenders and gothic *e*; its nine specimens include a plate of majuscule alphabet in both simple and flourished form and another of lower case. There follow 5 plates of *Abbreviature Cancellaresche correnti*, in the same style. *Lettera Cancellaresca antica nuovamente ritrovata*, is called 'antica' because it is written according to the same rule as the antique roman capitals which are, in a sense, its parent script. This is the 'novelty' which distinguishes it from the *formata* that in other ways it so much resembles. These specimens he shows will, Cresci says, refute the charge that he had merely copied the types (*stampa*) of Aldus and Griffo. The *antica* is shown in 9 pages of blocks, all of which are in large (i.e., not less than 30-point) size; the text used is Latin, either from the Vulgate or the liturgy; the script is in fact the equivalent of a sloped old-face, with bracketed serifs. Five are reverse blocks. If there is no reason why it should be called *cancellaresca* it was nevertheless obviously, in Cresci's mind, an 'italic'; the new form had a dominating influence on formal book-script. It was the basis of the *formata, formatella* and *formatellina* of all the subsequent writing books.

Lettera antica tonda is to Cresci the 'Queen of the letters'. It commands two pages of text and seven of specimens, all white on black and extremely well cut and printed. On account of its supreme excellence and dignity, he says, it is a true text of scribal ability, not at all so easy to write as some misleading teachers have vainly pretended. He has used the antique chancery, the antique capitals, and the antique round in large sizes and reverse blocks to show them off to best advantage. The *antica tonda* is the stylized humanistic roman of the late sixteenth century, with ﬄ ligature, and both forms of 'h': ƕ, h. Lower case 'k' has no ascender. Two pages of classical capitals complete the section.

Lettera Ecclesiastica comprises 11 pages of round gothic minuscule and majuscule appropriate to the writing of Missals, Graduals, and Antiphonaries. These, white on black, reproduce in large size Latin Biblical and liturgical texts. Unlike most others, Cresci does not recommend the use of the straight pen for this type of letter. *Lettera Bollatica* is used solely in Rome, by the Apostolic scriveners for the engrossing of Bulls. The specimen given, Cresci says, is the older form, rather than that in current use, and is the true *Bollatica*. There are five examples of this large legal gothic cursive, written with the pen fully slanted, followed by seven of *Lettera Bollatica Formata*: a large, formal but flourished legal gothic, including a minuscule alphabet and two majuscules, one of the latter, a highly decorated and very narrow version. *Lettera Mercantile Bastarda nuovamente ritrouata* is a compound of chancery, Italian gothic secretary, French gothic secretary and, according to Cresci, a dash (*alquanto*) of Spanish. It is useful, he says, for bookkeeping and correspondence on account of its ligatures. The specimens are bills of exchange, etc., with alphabets. *Lettera Francese* is used in Rome for legal and other business, Cresci says, and so he gives alphabets and two specimens, one *naturale*, the other *bastarda*. Part I concludes with a typographic colophon.

Part II, the same size and oblong format as Part I, has a typographic title-page within copperplate baroque scroll-work border. The prelims include a dedication to Mons. Salviati, '*Clerico*

della Reverenda Camera Apostolica et Presidente della Annona', followed by discourses on 'Maiuscole antiche Romane' and 'Maiuscole Cancellaresche a Groppi'. Cresci's antique capitals are
based, he tells us, on long and close study of the Roman monuments, certainly the best possible models; he has had the alphabet printed twice, one against a deep black ground for those
who have demanded this, a second time against a lighter inked,
grey black, which shows off the lines of the letters with greater
sharpness and clarity. The second set, his knotted chancery capitals, are a proof of virtuosity; all scribes wish to demonstrate
their ability to create new decorated alphabets, most of which
are poor; he has been the first to apply his ingenuity to the
adornment of the Chancery majuscules, and is pleased with the
result. He has had these engraved on copper and printed for
the benefit of painters and miniaturists, as well as goldsmiths,
sculptors, and kindred virtuosi.

The first alphabet of antique capitals, that on deep black
grounds, is surrounded with arabesque borders made up of fitted
sidepieces. Q and R are on a double page spread, the tail of the Q
extending well below the R; the whole is a single large block
whose cutting and printing are considerable feats of craftsmanship. The second alphabet, that on grey, has no borders; the Q
and R seem to have been recut (there may well have been an
accident to the other block) and are bordered with thick and
thin rules, cut on the block. The copperplate *entrelac* letters are
enclosed by elaborate baroque borders and printed on heavier
paper. They are, as Cresci intended them, a tour de force of calligraphic ingenuity. The plate for I carries the monogram of
Andrea Marelli in the border.

Almost another decade passed before the publication of Cresci's *libro terzo, Il perfetto cancelleresco corsivo*, which was printed
in Rome by Pietro Spada in 1579, 'ad instantia dell'Autore, e di
M. Pietro Paulo Palombo'. If the *Essemplare* was in the nature
of a revolutionary tract and *Il perfetto scrittore* an idealist demonstration, Cresci's third book was severely practical. He had

by now left the Vatican, but, clearly, without abandoning his Roman contacts. At the same time, he had obviously been struck by the more commercial needs of the industrial north. *Il perfetto cancelleresco corsivo* is addressed to the professional secretary: it advocates not merely the proper writing of the different hands for different kinds of document, but knowledge of different tongues, good draftsmanship, and other qualifications of the secretary, at court or elsewhere. The 52 examples demonstrate the *tondetta*, first elaborate and with multiple strokes, then simplified; next comes Cresci's 'invention', the *lettera corsiva*, and then, in succession, the *cancelleresca aperta*, the *corsiva senza tratti*, the *carattere trattegiato*, and the *formatella*. The results are not markedly different to the modern eye: in 1579, they must have struck the professional writers to whom they were directed as fine tuning of a high-powered instrument.

The need for this was emphasized by the *libro quarto*, published (significantly) at Venice and dated 1579, under the title *Avertimenti di Gio. Francesco Cresci, Scrittore, Gentilhuomo Milanese, intorno li errori, et false opinioni commesse nella professione dello scrivere, nuovamente posti in luce*. The printer was Pietro Dehuchino, once more 'ad instantia dell'Autore, e di M. Pietro Paulo Palumbo'; the dedication is to Bishop Antonio Maria Salviati. This is a straight-forward piece of letterpress, directed, as a series of punning references in chapter 8 make clear, at the new young star, Marcello Scalzini or Scalino of Camerino, of whom more presently. The odd thing is that Cresci's counterblast predates Scalzini's *Il secretario* by two years; evidently his methods were not unknown, book or no book. Scalzini's offence was to call in question not only the merits of the book scripts of which Cresci was master, but also the whole delicate apparatus of acceleration, the gradual diminution of strokes with increased currency, which constituted his 'method'.

There are, Cresci says, those who will offer to teach you all about writing in two or three months. Nonsense; writing needs practice, children must be started young: those whose *cartoni* advertise 15-20 day courses are liars. 'Trattegiare', the art of flourishing, is not the secret of success. It is not true that those who know many cannot be perfect in all styles of writing: mastery of the *formatella cancelleresca*, the *cancelleresca formata* and the *antica tonda* is no bar to writing *corsivo*. He asserts the advantage of technical aids such as prepared paper, and pours scorn on the irregular letters introduced by others as vile in form and inconvenient to use. He ends by commending a score of masters in different cities, among them, in Rome, the elusive but pervasive Cesare Moreggio, his own pupil Giovanni Luigi Mercato and 'M. Luca Orfei di Fano'.

There was also another Cresci *Quarto Libro di Lettere Formatello & Cancellaresche corsive*, printed in Rome by Pietro Spada in 1596 and published by Silvio Valesi. It contains a new alphabet of *lettera Ecclesiastica* credited to Fulgentio Valesi, a Cistercian monk. Cresci's examples show both formal and cursive chancery hands; a poor engraver, or perhaps Cresci's deteriorating skill, led in many instances to such gross exaggeration of the dotted heads that they became deformities. Several of the plates are dated 1579 and 80; there may have been an edition before 1596, but I have found no record of one. I shall postpone discussion of it until later, since it was obviously influenced by other masters whom we have not yet reached.

Despite the careful and stylish formality of the specimens labelled *Formata* or *Formatella*, Cresci's general practice was to turn away from the formal. The style which he practised with perfection and with which his name is identified is the *Lettera Cancellaresca corrente*. Cresci, it has been seen, was anxious to increase the speediness of the Chancery hand. Both the Arrighi of two generations before and his immediate predecessor Palatino addressed audiences made up of secretaries first and the general public second. All their chancery cursives were not only formal but exact. They were professionalised in such a way as to be, in fact, half-cursives. Cresci was the first to reach and exemplify a liberated Chancery cursive that would suit the free correspondence needs of the expanding writing public as well as those of the professional, i.e. writing masters. This was an aim in which he had been anticipated only by Amphiareo.

The latter advocated not the canonical chancery modified for speed but a mixed variety, a *bastarda*. In the mind of Arrighi, Tagliente and Palatino the *cancellaresca* was a vehicle for Latin written by professionals or those who wanted to be secretaries. Cresci made the secretarial, formal, Latin, Chancery cursive a vernacular medium. He did this, as has been seen, mainly by increasing its slope, therefore its flow, consequently its speed. Cresci, as a writer in the Apostolic Chancery, well knew that a Latin text required a formal type of chancery cursive if such a script was, in general, regarded as appropriate. But Cresci's specimens of current Chancery cursive are in Italian which quite properly may be written in a looser, faster hand. This is logical enough. But the extent – and it was far-reaching – to which the full cursive was used for vernacular purposes inevitably affected the semi-cursive used for Latin. In due time this presence of the vernacular induced Cresci's successors in the Apostolic Chancery to adopt the full cursive.

Thus for two generations after Cresci left Rome (about 1572), down to the turn of the century, the papal briefs were written in the style that Cresci himself had first taken so large a part in establishing and popularizing.

But the career of the Chancery cursive in the fully current style could hardly be arrested at the point of currency where *Il Perfetto Scrittore* left it in 1570. This was impossible, quite apart from the changes to be expected as a result of the emulation of scribes. Speed is a quality which inevitably accelerates once it is consciously sought, secured, and recommended on the basis of the kind of technical change which can be hailed as an improvement. Cresci yielded reasonably to the need and entailments of speed whereas his successors sacrificed much more in terms of form. If the master looped an occasional l *ℓ*, his pupils would loop frequently; if he permitted an occasional medial round d ꝺ, his pupils would make a feature of it. Worst of all, Cresci did not scruple to bastardize ℰ e, ſ h, ɩ r; Amphiareo had done the same thing, in a more conservative way, in his *cancellaresca bastarda* (Cresci, too, showed a *mercantesca bastarda* compounded of elements of Chancery, mercantile, and notarial). Both Amphiareo and Cresci were working in the same direction, that is, to extend the vernacular, domestic or commercial correspondence the rationalistic elements inherent in the Chancery script, originally limited to diplomatic Latin and classical texts.

How difficult it was to maintain even official Chancery script in the orthodox calligraphic formality exhibited by Arrighi may be seen if the briefs of Leo X are compared with those of Clement IX. It has been seen that in vernacular Italian writing Chancery formality was diluted or we might say, 'inflated'. It could hardly be otherwise. Writers of Latin were seldom called upon to write messages at speed, while writers of Italian were constantly called upon to accelerate. Thus the vernacular was bound to dominate a situation in which Latin, after Dante, receded before Italian.

Moreover, as seen by Amphiareo, being a teacher in Florence and afterwards in Venice (both commercial cities) the need was less for an extension of diplomatic Chancery than for a reformation of the hands habitual in commerce. His *bastarda*, bred out of crossing the old mercantile with the new Chancery, was a highly practical solution. Cresci's *Cancellaresca Corsiva Corrente* is a different *bastarda*, bred out of crossing the old gothic secretary with the new Chancery.

Of the two, it was inevitable that Cresci's version should win. Where Amphiareo had produced an acceptable mixture of the best parts of two kinds of writing, a good compromise in terms of what was currently available, Cresci had thought more deeply. His *corsiva corrente* dominates the host of writing books which poured from the press in Italy in the next eighty years. The influence in other countries of the 'Italian' hand, legible and distinguished, had been hitherto mainly restricted to documents and books in Latin. In 1560, the vernacular hands were still far from extinct for writing in the vernacular. Cresci, by producing a hand which was (in mass) as attractive as the original *cancelleresca corsiva*, but more self-contained and above all far faster than any other, forced the Italian invasion into the remaining vernacular strongholds. No commercial employer of scribes could afford to ignore it, and by 1640 this transformation of European hand-writing was almost complete, spreading even to the manner if not the letterforms of German. After 1640 the flood of Italian writing books, one of the vehicles of the transformation, began to dry up: no further development took place, and, the commercial battle won, the stimulus to change ceased. Many of the books published after 1560 have much to commend them, but Cresci's manuals decided the volume of examples of the main text hand (of which the majority consisted); they also dictated the nature of the other material shown. If Arrighi was the main force in the first half of this account, there can be no doubt that Cresci was an even more dominant force in the second.

Chapter 10

CHANGE AND DEGENERATION: 1565-1590

Some time after 1565 (the date on some of the plates) and before 1568 (when a second edition, with dated title-page appeared) a Carthusian, Don Augustino da Siena, published at Venice a book in the old upright format of Arrighi, Palatino, and Tagliente, thus rejecting the new oblong shape begun by the Franciscan, Amphiareo.[1] The Carthusian's Chancery hand is accompanied by engraved instructions as in Arrighi and Palatino. Unlike them, however, Don Augustino stresses the mercantile almost equally. He provides 26 specimens (the Chancery varieties are given 36) with copious instructions; he also shows the ecclesiastical hands, ribboned gothic, and bizarre and barbarous Beneventan-gothic of the sort that the scribes called *Lettera Todescha*. His *Cancellarescha da Notari* is a neat hand of the kind used for briefs, but with round d ẟ, gothic r ꝛ, gothic s ꞩ, and humanistic ɗ. This plate is signed 'Ego domnus Augustinus Senensis scripsi Tempore Papae Julii tertii', i.e., Pope Julius III, who died in 1555. Despite the wood-cut borders, made up of side pieces, and an attempt to decorate the plates with birds, flowers, and *trompe l'oeil* cherubs breaking through the page, this is altogether a mediocre book, even though printed in Venice which was certainly capable of producing fine work at the time, as may be seen from the bibliographies of the Duc de Rivoli.

The reader will have noticed the preponderance of two centres – Rome and Venice – in the publication of Italian writing-books to this date. Only Verini of the masters discussed (I exclude Moyllus, whose book is an architect's not a scribe's book) was published elsewhere. Throughout most of this period, Venice was the leading printing and publishing centre not only of Italy

1. *Augustino da Siena: the 1568 Edition of his Writing-book in Facsimile*, ed. A. Fairbank, (London, Merrion Press, 1975); Johnson, pp. 40-1.

but of Europe. Rome was also highly important, primarily because it was the centre of the Papacy and hence the seat of the Apostolic Chancery and Courts. It is odd that Florence, which according to Mr Johnson's figures, based on the British Museum collection, was far more active in general book publishing than Rome (while Venice produced as many books as the other two combined) should contribute no writing books.[1] One assumes that probably Venetian and Roman distribution methods supplied the Florentine market, as well as that of other provincial cities. Certainly Italy did not lack for provincial printers – F. Ascarelli lists more than 100 towns which had presses during the century;[2] many of these men working outside the largest cities possessed considerable skill, as the work of Petrucci at Fossombrone, or the Soncinos at Fano, will attest.

Among the more important publishing centres, naturally, was Bologna. During the preceding centuries it had been the home of the oldest and most important university in the peninsula, since the twelfth century the dominant school of jurisprudence. Its importance as a typographical centre is well indicated in Dr Curt Bühler's *The University & the Press in Fifteenth Century Bologna* (Notre Dame, 1958), and it provided a considerable market for books. It was also the home of an innovative calligrapher, Giuliantonio Hercolani, whose first book appeared in 1571. His book, however interesting for its place of publication, is more important for its introduction of a new engraving process into the Italian manuals of handwriting.

In Italy, skilled engravers had long been worked in copperplate, producing pattern-books, single prints, and occasional book illustrations, but above all maps. Copperplates had occasionally been used for book illustration in fifteenth-century Italian books (notably the 1477 Florentine *Monte Santo di Dio*, printed by Nicolaus Lorenz of Breslau and the 1481 Dante,

1. A. F. Johnson, 'Italian Sixteenth-Century Books', *Selected Essays on Books and Printing*, ed. P. H. Muir (Amsterdam, 1970), pp. 110-11.
2. F. Ascarelli, *La tipografia cinquecentina italiana* (Florence, 1953).

with engravings after Botticelli, from the same printer). This problem of double impression – relief for the type and intaglio for the illustrations – was too difficult, however, and so the printers soon turned to wood-cut relief blocks, type high, which could be printed simultaneously, except for unusual categories of books. Among the latter were the geographies – usually editions of Ptolemy – where they continued to employ copperplate for some time, printing the maps separately and binding them in, either as double-page spreads or together at the end. The first printed Ptolemy (Vicenza, 1475) had no maps; the second, printed at Bologna and wrongly dated 1462 (it is generally considered to be from 1477) had copperplate maps, as did that printed by Conrad Sweynheym at Rome the following year. There were two fifteenth century German editions of Ptolemy, printed at Ulm, which had woodcut maps, but the Italians continued to use metal plates for their maps until 1511, in which year a Venetian edition carried woodcuts.[1] Thereafter there was a considerable break.

The Italian printers, during the first half of the sixteenth century, were apparently of the opinion that cutting on hard wood offered a sounder printing surface than engraving on soft copper, and was more economical. Except for special subjects, such as maps, this had also been the consensus in the fifteenth century. Copper was useful, if at all, for single-sheet prints; at this period Italy virtually rejected copper-plate for use in books. Yet this was the process that was destined to take precedence over relief printing for book illustrations. In the struggle for the calligraphical fittest it was the intaglio technique, first used in Germany for the elder Neudörffer's *Gute Ordnung und Kurtze Unterricht . . . die Jungen Zierlich Schreybens . . .* (Nuremberg, 1538), that triumphed.[2] The Nuremberg master, it is relevant to notice, included two plates of Roman capitals and one of classical Ro-

---

1. T. Campbell, *The Earliest Printed Maps, 1472-1500* (London, British Library, 1987), pp. 122-141.
2. Doede, no. 3.

man Chancery, used for Latin texts in a sort of supplement to the body of the work, which was devoted to German Chancery scripts, with German texts, that originated in the court of the Emperor Maximilian. They represent a nauseous hybrid of gothic and baroque. The script is remarkable for the puerile degree to which embellishment is preferred to legibility; copperplate was a godsend to these artists even if at first it involved, apparently, highly complicated cutting and printing problems. Apparently Neudörffer's engraver could not master cutting in reverse, which is necessary for printing, and so the examples were transfer-printed on to another place for recutting in reverse. This is an operation rather like modern photography, which demands a negative master to provide a positive print. One reason for the greater use of copper in Germany than in Italy may have been the greater local abundance of the metal as well as of skilled metal-workers; Germany had been for centuries the European home of the metal trades.

In 1548 and thereafter we again find copper-engraving in Italian Ptolemies; the small Venetian edition of that year had skillfully cut maps whose inscriptions (in roman and an upright italic) were probably inserted from punches.

While it may have been the German printing technique that triumphed, it did so in association with the Roman chancery script; just as, in typography, it is the German invention that has come down to us while using the Roman letter and its companion italic, itself indebted to the Roman Chancery.

The spread and general progress of Roman Chancery script, the so-called italic hand, was less rapid in the sixteenth century than might be imagined from the number of manuals published. Certainly, the script in its several adaptations and variations found its way into many literary and domestic uses, but two generations after Arrighi's *Operina* were required to break the back of the old, Gothic, round, upright, looped and complicated hands familiar in the counting-houses of the merchants of Venice and elswhere in Italy. Even so, the adoption of the Chancery script by writers in Italian was a relatively easy transition. The supersession of gothic secretary by the Chancery script for the work required by French, Dutch, Netherlandish and English businessmen was a difficult process. Scholars and courtiers were easy to persuade. For one thing, the old Gothic secretary-commercial hands had, during their career, acquired a vast number of ligatures, abbreviations, and signs. The superior shorthand value of the old and familiar was valued, and there were tendencies at work in the circles that sponsored the new script that were unlikely to conciliate the conservatives. They thought the old gothic, whatever Petrarch might think of it, a practical script. Any decoration that grew out of it was welcome. Amphiareo had plenty of it for those who desired it, while his Chancery script was plain, like Arrighi's and Palatino's. As has been seen, Cresci began the tendency towards a decorative Chancery hand.

Hercolani had virtues other than his employment of the new technique which has evoked so long a digression. His *Essemplare Varie di Tutte le Sorti di L're Cancellaresche Correntissime* . . . (Bologna, probably 1571, the date of most of the plates) is the first Italian engraved manual of calligraphy[1] (I except Cresci's book of the year before, in which he had used copperplate for a set of interlaced initials large in size and abominable in design, intended to grace the introits in antiphonaries, etc.). The first edition is an exceedingly rare book; the Newberry copy and that recorded by Jessen (No. 5188) seem to be the only ones known. It is a most elegant production. As the title indicates, the author taught the 'most current' version of the chancery script. Its author was a doctor in theology in law of his university and Canon of Bologna. An artist of some modesty and yet a considerable innovator, he abstained fittingly from making any idle claim to be the 'inventor' of any new script. What he did was to develop the style of Cresci. The Canon's analysis of the full

1. Johnson, p. 41; Casamassima, pp. 75-6.

chancery cursive simplifies it into strokes and dashes. These he shows in a beautiful diagram which illustrates the correct holding of the pen. Similar cuts had earlier appeared in the books of Mercator and Fugger, in the Netherlands and Germany. Hercolani's is the first appearance in an Italian manual that I recall of the kind of diagram which is one of the stereotypes of the writing-book, surviving into the nineteenth century.

The three strokes thus formed according to the nature of the pen 'will produce a well-written chancery script'. In forming the *Cancellaresca Circonflessa* (his second and third plates), care is needed to see that it is rounded in body, in contrast to the '*acuta*' (plate 20), a polished version of Arrighi's hand.

The book is intended for secretaries and provides formalised specimens of the hands he found acceptable at the time in the Chanceries of the princes of Italy as well as of the Holy Roman Empire. It is uncertain whether the models put forward by Hercolani had widespread use in ordinary business. The specimens shown in Professor Vincenzo Federici's *La Scrittura delle Cancellerie Italiane dal secolo XII al XVII* (Rome, 1934) do not encourage the view that there had yet been anything like a widespread and standardised adoption of the Papal chancery script in the provincial chanceries.

The personal interpretation of the Chancery Script which the scribe describes as '*littere circonflesse del'Hercolani*' is rather more upright than Cresci's, slightly rounder in the body, not so heavily weighted in the serifs. As a piece of writing Hercolani's is a highly distinguished performance, given a brilliant setting by his fine anonymous engraver and first-class printer.

The sight of it would have astonished Arrighi who, half a century earlier, had felt the need to caution the reader that engraving (he meant engraving for surface printing) could not completely represent the living hand, a warning piously repeated by most of his successors. The time was approaching when the complaint would be that copper flattered the 'living hand', even enticed it – so that ultimately, in the 'copperplate hand', the acquired characteristics influenced the organism itself.[1] The conservative Silvio Valesi of Parma alludes to this danger in the preface to his 1596 edition of Cresci, where he argues that however pleasant to the eye copper may be it cannot give greater '*perfettione*', seeing that wood is '*piu al naturale*'. One would like to know the comparative costs of production to a publisher interested in the proposal to print, either by intaglio or relief. Valesi elected the method that Cresci had chosen in 1560 and 1570, and the 1596 Cresci is still printed from relief blocks. Hercolani's engraver, no doubt, flattered the living hand. By all appearances he was competent and probably well paid.

By this time engravers had vastly improved their skill in cutting, and their printers the art of reproducing, intaglio plates. The map-makers had much responsibility for the improvement. The engravers hesitated to give the cartographers the benefit of Cresci's 'baroque' Chancery; in small sizes it was wasteful of space, less legibile, and harder to read than the older *cancellaresca formata*. They used it for the legends in cartouches, and for large, swash inscriptions on seas, continents, etc., but where space was at a premium they recognized its unsuitability. In Rome, usually on large maps (as in those of the Lafreri atlas), cartographers occasionally imitated Cresci's heavily-weighted baroque serifs, although not in their most exaggerated form, for place-names etc. In Venice the older style (*cancellaresca formata*) always prevailed, and it was not long before cartography as a whole, even in Rome, reverted to the same style for the burden of its work.

The baroque letter won ground steadily, however, among the printsellers and illustrators, who saw its decorative possibilities to enhance title-pages, captions, borders, and the like. Obviously in maps legibility, plain and undefiled, was the prime virtue; even in Germany one finds, in the incunable Ptolemies printed

1. Cresci, *L'Idea*, p. 89.

at Ulm, not that the place names are delinated in gothic but in fere-humanistica. The second great requisite on a crowded map is spatial ecomony, and the cartographers used italic for the same reason that Aldus had – it took less room. In cursive writing, however, flourish was less out of place; indeed, it became difficult to separate the two. Moreover, the access to skilled copper-engravers, trained in the mapmakers' studios and capable of decoration when it was demanded, so tempted calligraphers, intent upon astonishing their rivals, into excesses of flourishing that legibility was sacrificed to expertise. It would be unjust to blame the copperplate engravers entirely for the situation; Tagliente, after all, had attempted it with woodblocks. Copperplate simply made it possible to carry the process further.

But the improved technique helped something more than the tendency to adorn. The engraver in relief who served Arrighi and Tagliente – or Cresci, for that matter – could never have produced the kind of diagrammatic plate made possible two generations later. Undoubtedly there were highly skilled engravers earlier – even in the fifteenth century, as we can discover in any Print Room – but for some reason (probably economic) they were not available to the printers and publishers of the books, especially of such cheap works as writing-manuals, until about this period. Ugo da Carpi and Eustachio Celebrino, working on wood, could not equal in minuteness and delicacy of engraving of, say, Martin van Buyten.

Hercolani's first edition, the *Essemplare Utile . . .*, is dedicated on the title-page to Cardinal Paleotti; next comes a splendidly ornamented Gothic L, with *putti*, mythological figures, etc., featuring a stalwart Hercules, the whole typical of the period's delight in visual puns; this serves as initial for *Lettori*; similarly decorated letters (M and G) are used as introductions to later sections of the book. Among the most handsomely engraved and laid out plates in the book are three pages of instruction which follow: the first two, on the Canon's *Cancellaresca Circonflessa*, are written in that hand and incorporate detailed instructions for cutting the pen.[1] Hercolani was particularly keen upon properly cut pens, and frequently includes an illustration of the appropriate nib when he discusses a hand. The third, previously mentioned, shows two fists holding pens, the 'courtly' (*signorilmente*) and common methods of holding the pen, and of making the three strokes employed in his method of writing. The bulk of the first section of the book is devoted to the *circonflessa*, a rounded and slightly inclined chancery script with normal-weighted *testeggiatura* heads to its curved ascenders. He provides minuscule and majuscule alphabets, abbreviations, and numerous plates of model flourished addresses with specimen epistles whose recipients range from the Pope and the Emperor down through other clerical dignitaries to members of his own family. These are all executed with a sure sense of style and layout. He also provided specimens of *cancellaresca acuta*, narrower in body, more sloped, and with slightly reduced ascenders and descenders; a plate demonstrates the differences of the two by means of ruled spaces, with model letters, for writing each. Hercolani's third chancery script, *lettera commune et corrente*, is highly recommended to secretaries, notaries, scribes, and merchants; it employs more ligatures than the other chancery scripts shown, has relatively more slope, and uses several forms from the gothic: *ħ*, as well as *h*; *ι* and *r*; *δ* (d). The various chancery scripts all demand the application of Hercolani's *Regole nuove* for good writing: the angle of slope must be the same throughout all the letters, and all the parts of each letter; if the body of a letter is upright (*diritto*), so must its ascender or descender be; if sloped (*pendente*), consistency must apply again.

Besides his three chancery varieties, Hercolani shows mercantile and notarial scripts, which do not much interest him; they are given the briefest of directions, and cursory demonstrations, as is his *Lettera da bolle*. *Lettera moderna*, on the contrary, does interest him, and he devotes three plates to round gothic minuscule, abbreviations, and ligatures; these are handsomely en-

1. Johnson, fig. 4, p. 42.

graved, broad outline letters with the delicate shading made possible by copperplate; a demonstration of the technique of interlacing ('groppi') is likewise enhanced by the engraver's skill. He also provides two majuscule alphabets: the first, in four plates, is an elaborate ornamented gothic, with grotesques, human figures, architectural details, etc., the first to be shown in an Italian printed writing-manual, although similar material had long appeared in the writing-masters' and illuminators' manuscript specimen books and been issued as collections of plates.[1] His classical capitals are outline letters, filled in with stippling. They are neither so free nor so sure as the decorated letters.

Hercolani's second book came out in 1574; *Lo Scrittor' Utile*... (can its title be a riposte to Cresci's *Scrittore Perfetto*?), is an expanded reissue of his first book. Apparently during the interval its author had consolidated his position, for this new venture appeared under the patronage of Cardinal Sansisto, and has a plate dedicating the work to two others: Cardinals Guastavillani and di Vercello. Most of the plates are the same, although many have either been altered or entirely recut to carry the date 1574. Some of the addresses have been changed or edited, several of the plates having been cut and reassembled to allow for this. Some of the changes are so minor that it is difficult to understand why either author or printer should have bothered, e.g. that demonstrating ruling sheets for practice, where the intervals between the lines have been filled in by cross-hatching, but the letters showing slope and size of ascenders and descenders remain the same. There are variant issues of the edition, one (at the Metropolitan Museum in New York and the Victoria & Albert Museum, London) dedicated to Cardinal Paleotti and having six more plates; another, also at the Victoria and Albert

1. H. Lehmann-Haupt and Norman Petteway, 'Human Alphabets', *Amor Librorum* (Amsterdam, 1958), shows several plates from Hercolani's ornamented grotesque alphabet, as well as a single letter from the alphabet of Paulini, dated c. 1570 – a set in which each letter is given a handsome emblematic landscape background. The article also shows a number of illustrations of contemporary manuscript alphabets very similar in style to Hercolani's.

Museum, has four leaves of italic letterpress with directions for making ink (*Giunta del Sig.* Giuliantonio Hercolani), with the imprint reading 'In Bologna, Per Alessandro Benacci.'.

Despite the seeming advantages of copperplate – the plates are less prone to damage than wood blocks, and give sharper reproduction – it did not take over the writing-book field immediately; Cresci's disapproval was not unique, and a number of manuals from woodblocks continued to appear after the publication of Hercolani's epochal book. The scarceness of copper in Italy may have made it an expensive process; the lack of engraving presses among the publishers may have been the explanation; or perhaps it was simply the innate conservatism of the book trade. Conretto da Monte Regale's *Un Novo et Facil Modo d'Imparar a Scrivere* ... (Venice, 1576) reverts to the old relief technique. Its author, who describes himself on the title-page as 'Scribe, Arithmetician, and Geometrician', a native of Piedmont, was Professor of Mathematics at the University of Paris later in his career, if we accept him as the 'Monte Regale, Piemontoise' who published a work on arithmetic at Lyons in 1585.[1] His prelims, set in italic surrounded by arabesque borders, include a dissertation on the best and most famous Italian scribes, among whom he ranks Vespasiano, Palatino, and Cresci, as well as a number of others who apparently published no work. The type-set materials also include directions for cutting pens, forming the letters, writing in gold, silver, and colours, and so forth. Conretto's blocks are heavily indebted to Cresci's example, but certainly not so well cut and probably not as well written. His *corsivo cancellaresco* has extremely heavily-weighted *testeggiatura* ascenders; in several plates the curved ascenders have been straightened and the dots exaggerated into filled-in loops, A number of the plates are signed as from Florence. Among the chancery scripts exhibited is a *moderna*, with gothic *a* and chancery *r r*, open o *o*, and almost complete ligaturing; *corsiva tonda*,

1. Johnson, pp. 41, 43; C. Marzoli, *Calligraphy 1535-1885* (Milan, 1962), pp. 46-7.

as its name suggests, somewhat less angular; and *formata*, a book hand with short ascenders and descenders, a few ligatures, and bracketed serifs. Mercantiles interested Conretto little, and received only four plates, as opposed to 26 for Chancery scripts. He also showed *Bolatica moderna*, an eccentric letter with flourished ascenders reminiscent of *fraktur*; *moderna formata*, a conventional round gothic; *antiqua tonda* in both ordinary and reverse blocks; a number of decorated alphabets, some of them of exceptional ugliness; and two alphabets of roman capitals, considerably better done.

Salvadore Gagliardelli's collection (Florence, 1583) of the methods of addressing dignitaries of church and state is also relief printed.[1] *Soprascritte di Lettere in Forma Cancelleresca, Corsiva* . . . was apparently highly successful, filling a definite need in a status-conscious age, for it went into a second, augmented edition the same year; the first edition gives the forms of address for 236 worthies, ranging from the Pope to mere *Signori*, all nicely graduated by rank and degree of formality; the second edition splits the hairs even finer, stretching it to 267 numbered titles and an odd blank for anybody omitted. The work is less interesting for any novelty in its script than for the extent of its text. Gagliardelli's 20 pages of type-set prelims (in the augmented reprint) include, besides the conventional Dedication and Epistle to the Reader, detailed annotation on each of the forms of address listed; they also provide a clearly set out and well reasoned table of the principal forms of letter in current use: Maiuscule Antiche Romane; Lettera Antica tonda; Lettera Formata antica; Lettera Formata da privilegi; Lettera Ecclesiastica over formata da libri di Chiese; Lettera Formata cancelleresca; Lettera Cancelleresca corsiva da principianti; Lettera corsiva graxiosa. Each is illustrated by key letters: G; C; M; O; B; F; S; Z, and the uses of each distinguished. He emphasizes the importance of inscriptional letters, and praises three of his contemporaries, Francesco da Monterchi, Cesare Moreggio and

1. Johnson, p. 43; Casamassima, pp. 76, 94.

Cresci. His own correspondence hand is closely related to Cresci and Hercolani. It is obvious that copperplate would have suited Gagliardelli's hand and book. The latter is sumptuous, with its borders specially cut for 'Il Gagliardello Scrittore in Fior.', but it had been far surpassed technically by Hercolani's printer and by the Venetians.

A book like Scalzini's *Il Secretario* (Venice, 1581) would have been unthinkable even to Cresci as a young man.[1] Scalino, as he later called himself, was an innovator in more than one respect; his innovations were partially made possible, and certainly exaggerated, by the possibilities inherent in copperplate printing. He received the bare rudiments of his craft, he tells us, from Scipione Cristiani, a superb writer unequalled in all Italy, according to his pupil, but otherwise unknown. Scalino came from Camerino (a town famous for its writing paper) to Rome at the age of twelve; his first book, printed by Domenico Nicolini at Venice in 1581, was dedicated to Cardinal Sirleto, prefect of the Vatican Library (was this carrying the war into Cresci's own ground?), and carried both Papal and Venetian privileges. A practical scribe, Scalino appealed to experience against theory; this, in his case, was equivalent to a championship of Cresci's method and style. Scalino espoused a variation of the style of Cresci (though not, of course, mentioning the master) as, indeed, any professional between 1560 and 1590 was bound to do. But there was a subtle and notable difference, how individual it is difficult to say.

There were at least eight editions of *Il Secretario*: despite the author's caution in obtaining double privileges, all those editions between 1581 and 1608 were piracies – 'copie false, stippiate, & difforme', he complains on the title-page of his *Regole Nuove* (Brescia, 1608, probably printed in Venice), the work of Madonna Elena Morosina, Tedesca, and her agents; he is bitter about the poor engraving of the plates and the vulgarity of

1. Johnson, pp. 44-5; Casamassima, pp. 76, 95; Marzoli, pp. 48-51. A. S. Osley, *Scalzini on Handwriting* (Wormley, 1971).

their decoration in these unauthorized and audacious counterfeits, which even reprinted the privileges to their rightful holder. The piracies are literal reprints of the originals, not as inferior as their author considered them. They even carry the praise given by Scalino to the engraver of the plates of the first edition, Giacomo Franco, himself the author of a later copy-book, who was probably not responsible for the new set.

Scalino tells curious stories about his prowess. At note 86, on page 12 of his 1608 edition (he tends to mix personalia and instruction in a rather haphazard fashion) he says that 'I even remember that when I passed through Milan in 1581, I argued with a famous old scribe, whose name I won't mention, so as not to injure him, who told me that he had taught *Il Camerino* to write during a three year period. This was the first time I had ever seen him, and I told him so, whereupon he blushed, for he certainly did not know me.'

In a later note, Number 166 on page 30, he explains the form of his name: 'The reason why I am sometimes signed as Scalzino and not as Scalino, as I now style myself, is this; when I first lived in Rome, a man from Venice of the same name – he is still living, and writes excellently – who is no relationship to me whatsoever, often came here, and the letters addressed to me from various sides by the ordinary post were often delivered to him, and his to me. So, in order to distinguish my name from his, I added the name of my illustrious country.' He adds that when he discovered that his family had been called Scalzino only from 1529, being named 'Scalino' in two old documents of his ancestors, one from 1377, the other 1461, he had gone back to the earlier form. The family originally had come from Germany. Marcello had a younger brother, Lucantonio, who formed 'exceedingly lovely letters which one day, by the Grace of God, he will communicate to the world.' If he did so, they cannot be found today.

It will be understood that *Il Secretario* in any edition, authorized or spurious, is an unteresting book. The novelty in Scalino's style, as compared with Cresci, consists of a certain contraction of the body. Whereas Cresci had been interested in making the 'acute' chancery of Arrighi and Palatino easier to write and therefore more expeditious, and Hercolani concerned to spread his speedier, or *correntissime*, chancery, Scalino pushed the process still further and taught a 'cancellarescha velocissima'. This, in sum, was a taller, narrower script than that with which his predecessors may be identified. The tendency towards lengthening the ascenders and descenders, and the compensation for the consequent loss of space by narrowing the width of the body, is not easy to trace before, say, 1580 or thereabouts. Plate 47 in Scalino's first book (*Il Secretario*, privilege dated 1580), plate 8 in the 1608 edition, analyses the new interpretation he wishes to propagate. Here it will be seen that he weighted the ascending strikes with a heavier, longer, and more tapered stroke than Cresci used or would, I venture to think, have approved. There came in at about this same time, whether by Scalino's invention is doubtful, but certainly by his precept, further distortions of the dotted serifs, particularly noticeable in the miserable deformation of *h*, as well as the pinched appearance of the narrow bodies in *m*, *n*, *h*, etc. The script with filled heads (*testi con corpi diretti* – Cresci's equivalent is *testeggiate*) is entitled 'carattere cancelleresco corsivo moderno del Secretario'. Scalino actually divides by *testi* into half-dozen categories. A further innovation is the elevation of gothic *ε* into a capital.

There can be no doubt that c. 1585, i.e., two generations after the printing of the first copy-book, the acute chancery cursive, started off by Arrighi, revolutionized by Cresci, continued by Hercolani, had entered upon a third and degenerate phase with Scalino. The matter is thus discussed by the judicious Servidori at page 29:

> *D. Juan*: Tell me, did Italy after Cresci make much progress with the chancery script or bastarda? Surely, with his example his followers should have attained perfection.

D. Anselmo: This should have happened but unfortunately did not. The Italians, indeed, blindly followed Cresci's rapid and curved hand, and acquired a manual speed far faster than that of other peoples; but since they did not take the precaution of using moderation and discrimination (and they would have become near-perfect if they had), they degenerated into a script made revolting by its excessive dryness (*degeneraron en una litra fastidiosa por lo demasiado seca*). And that is how Italian chancery script had continued to this day. Really, I would call this sort of script 'Bastard Chancery', because it is in effect the bastard off-spring of Aldus's beautiful type and of Cresci's hand.

When Don Juan asks, later, who it was that first used the new modern chancery, he is told that, so far as can be ascertained, it was Jacobo Romano, a follower (*discipulo*) of Cresci. Elsewhere (page 30) Servidori shows his knowledge of Scalzini. Later (page 142) he enters into a polemic with F. X. Santiago y Palomares, who, in the vitriolic style then common among calligraphers, had denounced Servidori as a boasting charlatan; Servidori objected because Palomares espoused, in his *Nueva arte de Escribir* (1776) the cause of Pedro Diaz Morante (d. 1632) who, in his *Nueva Arte* of 1616, was responsible, according to Servidori, for introducing Scalino's formula, which he dismisses as fantasy and charlatanism. This was obviously true, as may be seen if one compares the plates which Servidori cites in evidence, e.g. his 33, 36 and 37, which are to be compared with 19-22, 32 and 67. It is not our business here to deal at length with the influence of Italian writing-masters on Spanish style. It is only necessary to emphasize and elucidate the references to the Italian writers of the last quarter of the sixteenth century in Servidori, who had a wider and deeper knowledge of his predecessors than any other writer. If the Abate had compared more closely the manuals of Scalzino (1581), Romano (1589), and Curione (1590), all of whom he discussed, he would doubtless have more definitely credited Scalzini with the feeble, dry, modern Chancery from which Italy never recovered.

It should not be thought, however, that the manuals of these masters were restricted to the new hand. All the manuals present specimens of the more formal versions of chancery; but after Scalino they laid ever greater emphasis on the new, extra current fashion. Nor can it be said that all the writers of the period succumbed to it, at least in its worst form. Scalino was obviously not a great writer, despite his pretensions. He was certainly ingenious – especially in the form of flourishing called 'command of hand' – but he was not in the class of Cresci or Hercolani, and despite his anger at what others had done to his style he himself was not above such tricks as microscopic writing to be read with a glass. Curione, even, was a better calligrapher.

Ludovico Curione's *Del Modo di Scrivere le Cancellaresche Corsivo* (Rome, 1590), *Lanotomia delle Cancellaresche corsive . . .* (Rome, 1588), *Il Teatro delle Cancellaresche corsive* (Rome, 1593) and *Il Cancelliere* (Rome, 1582) are sub-titled, respectively, Books I-IV, despite their recorded order of appearance.[1] Apparently no copy of an earlier edition of Book I, referred to in the 1590 printing, has survived. They all contain good hands, well engraved, principally by Martin van Buyten. Curione, a Bolognese who worked mainly in Rome, was a gentleman. He dedicates a plate (Number 13 of *Lanotomia*) to his engraver, among others, and another (Plate 27) to Flaminian Finelli, explaining that he had decided to have his specimens engraved on copper to preserve 'la vivacita della mia lettera'. His first book, in which the blocks had been cut in the old-fashioned way, on wood, had apparently disappointed him. Certainly the hand is livelier – one might almost say flashier – in the copperplates. Plate 48 is an epistle to Salvatore Gagliardelli praising him as 'il primo homo del mondo nelle Majuschole antiche' – a refreshing change, considering the usual acrimonious manner in which cal-

1. Johnson, pp. 45-6; Casamassima, pp. 76, 95-6.

ligraphers of the period tended to speak of their contemporaries. Curione was certainly a competent judge, for he had to his credit a splendid A-Z roman alphabet in the forms that Sixtus V had approved (Plate 46). Curione also practiced a large upper and lower case roman, witness his text 'Gloriosa studiorum Mater Urbs Roma Quae inter omnes mundi Civitates, etc.' (*Lanotomia*, Plate 42), in 18 point. For collects in liturgical books he suggested a 36-point, and gives as an example the collect for the Dead, the 'Fidelium Deus Omnium'.

The third of the writing-masters blamed by Servidori for the debasement of the Italian script was Giacomo Romano, whose *Primo Libro di Scrivere* (Rome, 1589) was printed for its author by Pietro Spada, publisher of several other manuals as well.[1] Unlike Curione, who had at command all the benefit of Martin van Buyten's brilliant intaglio engraving, Romano used letter-press and his book has, in consequence, a somewhat old-fashioned look. But the contents are up to date, and the narrow *cancelleresca corrente, corsiva*, and *correntissima* of Curione are well shown in Romano's plates. He was a good scribe of the *Formatella*, *Formata*, and the *Antica tonda* book scripts, as well as of a handsome round gothic *moderna*; his mercantile is practical. Romano's specimen of the script 'Per Brevi', headed 'Sixtus Pap. Vs.', is good and conservative at such a date as 1588. Naturally, for the benefit of those looking for posts in the Apostolic Chancery, he gives a specimen and alphabets of *Bollatica*. The book ends with an extensive series of well cut and printed reverse blocks which include alphabets and texts in various sizes of upper and lower case roman, italic, and *rotunda*. The set of classical capitals are exceptionally fine, particularly the block which combines Q and R. In form these capitals are close to the old roman inscriptions but they manage to convey a contemporary, Sixtine, atmosphere. The whole provides a very useful manual for secretaries aspiring to act for eminent personages.

1. Johnson, p. 46.

Chapter 11

THE DEVELOPMENT OF THE CAPITAL
TO THE END OF THE ERA

Luca Horfei's book on the modern inscriptions of Pope Sixtus V is one of the rarest of all the works of the period relating to our subject.[1] It is what its title says, a collection of various inscriptions, not a writing-manual for secretaries or a text-book for pedagogues. It is rather an inspirational book for amateurs and practitioners of lettering and is intended to commemorate the work done under the great Pope who was responsible for the reconstruction of the eternal city. The full title of the book is *Varie Inscrittioni Del Santiss. S. N. Sisto V. Pont. Max. Da Luca Horfei da Fano Scrittore dissegnate in Pietra et dal medesimo fatte intagliare in Rame, Per Mostrare La Lettera Antica Romana In diverse grandezze & compartimenti Con alcune cancellaresche corsive variare et altre maniere di lettere necess. In Roma all'insegna del Lupo in Parione.* The title-page is excellently designed and engraved, with the arms of Sixtus above a baroque cartouche, against a background of Roman buildings. The book is a small folio, many of its 100 or more plates occupying almost the full page, $12\frac{1}{2} \times 8\frac{5}{8}$ inches. Only seven copies are recorded, at the B. N. C., Rome, the V. & A., Newberry, Fano, Texas (H. R. C.), Shrewsbury School, and Vatican (2) libraries.

The dedication, *Al Emo. Padre et Sig. nro. Sisto Quinto Pontifice Massimo*, is well written and engraved in *cancellarescha corsiva*. Luca, 'having by the special grace of your Beatitude designed with Roman letters in the antique style in various sizes and layouts (compartimenti) the noble inscriptions cut in marble on obelisks, aqueducts, the many magnificent buildings erected by Your Holiness, I wished to have these engraved on copper and published, since artists and gentlemen take pleasure in them,

---

1. Casamassima, pp. 77, 93-4; S. Morison, introduction to C. Marzoli, *Calligraphy 1535-1885*, pp. 21-7, 52-9; J. Mosley, 'Trajan Revived' pp. 17-48.

some for the gracefulness (*vaghezza*) of the antique style of lettering and its proportions, or the layout (*componimento*) of the lines (*versi*), others for the liveliness and vitality of the conception and phrasing [of the texts]; but all unite in admiration of the greatness of mind of Your Holiness who, in so short a time, has adorned in so many ways and thus renewed great Rome . . .'. The signature is 'Luca da Fano, Scrittore'.

The book consists of some fifty inscriptions in Sixtine capitals, interspersed with plates of comment by Horfei, who supplies details of the place, size and treatment of the letters of the respective inscriptions, and sometimes the name of the designer. Thus, of the text INITIVM SAPIENTIAE/EST/TIMOR DOMINI/ he says that the inscriptions were sculptured, under the arms of Sixtus V, over the main façade of the then Papal University of Rome, the Sapienza College. The letters were seven inches high, and after cutting were lined with gold laid on caustic (or 'size'). The letters themselves, he says, were designed by Cesare Moreggio the ecclesiastical scribe (*scrittore ecclesiastice*), one of those picked out for honourable mention by Palatino and Conretto, who affirmed their conviction that Moreggio justified his art with the very best proof (*con effetto valorosissimo*). It should be added that the inscription as it may be seen today on the facade of the Sapienza is enclosed within a beautiful cartouche not reproduced by Horfei (who also varies the text somewhat).

Lucas Horfeus was a cleric, a man of learning, a fine scribe in all the hands, e.g. *can. cors., can. cors. corrente, can. cors. correntissime, rotunda moderna, antica tonda* and *antica cors.* He was a musician, a singer in the Sistine chapel in 1594, and a transcriber of music, as is shown on plate 81, where he signs himself '*Lucas Horfeus Capello S'mi. D. N. musices scriptor scr.*'[1] Plate 88 is a specimen of his music for the chant of the Filioque in Latin and

1. Josephus M. Llorens, *Capellae Sixtinae Codices musicis notis instructi sive manu scripti sive praelo excussi, Studi e Testi* CCII (Vatican, 1960), records 11 MSS written by Horfei (nos. 29, 30-2, 54, 57, 62, 72, 76, 78, 153), executed between 1585 and 1599.

Greek. This is unsigned. The Filioque is included in a series of texts celebrating the ecumenical Councils. Thus plate 92 is a eulogy of the Fathers of the Council of Trent, set forth in a fine piece of open white rotunda: *Lutherani et alii heretici damnantur; Cleri populique disciplina ad pristinos mores restituitur*, which is signed *Lucas scr*.

The *Varie Inscrittioni* is an immensely desirable book, well arranged, handsome in form, beautifully engraved, by one of whom little seems to be known, since he is not mentioned by Servidori or other bibliographers. If a dedication copy to Sixtus V. exists, it must be a splendid possession. The title-page of the Newberry copy is endorsed in an illegible contemporary hand 'Sculpantur et imprimantur centum folia sequentia' and signed by Fr Thomas Pallain as *Sacr(i) Pal(atii) Ap(osto)lici Mag(iste)r*. Fr Thomas was one of the ten Frenchmen who, out of the ninety or so successors of St Dominic, according to a decree of the fifth Lateran Council (1513), were saddled with the responsibility of approving any and every book printed in Rome or its district. This regulation was made more rigid by later popes, notably Paul V, Urban VIII, and Alexander VII. Such regulations were largely responsible for the destruction of the printing and engraving arts in Rome, and are one of the reasons for the low state of the art practised in the Vatican Printing Office. When Benedict XIV in 1744 enacted that the imprimatur of the Master of the Sacred Palace must be got before publication was authorised, and that to secure the imprimatur, three printed copies must first be deposited, one for the Master, one for his assistant and one for the Cardinal Vicar, publishers inevitably migrated to Venice. It would appear, therefore, that the Newberry copy may be the imprimatur copy sent in by the author or printer to the Master of the Sacred Palace. We know little more of Horfeus, although he also produced at least two other, less impressive books; one was his *ALFABETO | Delle Maiuscole | Antiche Rome | Del Signor | LVCA HORFEI | DA FANO | Opera molt'utile | à Scrittori, Pittori, e' Scultori | Nella quale | Con ragione Geometrica | S'insegnano le misure di d.tte lte. | Si stampano in Roma all'insegna del Luppo in Parione.* The book is an oblong quarto, with 24 engraved leaves, in one gathering, including the engraved title-page. The pages, following the elaborate heroic-classical title, present a geometrical inscriptional alphabet A-Z in a style which, it is regrettable to say, reaches only a mediocre standard. There is no text and the title page is without date.

Horfei also produced *De Caracterum | et Litterarum | Inventoribus | Ex | Picturis | Bibliothecae Vaticanae |* likewise undated, and printed in Rome 'in Vico Parionis sub signo Lupi'. This is a modern, but still fanciful compendium of exotic alphabets; the same alphabets and attributions of invention re-occur, cut in wood or type metal, in the first specimen-book of the *Stamperia Vaticana*, issued in 1628.[1] Horfei shows Greek, Hebrew, Cyrillic, and other forms of lettering, all well engraved and befitting one who describes himself as 'Scriptor Capellae Apostolicae'. It is a noble memorial of the inscriptions in the Sixtine Vatican Library.

The masters in cities other than Rome and Venice found few engraving facilities. Alberto Mureti produced an intaglio book of some interest, with a portrait of the Archbishop of Siena to whom it was dedicated. The plainest of typographic title-pages reading, LIBRO | DI SCRITTURA | di A. MURETI | Siena | M.D. LXXXXIV., and a punning sonnet (*che crede Esser CRESCI-uto à secoli futuri*) introduce a number of mediocre essays in the Mureti-Scalzini-Curione style, all engraved and printed in Siena.[2]

Mureti was anxious not to follow some masters in this profession who believed that little or no esteem should be granted to works of that kind which have not been composed or en-

---

1. They were originally cut for Fr. Angelo Roccha's *Bibliotheca Apostolica Vaticana a Sixto V. Pont. Max. in splendidiorem commodioremque locum translata* (Rome, 1591). See H. D. L. Vervliet, *The Type Specimens of the Vatican Press 1628* (Amsterdam, 1967), pp. 19-20.
2. Johnson, p. 46.

graved in Rome or Venice. 'Not caring for these, I have had my book engraved in the illustrious city of Siena, and moroever even printed, in opposition to the judgment and advice of many ... I do not deny that with this choice I ran a great risk and that I had great good fortune; but even after I had given instructions concerning the rules, and prescriptions of my writing to the engraver, who had never really practiced this art, nevertheless, despite my assiduous diligence his imitation of me was but ... mediocre, yet he is not in the least to be blamed, rather on the contrary he is worthy of being excused and praised'. Mureti also alluded to the craze then prevalent of variety for variety's sake: 'I have been compelled, to my displeasure, to go out of my way and to vary my ordinary writing, so as to try to satisfy in part the many opinions and desires of others; because we are today arrived at such a pass that everyone wants characters in his own way, and some the more unfortunate since, in order to appear wise, they cause trouble imagining that the letter, if it is only joined and darkened by an abundance of ink, without any other art, or rule, or form, has merit above any other'. Mureti's is an individual performance, with little significance except, perhaps, in Siena.

G. F. Cresci's *Quarto libro di Lettere formatelle and Cancellaresche corsive* (Rome, 1596) is an oblong 7¾ × 5⅛ of 31 leaves of specimen printed letterpress with a 4 page title and preface. The book is of importance to the biographer of Cresci. He had left Rome, for his native Milan, sometime after 1580, it appears from the specimen at fo. 19 recto (i.e. E1) signed '*In Roma 1580 Il Cresci scrisse*'. The master's first book, the *Essemplare* had been published in 1560, i.e. 36 years earlier than the present modest production. Modesty had not hitherto been Cresci's distinction, but by 1596 he seems to have lost interest in calligraphy. *Il Libro Quarto* was published in Rome by Pietro Spada *ad instantia* of Silvio Valesi of Parma, who also wrote the Preface. His relative, Fr. Fulgentius Valesi, a Cistercian, contributed two leaves of large round Gothic which appear in advance of Cresci's chancery specimens, and two leaves of relatively inoffensive initials in the German style. Silvio Valesi explains that after sixteen years (he must have had in mind the date (1579) of *Il Perfetto Cancellaresco*, printed by the same P. Spada) the merits of Cresci had become overlaid by the books of inferiors, the grace and vivacity of his writing forgotten. Hence the new publication: though '*le sue cancellaresche, & altre fossero intaglate in Rame da valent' huomo, oltre, che demonstrarebbono più sotiliezza del legno, renderebbono anco l'occhio piu vago, ma non gia darebbono magior perfettione, essendo che il legno tira piu al naturale di esso Rame*'.

The specimens themselves do not add to Cresci's reputation; some are excessively looped and ligatured, others are over-artificial and ingenious; all are over-decorated except the cancellarescha formata antica. Even these, however, are more narrowly set than his earlier specimens. Obviously the vogue of the Scalzini-Curione type of modern Roman Chancery was too strong to be denied even by Cresci and, after 1580, he found himself accommodating his hand, much as Palatino did in 1560, to a trend he had reason to dislike and recommends, as Valesi says, a method to write quickly. However, the reputation of Cresci was not so weak that the 1596 edition, provided it was cheap, could not be made to pay. Somewhat unexpectedly Valesi adds that while engraving in copper adds subtlety to the strokes wood approaches nature more closely. The specimens signed by Cresci are dated 1579, 1580. A last edition was brought out in Milan forty years later by Cresci's son: *Caratteri, et Essempi | del Famoso Scrittore | Gio. Francesco Cresci | Nobile Milanese*, (Milan 1638). This is an oblong 6½×4½, miserably printed by Filippo Ghisolfi for G. B. Bidelli, who writes the preface addressed to '*Virtuosi giovani, et a qualunque, che desidera perfettionarsi nella scienza di scriver bene ogni sorte de Caratteri*'. It is quite unworthy of the master. The printer drags in a reference to Cresci's son, who is recorded as a worthy son of such a man and not his inferior in talent. The contents comprise 22 specimens, all badly engraved in relief letterpress, printed one side only, of G. F. Cresci's *Cancellaresca, corsiva* and *formata*, for the most part dated and signed 1580. The one novelty is the *Cancellareschina nuouamente dal Cresci posta in luce a. 1580, Il Cresci scrisse.* The book confirms Servidori's judgment of the influence, bad in nearly every respect, of Scalino: sixteen pages of his rules, set in type, bring the book up-to-date, and all the models are narrow and spindly. The whole is a disservice to the master's memory.[1]

Two books, *Il Franco Modo di Scrivere Cancellaresco Moderno* . . . (Venice, 1595) and *Del Franco Modo di Scrivere Cancellaresco Moderno Libro Secondo* . . . (Venice, 1596) represent the work of a prolific engraver and publisher, Giacomo Franco, who apparently decided to try his hand at authorship as well.[2] A versatile and skilful engraver highly in demand, he had earlier (1581) produced most of the plates for Scalino's *Il Secretario*; his own books are for the most part popularization of Scalino's and Curione's styles; there are also plates, engraved by Franco, signed by Fabio Tosta of Naples, Bartolamea Sopranini of Venice, *et al.* His own plates embody *ſ*, *đ*, *ſanno*, and other enormities by the full plate – a beastly book, deserving its failure. It marks the lowest point reached in the calligraphical publishing of the century.

The trade made a brilliant recovery in Marc'antonio de Rossi's *Giardino de Scrittori*, dedicated to Cardinal Aldobrandini, whose portrait is shown before that of the scribe. The *Giardino,* one of the great books of the period, was published at Rome, in 1598, *appresso il proprio autore,* of whom, also, there is a fine portrait.[3] It comprises a title and dedication, both engraved,

1. See above, p. 108.
2. Johnson, p. 46.
3. Rossi's book is an uncommonly rare one, of which no complete copy is recorded. The Newberry copy (formerly Destailleur-Ricketts) is the only recorded copy which has seventeen pages of letterpress dedicatory verses among its prelims, as well as an engraved title-page and dedication. It lacks 8 of the 119 plates; bound with it are the twelve plates of geometrically-constructed roman capitals A-Z, which were also issued separately with a letterpress title-

17 pages of letterpress, 119 numbered plates of calligraphy and 12 unnumbered of geometrically constructed capitals. Rossi is skilled in every type of letter and is, besides, a good showman. A feature of the book is the dedication of the plates, many of which are in his elegant, and on the whole conservative, version of the *cancellaresca corsiva*, to eminent personages. Plate No. 69, an excellent study of the restrained baroque chancery cursive, has only so much movement and decoration as, say, Cresci would have sanctioned. Rossi is expert with the big *antica tonda* he suggests for large liturgical books, and exhibits it (plates 71-90) in collects, the concluding numbers in the set being in letters half an inch high. The text of no. 89 *Exsurgat Deus et dissipentur inimici eius* is an exceptionally fine piece, the letters double that size. Plate 90 is a setting of the Psalm *Laudate Dominum omnes gentes* on five staves with diamond notes; and in no. 101 the introit *O Gloriosa Dei Genetrix* is on four staves. Other notable features are his Sixtine roman capitals, round gothic, decorated initials, bullatic (five plates), and pointed gothic. Of exotics he provides Greek and Hebrew. A series of fifty transcriptions of the *Pater Noster* in various languages is promised but does not appear to have been completed.

Scipione Leoni's *Mastro* [sic] *di Scrivere* (Bologna, 1606) supplies fifty plates, of, for the most part, fairly good *cancellaresca corsiva corrente*, interspersed with a number of the decadent hands alluded to by Mureti. Some of these, nothing more than scribble, make on copper a ludicrous appearance (plate 40, for instance). At his best Leoni is a fair practitioner of the speedy post-Curione style. It is not a good book, thought the format is sumptuous. A curious item is the dedication (dated 1605) to Ranuccio, Duke of Parma, engraved in imitation of the Garamond/Granjon italic. This was Leoni's most ambitious production; others included an unrelated *Quaranta Mostre Cancellaresche* and *Il Libro Primo di Cancellaresche Corsive* (Rome, 1601,

page as *Il Quarto Libro del Giardino de Scrittori* in 1598. The book is a large oblong quarto, excellently printed. For further bibliography, see Johnson pp. 47-8.

with dedication dated 1596). There is also a twelve page fragment in the British Museum which is apparently from none of these.[1]

Sempronio Lancione's *Idea Universale Delle cancellaresche Corsive, et bastarde Libro quarto* is a fine piece of engraving by Martin van Buyten (Naples, 1613).[2] The pages of *cancelleresca corsiva* within command of hand borders, are dedicated to various nobles; the ascenders are looped and well written, and of course well engraved; the borders are relatively restrained and avoid monsters. Plate 9 (numbered on copper) is an interesting progressive *cancelleresca corsiva* with double ascending characters, *bl*, *ll*, with the first unlooped and the second looped, but not *h*. His Pl. 10 *Regola mirabile per assicurare presto la mano* includes looped *h*. Significantly, Lancione provides at pl. 40 a 'Bastarda Testeggiata' with a Spanish text. This plate is headed SEMPRONIUS INVENTOR. The novelty appears to consist of distinguishing between the Italian and Spanish alphabet in point of pronunciation. An interesting book, well turned out and greatly superior to Scalino, though indebted to him.

The largest and most sumptuous of all the Italian books, to my knowledge, is *Dell'Idea/Dello Scriuere di/Giuseppe Segaro/Genovese/Intagliata Per lo Molto Reverendo D. Epifanio dal Fiano/Vallombrosano Priore dello Spirito Santo di Firenze/l'Anno 1607.*[3] It measures 14"×11" and is wholly engraved on copper, except for the dedication which is typographically set and enclosed in a border engraved in the style employed for the pages of the book. These are separately printed inside the borders. The date on the title-page is misleading for the book was published posthumously in Genoa by Giuseppe Pavoni in 1624, with a preface by Gio. Batt. Segaro for his father, who died in that year, suddenly if we may judge from the statement that Segaro passed from the pen to the tomb (*Calamo al tumulo*). Much use

1. Johnson, p. 47.
2. Bonacini, no. 1005.
3. Marzoli, no. 22, pp. 81-2.

is made of Chancery capitals for names, a solecism never committed except by Tagliente, and only by him as a stunt. Even Segaro's name, written in capitals on the title page, is almost illegible, but it is of the *Alfabeto maiuscolo d'inventione del Segaro* that the scribe appears most proud. His *alfabeto con corsivo facilissimo* is even narrower than Curione's or Scalino's but he does offer in pl. 10 a good conservative *cancelleresca corsiva*. This plate, and plate 15, are instructive, for the calligrapher printed texts in French, Latin, Italian and Spanish. The latter plate is dedicated to the Abbot (it was the Prior who engraved, in masterly style, the plates) of Vallombrosa. The dedication, in Latin, is in the old, most formal *cancelleresca corsiva* that Cresci would have approved. It is followed, very curiously, by a collect in his speediest cursive. That Segaro was predominantly interested in speed, as Scalino was before him, is clear. The majority of his plates are strongly cursive, except when he is engaged on Latin or Spanish texts. Even his *Formatella antica* (pl. 39), which is his broadest and plainest script, approaching most nearly to Cresci's early style, has the narrow g distinctive of Scalino and his followers. His *L'ra Formata* (pl. 40) is as narrow in the body as any to be found, but it avoids looping the ascenders. Plate 41 is described as a '*Letterina*', i.e. in scale equivalent to 14 pt., '*Velocissima et facile*' and is used for a text from the Vulgate. It comes towards the end of the book, whereas the plate of Segaro's '*Mercantile Velocissima*' occur at pl. 13. This is a fast chancery with one or two gothic vestiges, e.g. *p*, and abominably scribbled capitals of no pedigree. The essential fault of the script is the habit of keeping the pen on the paper as long as possible, joining every letter and stringing words together. Thus, Segaro's commercial hand is a dreary concatenation of letters. He was too clever by half.

A far better example of late Italian chancery is *Il terzo libro* of Francesco Periccioli, a scribe of Siena.[1] It is at first sight as

1. Marzoli, no. 20, pp. 74-7.

good as anything Cresci every did, and beautifully engraved. The eye is delighted more, perhaps, than it should be. The borders, unlike those in Rossi, are engraved on the same plate, and not printed separately. Great virtuosity is shown. Monsters, flowers, dashes, arabesques, and much other 'Command of hand' is exhibited. The engraver's skill renders in superb degree Periccioli's essays in the style of Curione whom, in fact, he surpasses. His large *antica tonda* roman is too spindly for general use as, indeed, is his Chancery cursive; but he performs a good large hand, and there can be no denying his elegance. He rightly praises the most illustrious Signor van Buyten, his engraver. I have never seen his earlier books and the Newberry (C. Ricketts) copy of *Il terzo libro* is incomplete. In the Destailleur copy there were 4 plates extra to the 48 in the Newberry copy. It is one of the few writing books to have been published in Naples, presumably in 1619, shortly after the date of the dedication to Cosimo II, Duke of Tuscany.

Tomaso Ruinetti's *Idea del Buon Scrittore*, engraved on copper by Christoforo Blanco in 1619 and published in Rome, is a handsome book which displays the speedy chancery style espoused by Scalino – years earlier.[1] The best piece of writing in the book is the privilege from Paul V. 22 November 1619, written in good conservative *cancelleresca corsiva*, on Cresci's model. The dedication to Cardinal Aldobrandini is in *cancelleresca corsiva corrente* with flourishes but without loops. The ligature 'ch' is used only occasionally. The layout is so excellent that it became a model for his followers. Ruinetti's formula was a command of hand border, enclosing a dedication or superscription to an eminent Cardinal, with fast writing of *cancelleresca corsiva corrente* The fast writing examples are well exemplified in plate 8, where is shows but he does not become addicted to looping until pl. 25, where occurs. His plate 31, *Alfabeti del Ruinetti per la l'ra Formatella* exhibits three lines of

1. Marzoli, no. 21, pp. 78-9.

capitals, swash and inscriptional, and three of lower case; six plates (32-38) provide a conservative *cancelleresca corsiva* (39), *cancelleresca corsiva antica*, a capital and lower-case sloped roman; 40 an upright *antica tonda*, which is quite tolerable. The book ends with a suite of the Latin capitals in the Sixtus V style. These were later printed separately. All are good though lacking in grace.

S. Giuliano Sellari of Cortona produced a *Laberinto di varii caratteri* in Rome in 1635, engraved on copper by Camillo Cungi.[1] It is a full folio of 32 leaves printed on one side. Sellari, who was obviously a good scribe, became instructor to the nephew of Cardinal Savelli, and was in a position to secure the services of a good engraver. The book is well done in *cancelleresca corsiva* of Curione's form, conservative, but strongly inclined. Evidently his Eminence did not wish his nephew to depart from the traces of Cresci still existing in the Roman Chancery. Sellari's inventiveness and flourishing are reserved to his entrelacs and borders. He has a good large specimen of the *antica tonda* within such a border.

The last great book of the Roman school, and a great book it is, was Leopardo Antonozzi's *De Caratteri* (Rome, 1638),[2] It is a full folio of 11½" × 8". This is the book of which Pepys, then busy collecting calligraphica, had heard. He thus wrote to his nephew John Jackson on 7 December 1699, 'What I have to add is the recommending to you the procuring for me a copy-book, printed at Rome in the year 1638 under this title: De Caratteri de Leopardo Antonizzi [sic]. And if there be anything in Italy of that kind more modern and extraordinary, whether at Rome or elsewhere, pray omit not to secure it for me.'[3]

1. Marzoli, no. 23, pp. 84-5.
2. S. Morison, 'Rare Italian and American Calligraphica', *Newberry Library Bulletin* I (1948), p. 20; Marzoli, no. 25, pp. 87-9.
3. *The private correspondence of Samuel Pepys*, ed. J. R. Tanner, I (London, 1926), p. 249. Jackson replied on 13 January, 'I have not been able to find the copybook you desire; but another I have of Il Curione's anno 1619' (*ibid.*, p. 273): this was *Il Cancelliere*, now in the Pepys Library at Magdalene College, Cambridge.

Antonozzi was a gentleman. His 4-page introductory epistle *A Lettori*, set in Granjon's Paragon italic, eulogises Cresci and justifies engraving on copper as reproducing the natural expression of the pen, but the roman capitals will be cut in wood as being suitable for that purpose. For these capitals he acknowledges the '*Iscrittione della superbissima e famosissima Colonna Traiana, le quali à giudicio di tutti gl'intendenti, tanto antichi quanto moderni, sono le piu belle, che siano al Mondo*'. He has also added specimens of the *Cancelleresca, formatella* and *bastarda*, and designed a figured alphabet. He would like to have added more specimens of characters, the *formata* and the *antica tonda*, engraved on wood; but left them out, since those that have been engraved have not attained, he thinks, the expression of his pen, as will be noted by anyone who will take the trouble to compare them, say with the books of the Papal Chapel to which he was Scribe and, in particular, the books with the three masses for the three principal days upon which his holiness sang the Mass, i.e. on the Nativity, the Resurrection and the Feast of the Apostles Peter and Paul, which His Holiness our Lord Pope Urban VIII was pleased to make him write. These books are in large format, and show the continuation of the *Caratteri*, well formed and uniform.

In accordance with now settled convention, the title-page on copper is signed *C. Cungius. Scul. 1638*. This plate is self-num-

Jackson was more fortunate in Naples, whence he bought back two copybooks, as he reported to Pepys on 12 March (p. 302). It is sad that he failed to respond to another request from Pepys (8 February 1700, p. 288):

> Captain Hatton (who was my gu[e]st to day, and your kind rememberancer) tells me of a printed booke of graveings don at rome about (as he thinks) 60 years agoe, finely don, of all the allfabetes of the severall languages in which there are any bookes extent in the Vatican Liberary; the same being taken from the paintings or drawings thereoff inscribed upon the severall int[e]r coulums in the same liberary, of which booke (if to be had) it would greatly sort with my Colection that I had a coppy of.

This can only be Horfei's *De characterum ... inventoribus* (perhaps somewhat confused with Roccha's *Bibliotheca Apostolica Vaticana*); would that a copy of Horfei were now at Cambridge.

bered 1. The name of the wood-engraver, who did the capitals, is not given.

Plate 2 is the dedication to Prince Maurice, Cardinal of Savoy, placed within a heavy border of cyphers, horses and leopards, done by command of pen, and enclosing text written in a fine *cancelleresca corsivo* of the style of G. F. Cresci, Sd. *Leopardo Antonozzi*.

Plate 3 is a similar dedication to Donna Olimpia Aldobrandini; *Cancelleresca corsiva corrente* with looped 1 in medial position. Sd. as pl. 2.

No. 4 is a plate dedicated to the Cardinal of Aracaeli; *Cancelleresca formata antica*, a true sloped roman excellently written and engraved. Sd. *Leopardo Antonozzi Osimano* (Osima is a place near Ancona).

5. Cardinal Biscia; as pl. 2.

6. Cardinal Pallotto; as pl. 2; sd. as pl. 4.

7. Abbot Ferdinande Deneufville; smaller *cancelleresca corsiva corrente* with stronger slope; *ff* medial or final; *h, l*, seldom looped. Sd. as 2.

8. Marchese Girolamo Mattei. Style as No. 3. *b, l* occasionally looped; sd. as No. 4.

9. Udalrico Barone di Kolourat. Style as No. 2. Sd. as No. 4.

10. Count Carlo Francesco Valperga; round and conservative version of No. 2 but with gothic traits. Sd. in small characters as No. 2.

11. Mgr. Bartolomeo Oreggi. Larger version of No. 7. Sd. as No. 2.

12. Sig. Andrea Trzebicki, style as Pl. 3. looped medial *l* only. Sd. as No. 2.

13. Irnerio Mattucci; in Curione's narrow-bodied *cancelleresca corsiva corrento* with looped and tied *bl*; large thin *m* for capital M. gothic *e* as in pl. 8, which is rare in Antonozzi. Sd. as 2.

14. Crescentio Saccardi; plain entrelac border; style as 8 with looped *b, l*, Sd. as No. 4.

15. Antonio Maria Candio; plain entrelac border; in *cancelleresca corsiva corrente* looped *b, h* (occasionally),; sd, as No. 4.

16. Santi Conti; plain entrelac border; style as preceding.

17. Ascanio Belmesseri, *maestro di Camero* to Cardinal Biscia (see No. 5) floral border; style as No. 12; looped *b, f, l,* occasionally *h*; sd. as No. 2.

18. Horatio Felici; figured border; style as No. 9; sd. as No. 4.

19. Aphorism on the four qualities of a warrior; style as No. 8. s. as No. 4.

20. Analogy of Rhetoric and Calligraphy; style and signature as preceding.

21. Aphorism on the merits of calligraphy; in strongly current *corsiva*, narrow-bodied but mostly unlooped, with only occasional looped *l*: Sd. as No. 2.

22. As preceding; signed as No. 4.

23. As preceding; Sd. *'Cancellaresca corrente Dell'Antonozzi Scrittore in Roma'*.

24. Progressive alphabet, showing the variations due to acceleration; Sd. *L'Antonozzi Scrivera*.

25. *Alfabeti di Lettere Maiuscole cancelleresche corsive*; One alphabet of capitals in three lines; followed by *Alfabeti di Maiuscole delle lettere Formatelle, bastarde, e Formate*: One line of smaller and plainer version of above; second line in plain italic caps; an alternative flourished as well as plain G is provided; sd. *Antonotius Scr*.

There follows the section of wood engravings of which Antonozzi entertained a poor opinion. They are printed with grey ink in Cresci's manner on what is certainly difficult paper for the work. Unlike the first part, the blocks are unnumbered; perhaps there should have been a title-page or half-title.

26. Is a scriptural text within a plain white line border, written in a plain large italic – what Cresci would call *cancelleresca antica*. Sd. *Antonot*.

27. As the preceding, but lettering slightly condensed; l.c. alphabet added; Sd. *Antonot*.

LIBER

PARTIVM NOMINA SVNT HEC.

Media Afta del quadro. Medio púćto. Punćto,e tefta.

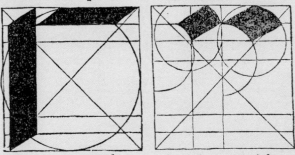

Afta naturale p il fcđo documéto de la.xxxvi. del prio.

Tefta dupla.   Tefta artificiale.

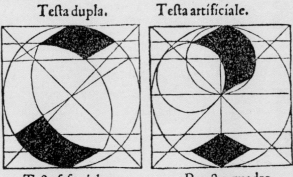

Tefta fefquialtera.   Punćto quadro.

Nota che ge fono multi altri effećti de péna.ma quefti
al propofito noftro baftano.

~: Al benigno Lettore :~

Pregato piu uolte, anzi constretto da molti amici
benignissimo Lettore, che riguardo hauendo al=
la publica utilita e comodo non solamente di
questa eta, ma delli posteri anchora, volessi
dar qualche essempio di scriuere, et regulata=
mente formare gli caratteri e note delle lre(
che (cancellaresche hoggi di chiamano) uole tier
pigliai questa fatica: E perche impossibile era
de mia mano porger tanti essempi, che sodisfa=
cessino a tutti, mi sono ingegnato di ritrouare
questa nuoua inuentione de lre, e metterle in
stampa, le quali tanto se auicinano alle scrit=
te a mano, quanto capeua il mio ingegno, E se
puntualmente in tutto nò te rispondono, sup=
plicoti che mi facci iscusato. Conciosia che la
stampa nò possa in tutto ripresentarte la vi=
ua mano, Spero nondimeno che imitando tu
il mio ricordo, da te stesso potrai consequire il
tuo desiderio. ~Uiui, e sta Sano:~

2. Ludovico degli Arrighi, *La operina*, [c 1525], f. 2.

3. Eustachio Celebrino, *Il modo di Imparare scrivere lettera Merchantesca*, 1525, f. 4v.

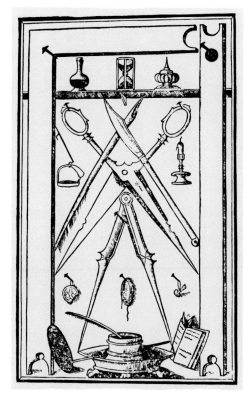

4. Giovan Antonio Tagliente, *Lucidario*, 1524, f. 14.

Lettera da Bolle antiche.

Clemens Epus seruus
seruorum dei. Ad perpetuam rei
memoriam
Lud. de Henricis vicetin

5. Ugo da Carpi, *Thesauro de Scrittori*, 1535, f. A[36].

LIBRO NVOVO

D'IMPARARE A SCRIVERE TVT,
TE SORTE LETTERE ANTICHE ET MO,
DERNE DI TVTTE NATIONI,
CON NVOVE RECOLE
MISVRE ET ES,
✤ SEMPI, ✤

Con vn breue & vtile trattato de le Cifere, Compolto per
Giouambattiſta Palatino Cittadino Romano.

Con Gratia, & Priuilegio.

6. Giovanbattista Palatino, *Libro nuovo d'imparare scrivere tutte sorte
lettere*, 1540, title.

IL PERFETTO SCRITTORE,
Di M. Gio. Francesco Cresci Cittadino Milanese.

Doue si veggono i veri Caratteri, & le natural forme di
tutte quelle forti di lettere, che à vero Scrittore
si appartengono.

Con alcun'altre da lui nouamente ritrouate.
Et i modi, che deue tenere il Maestro per bene
insegnare.

7. Giovan Francesco Cresci, *Il perfetto scrittore*, [1570], title.

8. Marc'Antonio Rossi, *Giardino de scrittori*, 1598, title.

9. Francesco Alunno, 'Scartafaccio', B.L. Add. MS. 27869, ff. 75v–76.

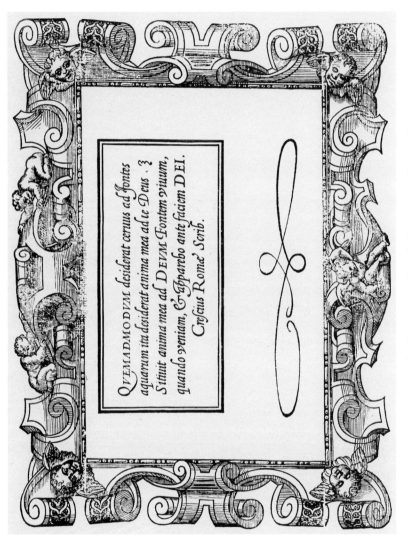

QVEMADMODVM desiderat ceruus ad fontes aquarum ita desiderat anima mea ad te Deus. Sitiuit anima mea ad DEVM Fontem viuum, quando veniam, & Apparebo ante faciem DEI.

Crescus Romæ Scrib.

10. G.F. Cresci, *Il perfetto scrittore*, [1570], f. A8v, cancelleresca formata.

11. G.F. Cresci, *Il perfetto scrittore*, [1570], f. C4, cancelleresca corsiva.

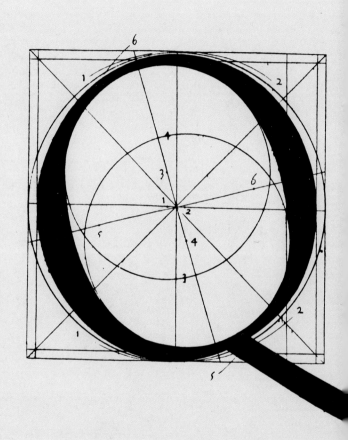

R

12. G. F. Cresci, *Il perfetto scrittore*, Parte seconda, [1570], ff. 8v-9.

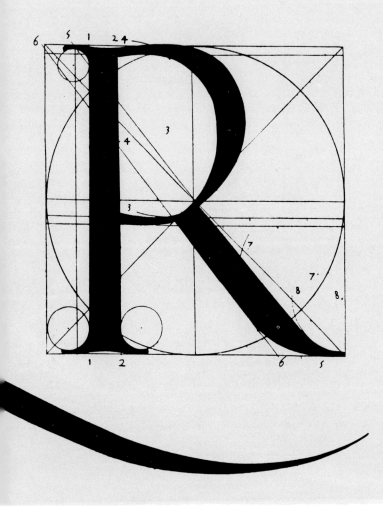

13. Marc'Antonio Rossi, *Giardino de scrittori*, 1598, [plate 9].

14. Marcello Scalzini, *Il secretario*, 1581, plate 47.

SIXTVS · V · PONT · MAX
OBELISCVM VATICANVM
DIS GENTIVM
IMPIO CVLTV DICATVM
AD APOSTOLOR · LIMINA
OPEROSO LABORE
TRANSTVLIT
A · M · D · LXXXVI · PONT · II

15. Luca Horfei, *Varie inscrittioni*, [c 1590], pl. 13.

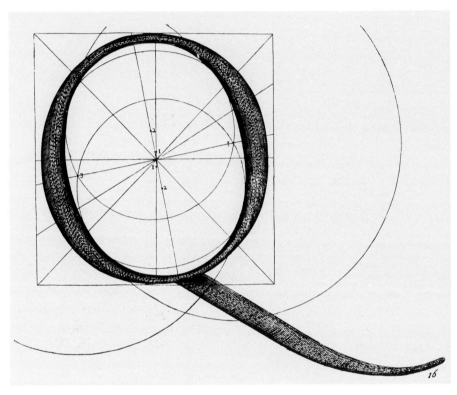

16. Luca Horfei, *Alfabeto delle maiuscole*, [c 1586], pl. 16.

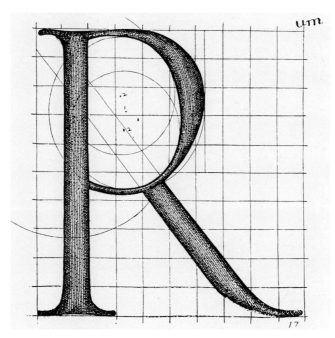

17. Luca Horfei, *Alfabeto delle maiuscole*, [c 1586], pl. 17.

18. Leopardo Antonozzi, *De caratteri*, 1637, f. 52.

IVLIANVS
SELLARIVS
CORTONEN
INVENT

19. Giuliano Sellari, *Laberinto di varii caratteri*, 1635. pl. 19.

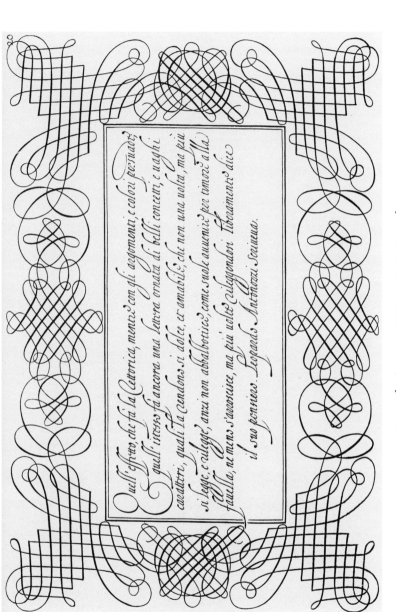

20. Leopardo Antonozzi, *De caratteri*, 1637, pl. 20.

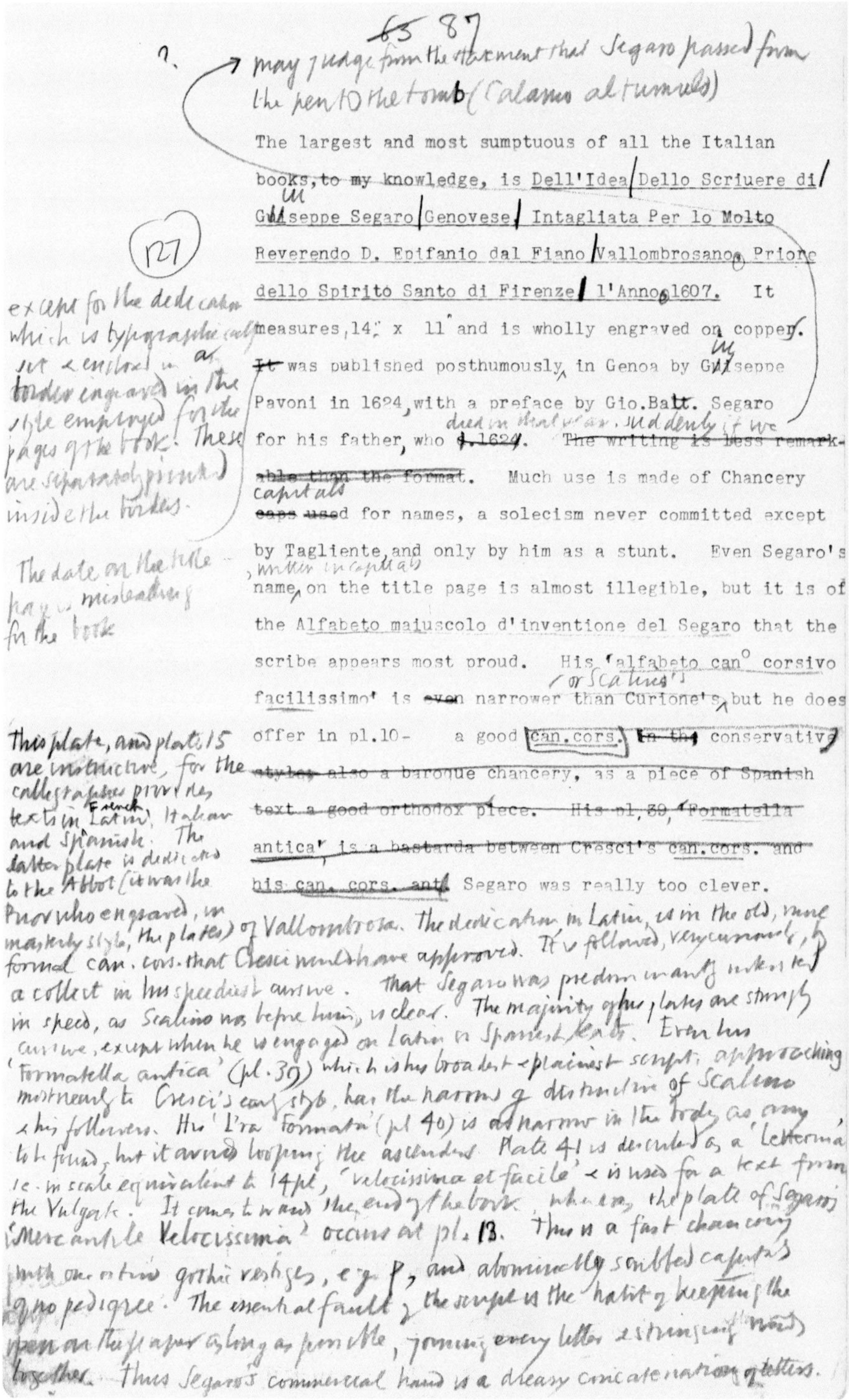

[handwritten top:] may judge from the statement that Segaro passed from the pen to the tomb (Calamo ad tumulos)

The largest and most sumptuous of all the Italian
books, to my knowledge, is Dell'Idea/Dello Scriuere di/
Giuseppe Segaro/Genovese/ Intagliata Per lo Molto
Reuerendo D. Epifanio dal Fiano Vallombrosano, Priore
dello Spirito Santo di Firenze/ l'Anno 1607.   It
measures 14" x 11" and is wholly engraved on copper.
It was published posthumously in Genoa by Giuseppe
Pavoni in 1624, with a preface by Gio.Batt. Segaro
for his father, who d.1624. ~~The writing is less remarkable than the format.~~   Much use is made of Chancery
caps ~~caps used~~ for names, a solecism never committed except
by Tagliente, and only by him as a stunt.   Even Segaro's
name on the title page is almost illegible, but it is of
the Alfabeto maiuscolo d'inventione del Segaro that the
scribe appears most proud.   His 'alfabeto can° corsivo
facilissimo' is ~~even~~ narrower than Curione's, but he does
offer in pl.10- a good can.cors. ~~in the~~ conservativa
~~style also a baroque chancery, as a piece of Spanish
text a good orthodox piece. His pl.39, 'formatella
antica' is a bastarda between Cresci's can.cors. and
his can. cors. and~~ Segaro was really too clever.

[left margin handwritten notes:]

except for the dedication which is typographical set & enclosed in a border engraved in the style employed for the pages of the book. These are separately printed inside the border.

The date on the title page is misleading for the book

This plate, and plate 15 are instructive, for the calligrapher provides text in Latin, French, Italian and Spanish. The latter plate is dedicated to the Abbot (it was the Prior who engraved, in masterly style, the plates) of Vallombrosa. the dedication in Latin, is in the old, more formal can. cors. that Cresci would have approved. It is followed, very curiously, by a collect in his speediest cursive. that Segaro was predominantly inclined in speed, as Scalino was before him, is clear. The majority of his plates are strongly cursive, except when he is engaged on Latin or Spanish texts. Even his 'Formatella antica' (pl.39) which is his broadest & plainest script, approaching most nearly to Cresci's early style, has the narrow g distinctive of Scalino & his followers. His 'l'ra formata' (pl 40) is as narrow in the body as any to be found, but it avoids looping the ascenders. Plate 41 is described as a 'letterina' ie. in scale equivalent to 14pt, 'velocissima et facile' & is used for a text from the Vulgate. It comes toward the end of the book, whereas the plate of Segaro's 'Mercantile Velocissima' occurs at pl. 13. this is a fast chancery with one or two gothic vestiges, e.g. p, and abominably snotted capitals & no pedigree. The essential fault, the script is the habit of keeping the pen on the paper as long as possible, joining every letter & stringing words together. thus Segaro's commercial hand is a dreary concatenation of letters.

21. A page from one of Morison's drafts of the present work.

28. Double alphabet, i.e. aa bb cc dd ee ff gg but *B*, etc, in large *tonda* finely done. Sd. *Antonotius S.*

29. Large single *tonda* alphabet; style as 27, 28; Sd. *Antonotius scriptor.*

30. Latin collect in style of preceding; Unsd.

31. Latin collect in round gothic; l.c. alphabet added; Sd. *Anton.*

32. Initials for the preceding, conservative.

The next section, as the Newberry, formerly Borghese, copy is bound, consists of twelve copper-plates, numbered 33-44, of figured 'cadels', the choir-book initials described by Antonozzi in his preface and favoured also by Cresci, A-Z, set two upon the page; all unsd. The next section comprises a suite of large roman capitals A-Z, printed from wood in grey ink, unnumbered, representing plates 45-56. They are 4¼″ high on a ground averaging 8″×6″. A larger suite begins at plate 57 and ends at plate 78. These are 5¹⁵⁄₁₆″ high on a ground averaging 8⅛″× 6¾″. Q evidently folded out to accommodate the tail which, since the scale of Suite 1 is nearly ¼″ more than the width of the O, must have swung out to a length of about 6⅞″. The Newberry copy, as cut, is only 4⅝″.

The point about the two suites of roman capitals is that the first, the smaller, is a scholarly reproduction of the Trajan model which preserves the M, N, without what Antonozzi calls the *capitelli*, i.e. serifs to the tops of the perpendiculars; the larger series is his invention, which he has constructed on a basis of 1:9, i.e. the height equal to 9 times the width of the mainstroke. He omits geometrical rules, or constructions.

The book as a whole is a magnificent achievement. It was never surpassed in Rome or elsewhere.

EPILOGUE

Antonozzi makes a fine triumphal end to the text, as Morison left it. But that was not his intention. He planned to extend it to the end of the seventeenth century, and the manuals of Honorato Tiranti (Turin, 1639-56), Francesco and Giovanni Battista Pisani (Genoa, 1640-1), Agostino Tensini (Verona, 1641-86), Giuseppe Maria Mitelli, (Bologna, c 1683) and Giuseppe Dolcetta (Venice, 1692),[1] with which the Italian tradition seemed to die out. This task was complicated by a number of factors. One was the rarity, obscurity and generally poor quality of the later books, a sad reflection, for the most part, of former splendour, a sign of the extent to which calligraphy had dropped in the scale of human importance in the later *secento*. Another was the extent to which primacy, in teaching the European world to write, had passed to France, to Holland, and, ultimately, to England. Whereas, in the sixteenth century, the calligraphers of other countries had been proud to copy the Italian models (Arrighi and Tagliente were reprinted in Antwerp), by the end of the next century there were signs that the direction of influence was in reverse.

Finally, the disappearance of calligraphy in Italy at the end of the seventeenth century was not so final as had at first seemed to be the case. The market for writing books appeared to go underground for a hundred years, only emerging at the end of the eighteenth century, when the Florentine master Gaetano Giarrè began to produce some entirely and refreshingly novel books, in a neo-classical style. (The revival of writing in Italy in the nineteenth century, a time of renewed invention and decorative sense, still awaits a chronicle.) But there were, in fact, a number of books produced in Italy. The Reycends

1. Some manuals printed in this period, e.g. those of Giovanni Battista Bonacina, (Milan, 1649), Marco Antonio Gandolfi, (Milan, 1660) and V. Spada, (1680 [1649]), are clearly reprints of plates engraved much earlier.

brothers in Turin produced a number of manuals by Peiraud and Pitois at the beginning of the century, all (significantly) engraved at Paris, and, in 1772, the large *Ammaestramenti teorico practici indirizzati ad agevolare il modo d'imparare da per se la scrittura moderna* of Decaroli. This too was engraved in France, and bears marked signs of French influence (the 'scrittura moderna' of the title). Finally, there was the Neapolitan *Essemplare* of Gennaro Tronte, reflecting the layout and interests of the previous century.

It is, perhaps, possible to draw some conclusions about this pattern. The most immediately striking fact is the collapse of the Rome-Venice axis, which so dominates the scene until 1640. The later books all come from the north, and more particularly the north-west (only one is from Venice), which prefigures the success of the Fratelli Reycends. It would be a mistake to generalize too much on so slight a foundation, especially while the resources, in terms of writing books, of Italian libraries are still far from fully explored. Equally, it would be a mistake to see signs of an economic collapse in this change. Italy was subjected to a variety of cultural as well as political pressures in the late *secento* and *settecento*. They did not make her poor, so much as offering a new market for imports, like French handwriting, from abroad.

On the other hand, it is significant that Pepys, an informed connoisseur of writing and writing-books in his time, had heard of no other books later than Antonozzi. What was 'more modern' was much less 'extraordinary'. It is vivid contemporary evidence of the decline of the home-grown article: it is also, unconsciously, evidence of a new and ultimately destructive trait, the passion for '*groppi*' or 'striking', elaborate patterns welcomed by the engravers as a chance to demonstrate their skill with the burin. Up to 1638, the prime object of the writing-masters' self-advertisement was letters, beautiful letters, speedily written. Increasingly, 'command of hand', the ability to build up elaborate patterns with a single, complex, controlled movement of the pen, dominated their minds and books, to the exclusion of the proper business of the formation of letters. The taste for the useless but spectacular calligraphic act goes back to Alunno: its dominance can be seen in Ruinetti. The later Italian masters pursued it, to the detriment of the art of writing, and also of the business of writing. The French and Dutch manner of laying out writing books, fused in the English style, was better designed, both economically and in terms of advertisement, to demonstrate the scribe's aptitude for all sorts of writing, from engrossing charters to double-entry book-keeping. The new style and needs implied rejection of the Italian style, 'remplies de hastes, accompagnees de grands poches et de traits trop longs, trop ennuyeux, et trop importuns a bien former'.[1]

In the sixteenth century, Italian handwriting was the cynosure of Europe. Morison owned the copy of Palatino that was inscribed by the great English mathematician John Blagrave 'Joannis Blagravi & amicorum liber. Anno Salutis 1580'. By then, it was the fashion to write the Italian hand, even in far off England. The revival of 'italic', which Morison and Fairbank did so much to stimulate, owes much to the fact that it grew out of a tradition that had already found roots in England. At the same time, most sixteenth-century Englishmen who could write 'italic' also wrote their own vernacular or 'court hand'. The fusion of the two in the seventeenth century led to the creation of English 'copper plate' script, which, popularized by George Bickham in the eighteenth century, appears as 'Carattere Inglese' in Giarrè's *Nuovo metodo per formare un bel carattere* (1801).

In a world changed by the invention of printing, the scribe could offer two advantages over the press, beauty and speed. Arrighi and Tagliente popularized the first; but Cresci combined it with speed. For Morison, he was the central figure of the Italian renaissance of the art of writing.

1. L. Barbedor, *Traité d'art d'escrire* (Paris, 1649), col. 28; quoted by Morison' introduction to A. Heal *The English Writing Masters* (Cambridge, 1931), p. xxx.

PART TWO

★

ITALIAN WRITING BOOKS 1522-39
An Attempted Chronology

PREFACE

The origins of this attempt to disentangle the complicated
threads that link the writing books produced in the 1520s have
been noted above (p. 16). The text which follows was completed
in the spring of 1967. As photocopying was still in its infancy
(and desk-top publishing undreamed of), it was duplicated, and
some 30 or 40 copies sent to those who had taken or might take
an interest in its subject. It is only fair to say that the response
was less than enthusiastic. Without the books in front of you,
without the chance to examine them in detail as I had had, it
was hard to visualize what was going on, to follow an argument
that linked the development of writing with xylography and
both with the technology of type-founding. Only Graham Pollard, with whom the work had been much discussed, and John
Oates, who came to it fresh, paid me the compliment of reading the script in detail, and providing the criticism that it needed.

I set the piece aside. None of my correspondents urged publication, and I had other and more pressing things to do. No
one, however, had questioned or upset the chronology I had
suggested or the interlocking influence of the books upon each
other. I felt that this was, perhaps, a story for which the world
was not yet ready, and I am happy to think that its time has
come now. I have re-read it, checked the facts, made some
necessary corrections, but have otherwise left it as originally
written. In particular, I have let the beginning stand, with its
notably difficult quotation from Giacomo Manzoni's *Studii di
bibliografia analitica*. The thought that Manzoni found so difficult
to express underlies the twenty-five years' progress of the present
work.

It has been a work of detection, or, as Manzoni says, vindication. The true story of the origins of the first printed manuals
of handwriting has to be uncovered from the confusion caused
by Ugo da Carpi. His attempt to retain a property that was not

really his, and then to annex that of others to fortify his position, has obscured the truth for a long time. If Arrighi had not died (as is likely) in the Sack of Rome in 1527 and Tagliente about the same time, all might have been clearer. As it is, their work, like that of Ugo da Carpi, fell into other hands, who had little sense of the purpose or integrity of their work, merely of its commercial potential.

This last factor explains what follows, and underlies what has gone before. Writing, and the teaching of writing, in a world now accustomed to the fact of printing, was suddenly seen to be good business, even big business. If printing had absorbed the scribe's main work of book-production, the need for an appropriate writing for special documents, charters, accounts, letters to monarchs and other notables, was thrown into sharper chiaroscuro. To Arrighi, from his vantage point in the curia, belongs the credit for first realising this fact. Tagliente, at the centre of the commercial universe in Venice, may indeed have come to the same conclusion independently. How right they both were can be seen by the cut-throat competition that publication induced, by the volume of reprints of their work (to which Fanti's was quickly annexed), and by the scarcity of surviving copies of them.

The business of writing (an art too, but it was its commercial aspect that made it popular) was an important Italian export for over a century. What follows can only be understood if it is understood as a battle for a market, as well as a style of writing which still has power today.

N. B.

152

Chapter 1

INTRODUCTION

'*It is my intention to illustrate a canon of analytical bibliography which I venture to call a canon of* vindication, *although I see that, by describing it so bluntly, its true value cannot be understood. On the other hand, it can be very easily understood that bibliography, more than any other, is the study best fitted to establish the precedence of authors and their works by whatever process of reasoning is called for. This assumption that it deals with points of precedence of this sort I call a principle or canon of vindication. In this work and, even more, in the course of time, it will be seen that though much has been written about literary or scientific plagiarisms, real or imagined – volumes could be written on the subject – little enough has been said about a very great number of cases of this sort. In these, the protestations of the plagiarists have been met without opposition and even with acquiescence. Capable as they were of deceiving others, their complaints that they have themselves been deceived have been accepted, and they have been given full credit in their attempts to convict their victims of deceit. I have, therefore, deliberately begun work in this field with the art of writing, with the books published about it, and with those who wrote them*'.[1]

In addition to the hazards of intentional deceit which exercised Manzoni, the history of the early writing books is much complicated by the limitations in the means of reproducing written hands and by the similarity of the finished books to those printed from movable types, from which, however, they differ in a number of important particulars. It may be useful to have the basis of these distinctions set out in detail, since they are axiomatic to the history of the individual writing books.

1. The accurate transfer of a written specimen on to an en-

1. Giacomo Manzoni, *Studii di Bibliografia Analitica* (Bologna, 1882), pp. xxi-xxii.

153

graved wood block requires great precision: the margin of error is infinitely less than that involved in similarly transferring a drawing. There the treatment of the subject can be varied slightly with the change in medium: with writing books, anything less than exact facsimile destroys the purpose of the original. It follows that there are at any time few craftsmen capable of such work; those that are will not be able to work very fast.

2. Unlike metal type, there is no satisfactory method of correcting inaccurate or damaged wood-cut blocks. Theoretically it should be possible to correct individual lines, but the problem of subsequent alignment, and the natural tendency of the calligrapher to connect one line with the next by means of flourishes, make this exceedingly difficult, if not impossible, in practice. Except in very rare cases, then corrections can only be made by deleting or by replacing the whole block.[1]

3. Letters printed from woodcut blocks are unique, and cannot be reproduced, as letters printed from metal types can be, by resetting. Even a faithful re-engraving of the woodcut image is bound to differ from the first engraving. It follows that the same book cannot be printed simultaneously in two different places. Any appearance to he contrary can only be explained by duplicate plant, and this, in view of the difficulty in creating it, can only be postulated sparingly. The blocks, however, once engraved are permanent, unlike the plant of books printed from metal type that can be distributed. Wood blocks, too, can be moved more easily than type, either in case or made up as pages.

4. Scribes of the first quality were as rare as engravers. The engraver is therefore unlikely to alter the scribe's work except in unusual circumstances, since he cannot rely on his own competence or imagination to provide the necessary copy. It follows that dates on engraved pages represent a *terminus post* for the book in which they appear, in normal circumstances: 'prophetic'

2. The only distinguishable example is the correction which marks the second issue of Eustachio Celebrino *Il modo d'Imparare di scrivere lettera Merchantesca* 1526; see below, p. 180.

dates are unnatural. A contrary case (that is, a book whose text pages dates later than the title-page date) requires special scrutiny, which is likely to show that the book was not issued until after the later date, the title-page remaining unaltered due to the difficulty of changing it. I shall avoid leaning on this argument without evidence from other sources, but the bulk of the evidence suggests that a page date should be regarded as a *terminus post* unless it can be proved to be otherwise.[1]

5. Imitation of one writing book in another, unless clearly determined by certain dates or a clear pattern of deterioration, can only be assumed in limited circumstances. If the same material appears in two books, the *terminus post* for each book can only be the previous edition of the same book that did not contain the material. There is, however, a strong probability that if two books contain the same material, neither will precede the last edition of either which did not contain that material. Imitation, however, need not be unidirectional. Calligraphers all imitate each other's book freely when it suits them to do so; but the engraver, if he lacks an original calligraphic source, must be dependent on existing printed examples.

6. Books in the making grow sheet by sheet: an inset imposition (that is, a book imposed as a single gathering) is therefore evidence of a pre-established extent. A copy of a book so imposed may normally be assumed to post-date a copy of the same book gathered in conventional quires.[2]

7. The use of metal type in writing books requires as careful study as the woodcut examples. Its total absence, and also its appearance on 'specimen' as opposed to 'text' pages, require explanation.

1. Within limits, it is possible to extend this theory to place as well as time. A clear distinction must be made between the place of the writer and the place of the addressee, where the document reproduced shows an address; the latter is obviously of no significance for this purpose.
2. No satisfactory collational formula has been devised for these impositions. 'A⁴⁸' seems an unnecessarily terse way of recording the make-up of a 96-page book. Perhaps 'A¹-A²⁴ (inset)' would be better.

Chapter 2

THE TRADITIONAL DATING

The accepted version of the chronology of the writing books produced in Italy in the seventeen years following 1522 is a fairly simple story. In 1522, Ludovico Arrighi published *La O-perina, da imparare di scrivere littera Cancellerescha* in Rome, probably late in the year since page 26[1] is dated 'in alma urbe' 7 August. On the subtitle *il Modo & Regola da scrivere littera corsiva over Cancellarescha*, Arrighi describes himself as 'Scrittore de brevi apostolici', a member, that is, of the branch of the papal chancery responsible for writing and despatching the 'briefs', letters elucidating the formal and often illegible bulls or of an informal nature. Between 1522 and the next year, Arrighi broke with the Curia, and went to Venice where he apparently became a public notary and published, with the assistance of the engraver Eustachio Celebrino, *Il modo da temperare le Penne con le varie Sorti de littere* in 1523. The internal dates of 18 September 1523 at Rome (p. 13) and 14 February 1525 at Venice (p. 10) must be ignored as fictitious. In 1524, Giovanni Antonio Tagliente's *Lo presente libro Insegna La Vera arte de lo Excellente scrivere de diverse varie sorti de litere* appeared in Venice, and was reprinted in the same year. By June, Arrighi was back in Rome, where he began a new career as a printer, not later than July, for a group of the cultivated humanist writers, all concerned in some way with the papal court. Arrighi's employment as a printer continued, with a curious gap from sometime after 12 April 1525 to a date fairly late in 1526, until May 1527, when it seems likely that he lost his life during the Sack of Rome.

1. All the works under description are unfoliated, and the system of nominal page numbering adopted here has been chosen for reasons of convenience. When, for example, the contents of a writing book do not change but the imposition does, it seems pedantic to refer to the same page in the same position in two different printings by reference to two different collational formulae.

Less than a month after the completion of Arrighi's last dated book in 1525, on 8 May, Ugo da Carpi, who cut the blocks for *La Operina*, obtained a privilege against Arrighi to print 'novas litterarum notas, et characteres', in which (he alleged) he had been obstructed by Arrighi. The privilege is attached to a new edition of *La Operina* printed from new and inferior blocks cut in imitation of the originals, but clearly without any assistance from Arrighi. In 1525, Ugo da Carpi also published the *Thesauro de Scrittori*, consisting mainly of plagiarisms of Tagliente's examples and text. In Venice in the same year, three more quarto editions of Tagliente appeared, and also *Il modo d'Imparare a scrivere lettera Merchantescha* by Celebrino, whose name had appeared as engraver not only in Arrighi's *Il Modo*, but also in Tagliente's second 1524 printing. This was followed before the year was out by a small oblong version of Tagliente.

There next ensues a gap of some three years until 1530-1, the dates (on title and colophon) of the next surviving issue of Tagliente; records, but no copies of editions of 1527, 1529 and 1530 survive. Other issues, all printed in Venice, of 1531, 1532, 1533, 1534, 1536, 1537 and 1539 are known. In 1532, also in Venice, Arrighi's two books were reprinted together in a slightly abbreviated form from the original blocks by Nicolo d'Aristotile, and re-issued in 1533. By 1538, however, the blocks had returned again to Rome, and they were reprinted, this time without any type-set text, by the D'Orico brothers, and reprinted again in the following year.

Chapter 3

THE DATE OF *LA OPERINA*

The are, it will be seen, a number of stumbling blocks in this sequence of events, notably the 'fictitious' dates in *Il modo*, and the unlikely gap in Arrighi's printing career. There is a further puzzle in the fact that the 'Venice' date in *Il modo* – 14 February 1525 – appears to fall in the middle of Arrighi's first prolific period as a printer, during which he produced 28 books in ten months. It is clear that there is scope for a detailed examination of the evidence on which the accepted version of the chronology is based. Where, moreover, such a detailed examination has already taken place, as in Mr Hofer's analysis of the surviving copies of *La Operina* 1522, it has been made clear that things are not what they seem.[1] Mr Hofer's discoveries are indeed a crucial part of this inquiry, and a brief recapitulation of them will serve to set the scene for what follows.

Eleven copies of *La Operina* 1522 are known to Mr Hofer. They divide themselves into three groups or states. Eight of the copies fall into the third group, which is differentiated from the second by signs of progressive damage to the blocks on pages 3, 17 and 32. The British Museum copy is one of two surviving of this earlier second state. The earliest state is represented by the Harvard copy only, which differs from the second and third states in two radical particulars which indicate that it is a separate issue from the other two. In it, page 17 is an entirely different block, with the words *Virtus* . . . . . . *profecto* on two lines in a poorly rendered extra-inclined cursive (not unlike Taglien-te's 'nodaresca'; and the cartouche lettered CUM GRATIA & PRIVILEGIO on page 32, which aligns poorly with the text above, conceals the fact that, beneath the words *Stampata in*

1. Philip Hofer, 'Variant Issues of the First Edition of Ludovico Arrighi Vicentino's "Operina", in *Calligraphy and Palaeography* (London, 1965), pp. 95-106.

Roma per inventione di Ludovico Vicentino scrittore, there followed originally *& Ugo da Carpi Intagliatore*.

At first sight, this all appears to fit very well with the accepted version. But it raises two questions which cannot easily be answered: what was it that caused Arrighi to take this offensive action against Ugo da Carpi, and why did Ugo da Carpi wait for some two and a half years before retaliating? It is clear that in publishing the 'copied' edition with the privilege dated 8 May 1525, Ugo was vindicating his rights: that it was also a direct retaliation against Arrighi can be seen from the colophon on page 32, which reads *Stampata in Roma per inventione No, Ludovico Vicentino. Resurrexit Ugo da Carpi*; the substitution of the word SEPULCHRUM on the cartouche below is an even clearer aspersion on Arrighi's action. A possible answer to both these questions is that *La Operina* was not published in 1522, but much later; that Ugo da Carpi was redressing a recent injury, and that Arrighi's exasperated action was due to protracted delay on the part of his engraver.

The immediate objection to this theory might run as follows: 'You are now asking us to disregard dates on title pages; you argued earlier that dates on any page were to be trusted implicitly, however improbable'. But there is a difference between accepting a date as absolute and a date as a *terminus post*; there are numerous examples in later printings of writing books with title page dates – even those already crudely corrected – remaining unaltered for one or even three years, although contradicted by a type-set colophon at the end. What evidence can we offer that 1522 is only a *terminus post*? What conjecture can be made about the *terminus ante*? In the first place the existence of three different states argues a certain passage of time. It is possible that a further examination of the surviving copies, particularly of those bound up with copies of *Il modo* 1523, might reveal more clearly how long that time was. The British Museum copy of both books together shows that they were printed on two different paper stocks: *La Operina*, which has horizontal chain lines (29 mm apart), was printed on half sheets, with a post-horn watermark close to Briquet 7855 (found in Rome and Bologna, c. 1513-15); *Il modo*, which has horizontal chain lines (35 mm apart), as is conventional in a quarto imposition, has a cardinal's hat watermark fairly near Briquet 3457 (found in Venice, Vicenza, Ferrara, Bologna, Cesena, Rome and Syracuse, between 1504 and 1517). The watermarks in the Harvard and Benson copies of *La Operina*, as recorded by Mr. Hofer (they represent his first and third states, respectively) are both different from that of the British Museum copy (second state). Moreover, since Mr. Hofer wrote his article, a fourth and still later state has come to light. This is described in the *Catalogue* 100[1] of Martin Breslauer. The collation given corresponds with the copy described by the Prince d'Essling as in the collection of Charles Fairfax Murray.[2] The colophon of *La Operina* and the title of *Il modo* are missing; and the extent is reduced by two leaves. But the paper stock is the same throughout, with the cardinal's hat watermark. This proves that Arrighi took all the blocks of *La Operina* with him to Venice, and printed it again, in a slightly different form, at about the same time as the first printing of *Il modo*.

There is evidence, too, that neither *La Operina* nor *Il modo* appeared in the form that Arrighi intended. The signature A in *La Operina* appears not on the first recto but on the first verso; it is woodcut and therefore presumably part of the block. The text of A 1 *verso* is the title *Il Modo & Regola de scrivere littera corsiva*: the wording here compares with *Il modo de temperare le Penne* which does appear on a 1 *recto*. It suggests that Arrighi planned his work to appear simultaneously in two sections, the title *La Operina* being perhaps originally destined for a preliminary gathering, the rest of whose contents never appeared. Some further evidence for this supposition may be deduced from the

1. London, 1965, no. 27A.
2. Essling, *Les Livres à Figures Vénétiens*, no. 2181. Although both Essling and Breslauer collate *La Operina* A-B⁴C⁶, probably both copies are imperfect.

text of page 13 of *Il modo*. This purports to reproduce three fragments of a notarial document, with the names of three witnesses, the place – Rome, and the exact date – Tuesday, 18 September 1523. Too much must not be made of this: 18 September 1523 was a Friday, not a Tuesday. Nevertheless, setting aside the problem this creates in the dating of *Il modo*, it seems improbable that Arrighi would devise a Roman document for publication in a manual that was to appear in Venice; that, in short, the pages of *Il modo* which are definitely Roman (the title and pages 13, 16 and 18-19; see Table, nos. 61, 64 and 66) were in fact designed for publication in Rome, and may well have been engraved there. (Had it been necessary, Arrighi could easily have adapted his originals for the Venetian market; the fact that he did not suggest that the blocks were in existence before he went to Venice). If therefore Arrighi was still on good terms with Ugo da Carpi, as late perhaps as 18 September 1523, such that Ugo was still prepared to cut blocks to his design, it can only mean that the first issue of *La Operina* 1522 was still unissued. If this is so, it follows from the first axiom that the fault is likely to lie with Ugo da Carpi rather than Arrighi, who was in any case unlikely to have specified a date on the title page of his book that he himself was unlikely to keep.

If then towards the end of 1523, Arrighi found himself still waiting for the completion of a work he had planned for publication in 1522, a work of 64 pages or more designed to cover every branch of the art of writing, his sense of frustration must have been extreme. Unwilling (unlike some of his less scrupulous competitors) to botch the job by attempting to rush it out in an imperfect state or by correcting the already mendacious date, he could only wait until Ugo da Carpi, a busy professional engraver, could find time to finish his work, an exacting, novel and not perhaps very lucrative task. At what point did Arrighi lose patience? The cutting of punches is a longer and even more exacting task than engraving wood blocks. If Arrighi was in a position to start printing by June or July 1524, he must have

set up his partnership with Lautizio Perugino some months previously. His own share of the undertaking, a press and paper,
need not have taken so long to provide and so he may have
found himself with a press and paper, waiting both for Ugo da
Carpi and Lautizio. Now it was noted above that the presence
or absence of metal type in a writing book requires scrutiny.
La Operina contains no type, a fact generally attributed to the
same taste which led Arrighi when he became a printer to have
an entirely new fount cut. But if Arrighi were really desperate,
as well he might have been if he knew that his Venetian rival
Tagliente was planning a similar book, he could always have
taken his blocks to an established printer who would have been
able to supply the missing material (however inadequately) with
types; this was the solution he finally chose for *Il modo*. The
absence of any type may then be an indication that Arrighi,
having taken as many blocks as were ready, but not (as we shall
see) his own designs, printed *La Operina*, a slightly imperfect
version of the first half of his full manual, on his own press in
the first half of 1524. Having printed it, he then decided to
disown Ugo da Carpi, first by obliterating his name on the
sheets already printed with a cartouche (perhaps originally part
of an unfinished preliminary page), and then by substituting
the cartouche for his name altogether in subsequent impressions.

A different hypothesis has been put forward by Mr. Graham
Pollard.[1] He suggests that the presence of the cartouche is evidence that *La Operina*, as well as *Il modo*, was first printed in
Venice. The argument stems from the similarity of the cartouche
to other white on black cartouches which can be certainly (as
in the 1525 edition of Tagliente in the British Museum) or
probably connected with Celebrino, and the assumption follows that all the *fond noir* blocks in Tagliente and Arrighi are
to be attributed to the same hand. This theory has a tempting
simplicity, but there are certain drawbacks to it. In the first

1. In his Presidential address to the Bibliographical Society in 1962.

place, it is improbable that the imperfections in *La Operina*, notably the misplaced signature A, would have been left unaltered in Venice, when Arrighi had access to printer's type. Again, it is unlikely that the two books would first have been printed separately on different paper stocks, and later together on the same. Lastly, Arrighi made a highly individual use of the decorative possibilities of the cartouche. This is already fully developed in his manuscript *Aristoteles Ethica* of 1517,[1] and the examples in *La Operina* and *Il modo* are in the same tradition. If, therefore, a similar treatment of cartouches is found elsewhere – and the only close parallel is in Celebrino's 'signature' in the 1525 Tagliente – it may be regarded as a sign of Arrighi's influence on Celebrino, not the other way round.

1. Amsterdam Universiteitsbibliotheek, Ms. II.A.19.

Chapter 4
ARRIGHI'S PRINTING TYPES

It is hardly necessary to emphasize that either argument is highly speculative. The only real anomaly in the accepted version is the length of the time between Arrighi's insult and Ugo da Carpi's retaliation. There could be other explanations than the one here offered, and all that can be said with any certainty is that if *La Operina* was printed after 1522, it is unlikely to have been printed later than June 1524. We come now to rather more certain ground. Arrighi's printing career is documented by a number of accurately dated colophons, relationships can be established between his various types which involve further conclusions, and the number of writing books issued both in Rome and in Venice increases, and with it the chance of making comparisons, and drawing conclusions based on them, about questions of priority.

There are a number of different ways in which types fundamentally the same can differ from one another. The same type in two different places may appear differently according to the degree of inking and impression given to it. Two different types cast from the same matrix may differ if the heat of the metal and the condition of the matrix differ. Two different matrices from the same punch may differ since no punch can be struck with the same impact twice. Finally, a punch may be modified by engraving or rubbing down between one strike and the next. These processes are here listed in ascending order of priority and of difficulty. Two types from the same casting can be taken out of the case simultaneously. Casting new type was a regular part of the business of any printing house. Striking matrices was a task requiring a steady hand and experience; it was not part of the ordinary printer's task, but (more probably) at this time, of the punch cutter's. Cutting punches was (and is) an immensely skilled form of engraving on metal, requiring skill, patience and experience: to engrave a homogeneous set of punches is a long task for a skilled craftsman of a kind never common at any period of printing history. Any estimate of the number of different 'types' held by a printer, in the sense of complete sets of upper and lower case letters derived from different punches, should be made in the knowledge that a complete set of punches can take months, even years, to engrave. Another reason for caution in distinguishing independent 'types' is the fact that the alteration of only a few characters can radically alter the general appearance of a type in mass.

The actual number of 'types' owned or used by Arrighi is hard to determine, and only the barest indication of the problem can be given here. Five 'types' have been distinguished, of which three were extensively used by Arrighi for book-printing.[1] Of the latter, the first is assumed to have been cut for Arrighi by his partner Lautizio Perugino (who is generally equated with Lautizio Bartolomeo dei Rotelli, the goldsmith praised by Cellini). It contains a large number of variant sorts, including a number devised by Arrighi's patron Giangiorgio Trissino as part of his phonetic spelling reforms. These make detailed analysis difficult, but a distinction can be made between the earlier form (Casamassima I.a), found in 14 books printed between July and December 1524, and the later form (Casamassima I.b), also found in 14 books between July 1524 and 12 April 1525. The division, which is not hard and fast, is founded partly on subject matter (the earlier group is largely vernacular, the later mostly Latin) and partly on time (poor sorts were to some extent replaced during the nine or ten months during which the type was used). The first form is characterised by curved descenders, the predominance of cursive *g* and formal capitals; the second by

1. The best and most up-to-date account of them is given by E. Casamassima, 'I disegni di caratteri di Ludovico degli Arrighi Vicentino', in *Gutenberg-Jahrbuch 1963*, pp. 24-36, and 'Ancora su Ludovico degli Arrighi', *Gutenberg-Jarhbuch 1965*, pp. 35-42. See also A. S. Osley 'The Origins of Italic Type' in *Calligraphy and Palaeography* (London, 1965) pp. 107-20.

seriffed descenders, more frequent *antica g*, and some informal capitals: *d*, *b* and *l* were noticeably improved.

The second type is altogether different. If the first is what one might expect from a goldsmith instructed by a calligrapher, elegant in mass but irregular and uncomprehending in detail, the second is a thoroughly professional design, with a sharper angle of stress and seriffed ascenders and descenders (including long *s* and *f*). It is used in five books all dated 1526, without day or month. The third and last type, closely related to the second, has hitherto been known by only four productions between November-December 1526 and June 1527 (the last perhaps posthumous), but several additional examples can now be added which extend its period of use. 'Arrighiesque' types are also found in a number of places after the supposed date of Arrighi's death. These will require investigation later.

The other two types are that of the text part of the first edition of *Il Modo*, and that of a later edition, generally dated *c* 1525,[1] although the colophon reads *Ludo. Vice'tinus Rome in Parhione scribebat ANN. MDXXIII*. Let us dispose of the latter first. The edition is known by the unique copy in the Newberry Library, Chicago. Doubts have already been expressed on its authenticity by Mr Hofer, which have been echoed by subsequent writers, notably about the first and last leaves which are not conjugate, and appear to be on different stock from the rest of the book. It is imposed inset as a single gathering, signed A(I) – XV, which by our sixth axiom ought to be an indication of late date.[2] Its text pages are set in an italic type, with some general resemblances to Arrighi's types, which does not appear to have been used before 1532. It is printed from Arrighi's own blocks, not Ugo da Carpi's (which were in existence from

1. E. Casamassima, *Trattati di Scrittura del Cinquecento Italiano* (Milan, 1966), p. 57, n. 20; A. F. Johnson, *Type Designs*, 2nd ed. (London, 1959), p. 100.
2. Philip Hofer, op. cit. p. 105. Note that the collation formula given by Hofer is that of Essling no. 2181, not the Newberry Library copy, which immediately precedes it in A. F. Johnson's *Catalogue*.

c. 1525 onwards), and the block on page 17 is the first state found only in the Harvard copy of *La Operina* 1522. These circumstances suffice to prove that the middle 28 leaves of this copy are from a copy of the reissue of both of Arrighi's works put out in 1532 and again in 1533 under the title of *Regola da imparare scrivere,* by Nicolo Zoppino d'Aristotile. Whether he printed it himself is difficult to say. The Venetian printers of the time regularly took in each other's work, but I have been able to find only one other usage of the types used in it, either in Zoppino's work, or that of his contemporaries. There is one anomaly, in the text pages – the fact that the border of the cartouche on page 32 is perfect in the two places where it is found broken from the third state of *La Operina* 1522 onwards, including *Regola* 1532. This could be the result of careful restoration. The first and last leaves are a different problem. The colophon reproduces the lower half of page 24 too accurately (judged by Ugo da Carpi's or the Antwerp recutting of 1543) to be anything but a facsimile produced by lithography or a process line block. The title page was probably reproduced by the same means from a redrawing of the 1522 original.[1] It is clear that a deliberate attempt has been made to 'perfect' the book at some time after, say, 1870. It is not clear whether the object was only to produce a perfect copy from an imperfect one, or whether it was constructed to provide an 'earlier state' than the existing copies of *Il modo* 1523, lacking some of the material and therefore presumably printed before Arrighi left Rome. But we can safely reject the type of this counterfeit from the sequence of those with a claim to have been designed by Arrighi, although, as we shall see, it has some claim to examination on its own account.

We are left, then, with the first type and its variants, cut for Arrighi by Lautizio, in use between June 1524 and April 1525,

1. It would be interesting to know what copy of *La Operina* was used as copy for the redrawing. No facsimile had yet been published which a draftsman might follow; the drawing itself is poor and lifeless, revealing no comprehension of calligraphic methods.

the two related types in use from late 1526 to May or June 1527, and the type of the true first edition of *Il modo*. I hope to show that the last is the first attempt of a new punch cutter to follow the same, or a similar, model as that given to Lautizio, and that the 1526-7 types contain improvements and modifications of it, some sorts remaining virtually unchanged. The following table indicates both the progression of the design, and the identical sorts.[1]

TYPE IB	*a b c d e f g g h i l m n p g q r s ſſ t u y z*
IL MODO	*a b c d e f g h i l m n p g r s ſſ t u y z*
TYPE III	*b d g h l p q q r ſſ u y z*
TYPE II	*a f ſ y*

TABLE: All the critical characteristics of each sort are exaggerated.

It will be seen that none of the actual sorts of the first type appear in the subsequent founts, although in *Il modo* the rounded ascenders and descenders and tailed g are carried on. The angle of slant is made more regular – in the earlier type some ascenders, notably b and d, were too vertical, whereas others, like *i, t* and *s*, were too inclined. The protruding head of *a*, the flattened top of *f*, the reverse curve at the foot of *l*, are all modified. On the other hand, *c* and *r* are not modified; *h* is an obviously unsatisfactory character. The most noticeable feature, however is the general sharpening of contrast, accentuated in the substitution of a point for a curve in *b, c, d, e, h, p, g*. This last characteristic is even more marked in type II, even allowing for the extreme

1. The numbering is that of Casamassima in *Gutenberg-Jahrbuch 1963* and *1965*.

number of serifs on ascenders and descenders, which superficially alter the face.

If, on the other hand, comparison is made between the type of *Il modo* and Arrighi's last types, a startling number of similarities appear that belie the incidental characteristics – the curved ascenders and descenders and tailed *g* – which seem to connect it more closely with the earliest type. In one place only, line 10 of page 3 of *Il modo*, is there a seriffed ascender. It confirms at a glance the resemblance to the later types. In fact, only five sorts in *Il modo* – *g*, *h*, *r*, *u* and long *ss* – differ in form from those of the later types. Of these, *r* and long *ss* can be seen to be an intermediate stage between the earlier and later types; *h* is a poor sort, which might well have been rejected later; *u* with its pointed curve and exaggerated up-stroke may well have been rejected also since it fits so badly with *m* and *n* (its characteristics suggest a copy of one of the Griffo italics, particularly the first); only *g* is a satisfactory design with no obvious connection with either the earlier or later types, although parallels could be found in other contemporary Venetian italics. In every other respect – the incidental seriffing apart – the type of *Il modo* resembles the later types, and *a*, *c*, *e*, *f*, *i*, *m*, *n*, *s*, long *s* and *t* in *Il modo* are unchanged in the later types – a substantial proportion. We shall return later to the evidence on the date of *Il modo* which can be derived from this typographical evidence. The later history of Arrighi's types is a very much more complex business, which has a direct bearing on the chronology of the writing books, since the earliest date by which they are used must provide some indication of the date of the type of *Il modo* and therefore of *Il modo* itself. Successive studies of Arrighi's types have tended to reduce the number of independent faces found in his books, but even in the most recent[1] the last two are treated as separate designs. But apart from the foot serifs of *f* and long *s*, the similarities are far too close for it to be possible to treat the types as

1. Casamassima, loc. cit.

independent designs – that is, derived from separate sets of punches.¹ The main difference – characterized by Dr Casamassima as 'less stylised, more fluent and more open in appearance' – is largely a question of contrast of thick and thin strokes, rather than the actual shape of the individual letters. Only one letter – *a* – is different in this respect, that of type II having an almost vertical counter while that of type III is angled – as is the *a* of *Il modo*.

The dating of the two types – or versions, rather – has hitherto been treated as self-evident. The five short books in type II – similar in appearance to the productions of 1524-5 – are all dated 1526; none has a month date. (It is worth noting that by the standards of 1524-5 these might all have been printed within a month or two). The four recorded productions in type III are spread over a long period, and vary in extent from a single broadside, the brief *Cum nuper exercitus*, dated 8 June 1527 (perhaps after Arrighi's death) to the *De arte poetica* and other tracts of Marco Girolamo Vida, one of Arrighi's longest books, dated May 1527. The third is the first edition of a work by Marco Fabio Calvo, scholar and antiquary, who perished during the Sack of Rome. This was *Antiquae urbis Romae cum regionibus simulachrum*, April 1527, a large folio (Arrighi's only production in such a grandiose format) chiefly occupied with the magnificent woodcut plans by Tolomeo Egnazio, lettered in a chancery script which can be confidently ascribed to Arrighi and is as impressive a tribute to his skill as *La Operina*.² The last of the four is the sixteen page *Perpetuatio officiorum etiam Romanae Cunae* of Clement VII, usually dated November-December 1526; it must, however, be after 26 November, the beginning of the

1. The types are cast in different bodies which increases the difference of appearance. The measurements are: type II, 20/11 – 142/3 mm; type III, 20/11 – 129/30 mm.
2. See A. Jammes, 'Un chef-d'oeuvre méconnu d'Arrighi Vicentino', *Studia bibliographica in honorem Herman de la Fontaine Verwey* (Amsterdam, 1968), pp. 297-316.

fourth regnal year of Clement VII, in which it is dated.[1] To these can now be added a fifth example, also printed for the Curia. This is also a quarto of 16 pages, *Bulla erectionis Montis Fidei et illius Collegii ac Venditionis & assignationis Dohannae Mercium Sancti Eustachii de Urbe*, dated the fourteenth before the Kalends of November in the third year of Clement VII; that is, 18 October 1526.

This addition gives some reason to alter the traditional order of the two versions of Arrighi's last type. Before, there was a group of four works, one long and one which with its many maps may have drawn extensively on Arrighi's time as a calligrapher, in the period December 1526 – June 1527, before which the five works of the other group were presumed to have been printed. Now the beginning of the use of type III can be put back to October 1526, and there is no reason to exclude the possibility that the two versions were used simultaneously, as were the variants of type I.[2] It is difficult to gain an accurate impression of the exact appearance of type III. The three papal documents are printed on poor paper, the *Antiquae urbis simulachrum* on thick but soft paper, and the Vida (in the copy most frequently reproduced, that from George III's library in the British Museum) on vellum. It is possible that the difference from type II are merely differences of impression. If however it is 'thinner' than type II, it must represent an earlier state of the punches, which could only be altered by rubbing down to produce a thicker image. If this process did take place now (and it can be demonstrated that it did take place again some years later) the variation in the form of *a* would indicate that type III preceded type II.

It is probable that more detailed examination of papal printing of the period 1526-7 will reveal more examples of the use of

1. A. Pratesi, s.v. 'Arrighi, Ludovico' in *Dizionario Biografico degli Italiani*, IV (Rome 1962), pp. 310-3.
2. A. S. Osley, loc. cit., p. 119, notes the appearance of the Type III long *s* in the last two signature of Collenuccio *Apologi*.

type III which may establish the dating more exactly. A fully dated example of type II, even more desirable, is less likely to be found. We must now turn to the history of Arrighi's types after the Sack of Rome. Printing, like every other civil activity, was brought almost to standstill by this cataclysm. All trace of Arrighi's type is lost until 1530. In that year Antonio Blado printed in Rome an edition of Sannazaro's *Sonetti* entirely in an italic type that is clearly produced from new matrices struck from the same punches as type II & III, rubbed down (perhaps for the second time) to produce a bolder letter. Two sorts in particular need notice: *a* has the slanted counter, and there is an occasional chancery *g*, which corresponds exactly with that in *Il modo*. This version is the most regular and imposing of all the variants. It was used for years to come in the series of editions of vernacular texts which, with his work as printer to the Curia, have made Blado famous. If he bought or acquired the punches of Arrighi's type, it is clear that he also obtained other printing material from the same source. One of the difficulties of identifying Arrighi's work is the almost complete absence of decorative material or display types: only the type III productions have any of either, *Il modo* always excepted.[1] Among a number of fine decorative initials in *Il modo* is a fine 'lettera a groppi' E in white on black within a rule border. This also appears in *De sacrificio missae adversus luteranos* by Thomas de Vio (better known as Caietan), printed by Gherardo Blado and dated 3 May 1531. Some of Blado's other books[2] in the Arrighi italic also contain two fine outline decorated initials C and H just over an inch deep. These were evidently considered appropriate with italic, because apart from their use with the Arrighi italic they seem only to be found in the three books, dated 1525-6, which Blado printed in a curious large italic (the only one he

1. It is possible that the *moderna* types shown in *Il modo* and used for display in Arrighi's 'type III' printing may be identified elsewhere.
2. E.g. Thomas de Vio Caietan *De Communione . . . adversus luteranos*, dated 25 August 1531.

seems to have had before he acquired Arrighi's), to which we will return later. These initials are very close copies of a set of three (A, C and H) much used in Venice at the time, and may have been originally cut by the same hand that cut the blocks for Tagliente's books, in which they are also found from 1525.[1]

The printing connection between Venice and Rome was a strong one. Apart from the sons of Eucharius Silber, who set up the first permanent press in Rome in 1480, almost all the printers in Rome came from Lombardy: the Blado family came from Asola, Mazzocchi from Bergamo, Calvo from Como, and Valerio D'Orico from near Brescia.[2] The last named and Blado were the only printers working in Rome in the 1530s (except that in 1538 Valerio D'Orico was joined by his brother Luigi) until 1540, when Baldassarre di Francesco Cartolari of Perugia inaugurated his press with Palatino's *Libro Nuovo* and Stefano Nicolini da Sabbio left his many printing relations in Venice to share the papal printing with Blado (books in Arrighi's type are also found under his imprint in the 1540s).[3]

For a period, then, Valerio D'Orico was the only other printer in Rome apart from Blado, and he inherited another part of Arrighi's printing material. He had come to Rome in 1526, but ceased work from 1527 until 1531, perhaps returning to his native Lombardy to avoid the *Lanzknechts*, who killed Marco Calvo and may have killed Arrighi. In 1534 he printed the second edition of Calvo's *Antiquae Urbis Romae simulachrum*. It is probable that the Sack of Rome interrupted the printing of the 1527 issue; it is now very rare. At any rate the second

1. These are copied so accurately as to make it possible to distinguish the source as the Venetian set, rather than Blado's, in a manuscript list of benefactors of Trinity College Cambridge, written in 1563 (A. Fairbank and B. Wolpe, *Renaissance Handwriting*, plate 48; see also pp. 25, 31, 78). An imperfectly realised O in the same style begins the subtitle of the *Thesauro de Scrittori*.
2. F. Barberi, 'I Dorico, tipografi a Roma nel cinquecento' in *La Bibliofilia*, LXVII (1965), pp. 221-61.
3. See Stanley Morison, 'The italic types of Antonio Blado and Ludovico Arrighi', in *The Monotype Recorder* XXVI (1927), No. 217, fig. 12. Morison's text is the only authority on the use of these types after 1527.

edition repeats the layout of the first very closely,[1] and the type is clearly the same (Type III, that is) as the first. The privilege of the 1534 edition was granted by Clement VII to Timoteo Fabio, grandson of the author. He presumably inherited the plant of his grandfather's book and brought type as well as blocks to D'Orico. Among the decorated initials used by D'Orico is an outline lombardic decorated Q in white on black which corresponds exactly with that in the set of initials on pages 18-19 of *Il modo*, and a S from the same set as the E mentioned above. The D'Orico brothers continued to use Arrighi's type for many years; the type of Ruano's *Sette Alphabeti* which they printed in 1554, consists mainly of Arrighi's type III, although some sorts have been replaced. It seems unlikely that they had matrices. The brothers had a further connection with Arrighi, because they were responsible for the third separate reprinting of Arrighi's blocks for *La Operina and Il modo*. As with the Zoppino reprints, there were two issues, one in 1538 and another in 1539. Arrighi's type was not used.[2] It is possible that the return of the blocks from Venice to Rome is connected with the fact that Luigi D'Orico came down to Rome in the same year, and may have acquired the blocks from Zoppino before he left.

There are only two other places where Arrighi's types are found after 1527. The first is at Vicenza, where in 1529 Tolomeo Janiculo printed a number of books for Giangiorgio Trissino in a type which consists almost entirely of sorts from Arrighi's improved type I. It is generally assumed that when Trissino left Rome for Vicenza (he left after 17 September 1526, the date of Clement VII's letter of safe conduct, and arrived before 10 October, when he wrote a letter dated from Murano; the

1. I have not seen a copy of the first edition and derive this statement from Barberi (loc. cit.), who says that the decorative material only is different. The page (f. IV) reproduced by Casamassima, 'Ancora su Ludovico degli Arrighi', p. 39 (fig. 3) corresponds exactly with the 1534 printing; it also shows the initial Q referred to below.
2. Both the earlier and the later blocks of the *& accio che* page are used, the former in place of the text of *Il modo* (see Table, no. 87).

exact date is important),[1] he took with him matrices, and possibly type and punches as well, of Arrighi's first type. He used them only for a brief but prolific period, during which Janiculo produced some small folios (Dante's *De Vulgari eloquentia*, Trissino's own *De le lettere*) which are perhaps the best-designed books printed in any of Arrighi's types. After 1529, the types disappear. Three letters of the fount used by Janiculo need attention: *g*, *k* and *p*. The *g* differs from the normal type I *g* in the same way as that in *Il modo*: that is, the down stroke is straight, not concave, and the tail ends straight, without the reverse curve into the outer edge of the bowl. It is not however the same sort as the *g* in *Il modo*, and a similar *g* can be found in an italic used by Marcolini at Venice in the 1530s. The *k* and *p*, however, are more obviously part of the fount of *Il modo*; the *k* not quite certainly (it only appears once in *Il modo*, in a blurred line), but the *p*, which appears in Janiculo's specimen and as an alternative in *De le lettere*, is unmistakeable. It seems likely that Arrighi discarded the curved ascenders and descenders before he left Venice, and that Trissino had access to Arrighi's abandoned material when he arrived there.

The other example is the type used in Zoppino's *Regola da imparare scrivere* (Venice 1532 and 1533). This is sufficiently like type III (it is cast on the same body) to be confused with it, if the means of direct comparison are not available. On close inspection, however, it can be seen to be a very mixed fount. Only *b*, *d*, *l*, *p* and *g* seem certainly from type III; *a*, swash *e*, *r*, *s* and *t* may derive from Janiculo's types,[2] *e*, *i*, *m*, *n*, *o*, *u* are not immediately identifiable, though similar to other contemporary Venetian italics; the curious bottom-heavy *c*, *f* with its long bent right-hand bar, the ill-fitting *g* with its sharply-angled junction between the two bowls, and *h* seem to be peculiar to this fount, and might serve to identify it elsewhere. I have seen

---

1. B. Morsolin, *Giangiorgio Trissino* (Florence 1894), pp. 132-3.
2. Janiculo ceased to use them after 1529, and the subsequent history of the fount is unknown.

it nowhere else, either in Zoppino's books or those of the Da Sabbio family, except in *Eunuco*, an anonymous translation of Terence printed by Zoppino in July 1532, in which it is used for the title, 'Interlocutori' and 'Argumento'.

The evidence to be derived from Arrighi's types can be briefly summarised. Only two distinct types from two separate sets of punches existed, although there were many variant sorts in both. The type of *Il modo* is a prototype of the second of these. *Il modo* itself must therefore have been printed after 12 April 1525 (the last date in the first period of printing) and before 18 October 1526 (the first date in the second). If, as further evidence will show, it was printed later rather than earlier in this period, it might be conjectured that Arrighi returned to Rome not long before 18 October 1526, since there is no evidence of renewed contact between Arrighi and Trissino before the latter left Rome soon after 17 September 1526 (an *argumentum ex silentio*, but not perhaps implausible). Who cut the punches for the types? The evidence that Lautizio cut the first set remains unaltered, and is convincing both in terms of style and of the documentary evidence. The possibility that Eustachio Celebrino cut the second remains so far unexplored, and it is time now to return to Venice, where Tagliente's writing books appeared. The evidence that connects Celebrino with those, if only as an engraver of blocks, is certain. Further investigation depends now on a detailed examination of the contents of Tagliente's books in comparison with those of his contemporaries.

Chapter 5

TAGLIENTE: *LO PRESENTE LIBRO*

The exact sequence of editions is not as self-evident as might at first sight appear, nor, since all the books are rare, is it easy to distinguish one from another and to realise when two imperfectly recorded editions are copies of the same book. When to these difficulties is added the unreliability of title page dates, one can only echo Manzoni's description of the bibliographical analysis of writing books as a work of vindication. But one important division of our material can be made at the outset, between the books published by Ugo da Carpi and the rest. Although the falsehood of almost all the information provided in the *Thesauro de Scrittori* was pointed out as long ago as 1927 by Raffaello Bertieri,[1] the scholarly printer of Milan, it has been left to Dr. Casamassima[2] to demonstrate convincingly that Ugo da Carpi, expert engraver and publisher of prints,[3] was no scribe; any original material in his books derives from the work of other hands: he is, in Dr Casamassima's appropriate phrase, the 'cornacchia d'Esopo' of sixteenth-century calligraphy. It will make subsequent investigation much easier if it is understood that the source of any material shown by Ugo da Carpi must be sought elsewhere, and that any statement in his books must be treated with suspicion. Thus, if Arrighi and (so far as can be seen) Celebrino were careful not to put out any specimen or information below a very high standard, Tagliente was rather less so, the text in successive editions being 'cut to fit' so that it sometimes hardly makes sense, and the blocks roughly treated; a similar

---

1. R. Bertieri, 'Calligrafi e scrittori di caratteri in Italia nel secolo XVI', in *Il Risorgimento Grafico*, XXIV (1927). The series of studies put out by Bertieri in this periodical, which was printed and published by his own firm, were an important addition to the subject and deserve to be better known.
2. Casamassima, *Trattati*, p. 48.
3. L. Servolini, 'Il maestro della xilografia a chiaroscuro: Ugo da Carpi', *Gutenberg-Jahrbuch 1934*, pp. 107-14, provides a useful account of his activities.

carelessness is seen in matters of date. But Ugo da Carpi had no interest in and no apparent knowledge of calligraphy. Accidentally involved in the business through his connection with Arrighi, he seems merely to have been anxious to capitalize on what he may have considered dear-bought experience; the order and significance of the material clearly meant nothing to him; he was equally careless of dates.

So far we have dealt only with Arrighi's two books, of which, although several states are known, there was only one edition each before the 1530s; the first seems to have appeared before June 1524 and the second after 12 April 1525. During the same period there were many editions of Tagliente's works, differing considerably in content and extent; some of these are only known by descriptions in catalogues and works of reference, which are not always exact enough for precise identification; sometimes such descriptions can be shown to have raised a 'ghost' edition, but more often than not there is no reason to doubt them; one can only hope that the missing editions listed, for example, by the Prince d'Essling and in the Yemeniz catalogue will reappear. The following summary is based on the order of Mr A. F. Johnson's 'Catalogue of Italian Writing-books of the Sixteenth Century',[1] unsurpassed as a bibliographical guide to the subject.

There is no reason to doubt that the shorter is the earlier of the two editions of *Lo presente libro Insegna La Vera arte delo Excellente scrivere de diverse varie sorti de litere ... Opera del tagliente nouamente composta cum gratia nel anno di nostra salute* MDXXIIII. It contains 24 leaves; the other edition has 44, the increase being mainly due to the insertion of 11 leaves showing the geometrical construction of two alphabets, quite carefully copied from Sigismondo Fanti *Theorica* 1514, book III, where they are described as 'fermata moderna' (round gothic) and 'gallica' (angular gothic). There is also a new title on the verso of the original

1. In *Signature* 10 (N.S.), pp. 22-48.

title, in which the book is entitled '*Lucidario*',[1] and some textual changes. The editions of 1525 are more complex: there are records of an edition of 24 leaves with Celebrino's 'signature' block on F4 *recto*, an edition nominally of 40 leaves with Celebrino's signature on G4 *recto* (Essling 2184), an edition of 28 leaves without Celebrino's signature, and a small oblong edition of 16 leaves. The British Museum copy of the first was destroyed in the war, and I have only seen the second and a facsimile[2] of the fourth. A 40-leaf edition (which clearly corresponds with Essling 2184) has been acquired by the British Museum since the war. It is, in fact a composite work, consisting partly of a complete edition of Tagliente (28 leaves, signed A-G) and 13 leaves, signed H-K, containing three examples and the text of Tagliente, which come from the *Thesauro de Scrittori* of Ugo da Carpi, printed in 1525 by Blado, whose mark appears on K4 *recto*. As the signatures run on, the Prince was pardonably misled, but the confusion so caused is a typical product of the genius of Ugo da Carpi. The small oblong edition is known by the unique copy in the Newberry Library. It is made up from material used in the quarto editions, full-page blocks being cut in two to fit the smaller format. The text is very condensed. The cut blocks were joined together again for subsequent quarto editions: in these, the joins are clearly visible – a convenient means of identifying later editions. On page 2 appear the two blocks of the writer's tool and a hand writing from Celebrino's work, but with Celebrino's name removed from both. This presents a considerable problem of dating. It is probable, to, that this single surviving copy is incomplete, or an unfinished record of an abortive plan: folios 3-8 are signed '7'-'12'. No other

1. This type of title was evidently popular at this time: other examples are Verini *Luminario* 1527, Tagliente *Lucidario di arithmetica* 1525 and Bordone *Isolario* 1534.
2. *Opera di Giovanniantonio Tagliente 1525*, reproduced in facsimile with an introduction by James Wells, Chicago. Newberry Library, 1952.

blocks appear to be split, so it is impossible to conjecture what else may have been intended for inclusion.

In 1525 also the first of two issues of Celebrino's *Il Modo d'Imparare di scrivere lettera Merchantesca* appeared, dated in 'the holy year', the jubilee decreed by Clement VII.[1] The second issue, known only by the unique copy in the Biblioteca Alessandrina in Rome, is printed from the same blocks, which have been – uniquely – carefully and almost imperceptibly altered. Where in the first issue the date was followed by a colon and flourish, in the second the colon has been apparently changed to a '1'. The indication is that the colon was cut away and a new small piece of wood inserted and cut to shape. The last two writing books dated 1525 are those published by Ugo da Carpi: the re-cut *La Operina* and the first version of the *Thesauro*. It is probable that the first is correctly dated, but there is good reason to suppose that the second appeared as much as a year after the title date.

There now ensues an irritating gap. Between 1525 and 1530, there seem to have been at least two, perhaps four, editions of *Lo presente*, of which records, but no copies survive. Essling (2185) records an edition of 28 leaves dated 1525 on the title page and 1527 in the colophon – a classic example of *insouciance* in the matter of title page dates. Manzoni, quoting Zeno's edition of Fontanini *Biblioteca della Eloquenza Italiana*, records an edition of 1529 printed by Giovanni Antonio and the brothers da Sabbio. In the Yemeniz catalogues (637) another edition of 1529 is recorded as printed by Giovanni Antonio alone. Finally, Brunet records an edition of 1530. The earliest accessible copy after 1525 of *Lo presente* is the Newberry Library copy, which is dated 1531 on the title page and 1530 in the colophon.[2]

1. On Celebrino, see Stanley Morison, *Eustachio Celebrino da Udene, calligrapher, engraver and writer for the Venetian printing press* (Paris 1929), and L. Servolini 'Eustachio Celebrino da Udine intagliatore, calligrafo, poligrafo ed editore', *Gutenberg-Jahrbuch 1944-9*, pp. 185 ff.
2. Reproduced in Oscar Ogg, *Three Classics of Italian Calligraphy*, New York, 1953.

This is the first surviving edition to be imposed inset as a single gathering, evidence that the contents were now stabilised. It contains only one new block not in any previous edition, an example of a conventional *cancelleresca* hand. Its abrupt opening reveals it as the end of the dedication, which appears in full in typeset form at the beginning. There must in fact have been two other full page blocks to complete the dedication, which may have appeared in this form in one of the missing editions of 1527 or 1529. The second block of the set appears only (among copies seen) in the Rampazetto edition of 1560, in which the first page alone of the dedication is set in type. It would be interesting to discover a copy with the first dedication page in woodcut form, in case the initial could be connected with those used in the type-set versions. Another edition of *Lo presente* in the British Museum is dated November 1531; in it, several plates have been omitted, and the number of leaves is reduced to 26. There are two editions of 1532, both dated November, apparently printed (at least as far as the text is concerned) by two different branches of the da Sabio family. That printed by Stefano da Sabio is 32 leaves long (the other is 28), the increase being accounted for by the insertion, rather jammed together, of the blocks of Fanti's 'fermata moderna' from the second edition of 1524. Between 1534 and 1539, Tagliente was reprinted at least five times, variously in 28 and 32 page editions.

It is obvious from this brief summary that the addition of original material to any of the writing books ceased by about 1530, and detailed investigation may be restricted to those which appear before that date. This investigation should ideally take two forms: first, a detailed analysis of the examples by pages or (where several blocks appear on one page) parts of pages; and secondly, a similar analysis of the texts. The first, although spoilt by the omission of the Tagliente editions of 1527 and 1529, can be attempted from existing copies with some success. The second requires examination of all the surviving copies, and this has not proved possible. Some general observations can be made, based on the copies accessible, which help to confirm the conclusions of the first part of our investigation, but the main task is yet to be done. The results of the analysis of the examples of script have been set out in a table. This provides a convenient form of reference to the material in each book, and illustrates where and how far different books have followed the order of contents of previous editions, or copied their examples. The principle has been to list the contents of the first to appear and thereafter the additions made in subsequent books. This order follows the order of priority indicated by the contents, as far as this can be deduced from the contents (see axiom 5). If logically applied, the evidence derived from this analysis should provide final proof of the order of appearance of the material.

Analysis of the examples in the first two editions of Tagliente is a relatively simple task. The 38 items which appeared in the first edition all re-appear in the second, with seven additions. These include the new title page, which only temporarily ousted the first,[1] an expanded series of type-set specimens in roman and italic, type set specimens of greek and hebrew, with phonetic renderings of the names of the letters, the two fine alphabets of roman capitals in white on a criblé background, and the series of geometrical constructions, fairly accurately copied from Fanti. The order of the material is changed so as to present (for the first and last time) a logical arrangement. It begins with the chancery specimens, continues with the merchantesca, followed by a page of miscellaneous pieces, including some display lettering suitable for both the preceding hands. Then come the italic and roman type-set examples, followed by the more exotic vernacular hands, *antiqua tonda*, *bollatica* and so on, with a page of chancery capitals, the only specimen which seems a little out of its proper place. Then follows the elaborate design of inter-

---

1. Changing the title was not uncommon. Tagliente clearly regarded his titles as part of the text rather than as an immutable name. Similarly, *Il modo de tenere conto*, as it is called at the beginning, becomes *Luminario di arithmetica* on the last leaf.

laced capitals, whose precise reading is not quite clear: Manzoni[1] took it to be *in primo nome de Ydio è gran secreti*; it might equally be *IHE primo nome d'Ydio gran secreto*. Next come the specimens of exotic letters, which vary from the fine reversed hebrew, to the small persian, chaldean, and so on. Lastly, there are the decorative letters, *francesca*, the elaborate penwork initials called *lettere a groppi*, and roman capitals, followed by the constructions borrowed from Fanti. The final text is four pages longer than in the first edition, but like it is set in simple form with a plain large type initial at the beginning.

But this logical arrangement was not to last, although with two of the known editions missing it is not possible to say when the alteration was made. It is not perhaps beyond the bounds of conjecture to try and work out the order of the editions. Of the four, two have a direct acknowledgment to Celebrino, which in a third (the small oblong) appears to have been withdrawn, since it contains both the blocks (or perhaps more likely copies of them) from Celebrino's own book, but with his name removed. The reasons for Celebrino's appearance and disappearance will be considered later; at the moment it suggests that the 28-leaf edition without Celebrino's name follows directly on the 1524 editions, followed by the 28-leaf and 24-leaf editions with his name, probably in that order,[2] and that the 16-leaf oblong edition came last. The earlier surviving 1525 editions shows considerable departures from the 1524 plan. Some pages remain in the same order, & some even appear in the same place. The pattern is principally disturbed by the breaking up and reassembly (in part only) of the three composite pages (pages 10, 18 and 22 in the first edition). The two cartouches showing *mercantesca* and chancery in white on black (Table, nos. 9 and 12)

1. Op. cit., p. 120. It must, in fact, stand for HIERONYMO DEDO GRAN SECRET., the dedicatee.
2. The description of the copy of the latter (now destroyed) in A. F. Johnson's Catalogue suggests that the order, already disturbed in the 28-leaf edition, was further changed in the 24-leaf edition (see Table, where the position of the leaves mentioned in Johnson's description is indicated).

disappear completely, as do the examples of exotic alphabets (only the Persian reappears later), and the italic and roman type. The additions are six in all: a new *mercantesca* page, a fine decorated specimen of 'French' gothic, 3 new and more striking cartouches, and – most significant – a type specimen of two sizes of *rotunda*, headed 'Lettera formata'. The two collects which provide the text for the last may well have been chosen to demonstrate the A and C from the initial set mentioned above, which here makes its first appearance in any edition of Tagliente. The initial C also appears in the dedication and in the text, at the head of the third paragraph, beginning 'Conveniente'. Immediately above this paragraph there is another new insertion: the heading 'Modo di temperare la penna'.

In the oblong edition, the text is very much condensed, but the first paragraph (beginning 'Havendoti') begins with the H, the last of the initial set to appear. The third paragraph is omitted, initial and all, and does not return in subsequent editions, but the original fourth, beginning 'Piglia', now has an ornamental initial, though of a different design. The heading 'Modo . . .' appears above it. The dedication is equally condensed and transferred from Dedo to the 'benigno lettore'. In the examples, apart from the cutting of the blocks, the only innovations are the fine new title border (the text is type-set), the Celebrino blocks, and a set of type 'lettere Greche' which are all that is preserved of the original exotic alphabets. In later editions, the same greek letters and the two pages of hebrew appear; the other exotics (other than the Persian) do not.

Chapter 6

ARRIGHI: *IL MODO* AND THE LATER REPRINTS

It is at this point that the gap in available editions of Tagliente occurs, and it is high time that we considered the contents of *Il modo de temperare le Penne con le varie Sorti de littere ordinate per Ludovico Vicentino*. There are twenty separate items, which complement *La Operina*: instructions on cutting pens, more careful and carefully illustrated than those in Tagliente, four pages of mercantesca, the specialist hands for notaries, papal bulls and briefs, and a page containing some small roman capitals on a characteristic cartouche, with below it a highly individual *antica tonda* with exaggeratedly curved *f* and long *s*. These unusual characteristics must have a bearing on Dr Casamassima's attribution to Arrighi of a manuscript of an unidentified vernacular dialogue, recently acquired by the Biblioteca Nazionale Centrale at Florence. If the attribution is accepted, this is another example of Arrighi's non-italic hand, the *formata* in which he wrote the Missal for Cardinal Giulio de' Medici, now at Berlin.[1]

Il modo concludes with several varieties of ornamental letters, and some pages showing different sizes of printer's type, roman, italic and *rotunda*. These may have been inserted to fill out the final sheet. The first specimen of roman and italic is found in two states, one with six units of type, in the separate printing of *Il modo*, and the other with seven, in the combined printing with *La Operina*. The extra unit in the latter is a Latin couplet, set in roman capitals:

VIXI QVOD POTVI, SEMPER BENE, PAVPER HONESTE.
FRAVDAVI NVLLVM, QVOD IVVET OSSA MEA.

1. Cod. Nuovi Acquisti 1090, and Berlin, Kupferstichkabinett, MS.78.D.17. See also, now, V. Law, 'About a rare manuscript', *The Scribe*, no. 28 (1983), p. 16.

It is tempting to see here a modest rejoinder to the insulting additions appended by Ugo da Carpi to his imitation of *La Operina*. The other examples are all standard classical tags from Vergil and Ovid, only remarkable in a writing-book; writing-masters in search of a text seldom strayed beyond the demands of commerce, correspondence and the church into the realms of literature. The *rotunda*, like Tagliente's page in the 1525 edition, is labelled 'Lettera formata': the larger type, on about 20pt body, is exactly the same as that used by Tagliente, and the text used for the smaller size, the collect *Actiones nostras*, is exactly the same in both, though the types themselves are different. This is proof of an unmistakeable kind that one is imitating the other: further, one might hazard the guess that if Tagliente's choice of collects was determined as much by a desire to show off his two new initials as to illustrate the *formata* letter, so Arrighi chose a different collect – *Deus in nomine* – to display the fine delicate initial *d*, an enlarged variant of the *d* in the last series of *lettere a groppi* (Table no. 73), which also provided the model for similar if smaller initials (see pp. 172, 174 above).

There is another instance of imitation beside this, namely, the introduction into the 1525 Tagliente editions of the heading 'Modo di temperare la penna', which can hardly be an uncon-scious echo of the title of *Il modo*. It is possible too that the title of Celebrino's manual of the *mercantesca* hands is derived from Arrighi. Titles at this time were not (as the example of Tagliente shows) necessarily short and pithy, and Arrighi's ability to com-pose them so may have been novel and worth imitating. But who, one may ask, is copying whom? By axiom 5, the mere fact of simultaneous appearance conveys nothing except the vir-tual certainty that both books must be after 1524, the date of the last Tagliente manual without the *formata* specimens. There is, however, another important piece of evidence: the second example of *mercantesca*, which takes the form of a bill for 40 ducats drawn by Arrighi in favour of Marco de Lucha da Ra-gusa, dated 14 February 1525. This date is at first sight very baffling: in February 1525, Arrighi was hard at work printing in Rome. The solution lies in the various forms of dating in use in Italy in the sixteenth century.

In Rome, Milan, and many other cities the year began at Christmas. At Florence down to 1749 or 1750 the 25th of March was New Year's Day, and at Venice, though the common use was to treat the year as beginning with the 1st of January, the legal year which was used in all public acts and official documents was reckoned as beginning on the 1st of March down to the fall of the Venetian Republic in 1797.[1]

Thus 14 February 1525 *more Veneto* is in fact 14 February 1526.

This piece of evidence for the late dating of *Il modo* has already been advanced in an article by Lamberto Donati,[2] and rejected by A. Pratesi in the entry for Arrighi in the *Dizionario Biografico degli Italiani*,[3] on the ground that dates on sample pages, unlike colophon or title dates, should be considered merely as examples, analogous to the title of 'notary' which Arrighi adopts on another page. Admittedly, an unsupported date on a single page is little enough to build a theory on, but both these statements merely express an opinion. In the present case, the determining factor is the coincidence of material in *Lo presente* 1525 and in *Il modo*; but the page beginning *Pagareti*, with its very Venetian detail, adds further evidence to date *Il modo* after 14 February 1526. This late date suggests that in the specimen of the *lettera formata* it was Arrighi who followed Tagliente. It is not unlikely that the name of Arrighi's book was known to Tagliente, especially if Celebrino was working simultaneously for both calligraphers. If the 28-leaf edition without Celebrino's name does not contain the

1. R. C. Christie 'The Chronology of the Early Aldines' in *Bibliographica* I, p. 196.
2. 'Un nuova bolla zilografica', *La Bibliofilia* LII (1940), pp. 154-65.
3. IV (1962), pp. 310-13.

heading 'Modo . . .', it would confirm that this edition was the earliest of the four, printed before Arrighi's arrival in Venice.

If, then, we can safely believe the essential details of the text on Arrighi's pages, what inferences can be made about the rest? The title and three specimens (nos. 55, 62, 65 and 67) are written as at Rome, the *littera per Notari* being dated 18 September 1523. There seems no reason to doubt that these specimens were written and engraved in Rome before Arrighi's quarrel with Ugo da Carpi, and that Arrighi, when he left Rome for Venice about the middle of 1525, took not only the blocks already used for *La Operina* (including, for some reason, the earlier and apparently rejected block for page 17), but also part of the set of blocks for *Il modo*, as yet unused. If, subsequently, Arrighi completed (after a fashion) his plan for *Il modo* by having extra blocks engraved in Venice, we can almost certainly add to the *Pagareti* block and the colophon acknowledging Celebrino as the engraver the other three blocks showing the same *mercantesca* (nos. 58, 60 and 61); it is possible that Ugo da Carpi, whose own imitations of the printed *mercantesca* specimens of Arrighi and Tagliente are unsatisfactory, was also unsuccessful in his attempts to reproduce Arrighi's original specimens of the hand, and that this was an additional cause of the breach. This leaves ten blocks (including two pairs) unattributed, and at present, no other basis for identifying their engraver seems to be available.

One conclusion from the late dating of *Il modo* is that Celebrino's own specimens of *mercantesca* precede those he engraved for Arrighi, and this suggests two questions. What need was Celebrino supplying which was not supplied by the fine range of examples which he (if it was he) had engraved for Tagliente? What is the relation of Tagliente's half-size pocket *Opera* to Celebrino's even smaller manual? To these may be added two others. What was Arrighi doing in Venice from his arrival before the middle of 1525 to at least spring 1526, beyond writing, which brought the title of his still unpublished second part to the notice of his rival? And what (generally speaking) was the relationship of Tagliente, Celebrino and Arrighi?

Nothing but conjectures can be offered in answer. It is possible that by 1525 Arrighi was no longer greatly interested in printed writing manuals. He may have regarded his experiment with Ugo da Carpi as a complete failure, while the experiment with Lautizio Meo was a success, although one which could be improved on by a more expert punch-cutter. Common prudence would make it worth his while to take the blocks of his manual with him to Venice, and printing them there gave him an opportunity to try out what may have been a greater preoccupation. This was the cutting of the new type, and it seems more than likely that he went to the punch-cutter who engraved the punches for Tagliente's calligraphic italic of the previous year. The evidence for this lies more in the indefinable quality of style, but one may perhaps point to the straight backed cursive *g*, the narrow upper bowl of *antica g*, with the lower bowl and junction in line with the angle of slant, and above all to the contrast provided by the pointed tip to the curve in *b*, *c*, *d*, *e*, *h*, *p*, *q*, all marked features of the type of *Il modo*. The main difference is that whereas the Tagliente italic has a pronounced slant, so much so that Graham Pollard thought that it was cast on a parallelogrammic body,[1] the type of *Il modo* is more upright and is cast on a rectangular body.

Whether the punch-cutter was also the engraver of the blocks must remain uncertain. There is at least a possibility this was so, a possibility increased by the evidence that suggests that Arri-

1. Graham Pollard suggested this in 1962 in his Presidential Address. He saw evidence of it in the anti-clockwise twist visible when the lateral pressure exerted on a line in locking up is greater than the longitudinal pressure. This can be clearly seen on line 3 of page 39 of the copy of the 1530-1 edition reproduced in Ogg, op. cit., p. 103. The theory is, however, disproved by raised spaces (to be found on k2 and k3 in S.M.'s copy). These are vertical and show that the type was cast on a conventional rectangular body. Asymmetric type-bodies were introduced for the even more slanted script types developed in the nineteenth century to simulate 'copperplate' engraved script.

ghi's acquaintance with Celebrino began from his earliest days in Venice. If therefore Celebrino cut some if not all the blocks in Tagliente's first two editions,[1] the presence of the cartouche with 'Intagliato per Eustachio Celebrino da Vdene' on it in at least two editions of 1525 might be explained by the arrival of Arrighi, anxious to get Celebrino to work for him and promising that if he did his name would be properly recognised, as Ugo da Carpi's would have been if Ugo had fulfilled his side of the bargain. If, further, at some point in the summer of 1525 Celebrino was working for Arrighi on the cutting of the type, he might have gathered something of Arrighi's plans for a systematic manual of writing, and had the deficiencies of *Lo Presente* pointed out to him, both in the nature and the order of its examples and the rather inconsequential text. This might have produced *Il modo d'Imparare di scrivere lettera Merchantescha*, which, though short, is both lucid and comprehensive, certainly, in its unity of purpose and absolute certainty of both style and execution, it has, as Dr. Casamassima rightly observes,[2] only one parallel among the writing books of this time, namely, *L'Operina*.

It is difficult to imagine Celebrino's *Il modo* to have been uninfluenced by Arrighi. It is equally difficult to see what Celebrino's further relations with Tagliente were. It is possible that the oblong *Opera*, with its fine title border and the two blocks copied (more likely) or taken from Celebrino's *Il modo* but without Celebrino's name on them, is not an offensive gesture, inadvertent or on purpose, by Tagliente to Celebrino,[3] but a rather perfunctory expression of continued interest by Celebrino in Tagliente's successful work, an expression perhaps suggested by his own plans for a pocket writing manual. At any

1. It is possible that the leaf ornament on the *Beat*mo page (Table, no. 15) may be a 'signature'. It also appears reversed black on white on the elegant title-block of Hieronymo Tagliente *Opera che Insegna A fare Ogni Ragione di Mercantia* 1525. Other examples of its use might be revealing.
2. *Trattati*, p. 50.
3. As suggested by Morison in *Eustachio Celebrino*.

rate, Tagliente was still able to have first-rate blocks engraved after 1525 and before 1530. It is possible, too, that Tagliente like Arrighi had discovered that lettering maps and diagrams provided another outlet for his gifts. Both Ludovico Foliano da Modena *Musica Theorica* (Venice, de Sabbio, 1529) and Benedetto Bordone *Isolario* (Venice, Zoppino, 1534) contain maps and diagrams lettered in a fine confident *cancelleresca* comparable with the similar work of Arrighi and Palatino. Book II of the latter, which begins (like Tagliente's text) 'Havendo io' employs the H of the initial set that Tagliente seems to have designed or commissioned. It is, finally, certain that Arrighi's *Il modo*, with its trial usage of the second type, bears every sign of being an amicable joint enterprise. Its exact date of publication remains uncertain, but it probably came out in the summer of 1526. If 14 February is the terminal date for the copy, there would have been time enough before 19 October, when Arrighi was back in Rome, in the *rione* of Ponte, where his presence is recorded with a household of four persons in the census made between 14 November 1526 and 30 January 1527.[1] It is possible that he was back in Rome before October, since Trissino (who returned to Vicenza in the latter half of September) does not seem to have made contact with him again. If Arrighi had time to have the type of *Il modo* adjusted after publication to the forms which he used on his return to Rome, *Il modo* cannot have been printed long after the middle of the year.

Variations in the succeeding editions of Arrighi's works are few and unimportant. The curious reversion, in the Nicolo d'Aristotile reissues, to the first state of the block beginning & *accio che* on page 17 has already been noted. This may have been due to no reason at all – a random choice between two similar blocks. The alteration of the text type has already been discussed. The type specimens are all dropped, and a brief *recetta da far inchiostro* substituted (in the 1533 issue only) on the

1. Pratesi, loc. cit.

last leaf. The new title page in addition to a border has a block of a hand holding a quill. Dr Donati, comparing this with the block in Celebrino's *Il modo* (to which it has no resemblance, save the subject), suggests that the device is Celebrino's 'trademark', and further evidence of his connection with Arrighi. It is indeed possible that Arrighi left his blocks with Celebrino when he returned to Rome, but the point remains unproven. The 1538 and 1539 printings differ only in the colophon date. All the type-set text is absent, but both the *& accio che* blocks have been included; the second state block returns to the proper place in the text of *La Operina*, while the first state block appears in the preliminaries of *Il modo* on page 35.

Chapter 7

UGO DA CARPI: *LA OPERINA*
AND THE *THESAURO DE SCRITTORI*

The last group of writing books produced before 1540 is at once more complex and easier to comprehend than any of those hitherto described. Ugo da Carpi produced two books, the imitated *La Operina* and the *Thesauro de Scrittori*. Neither is easy to find in any state or edition, and no two copies, even of the relatively common 1535 *Thesauro*, seem to be exactly alike. But complex and various though the arrangement of their contents may be, the amount of original material to be found is very small indeed; most of the blocks are copies of existing material in other writing books. Moreover, the copies once made do not change, since there was no incentive to make changes, as there was in the books put out by writing masters.

Of the two works, the imitated *La Operina* is, or appears to be, the simpler, but since only four copies are recorded and only two are known to exist, it is difficult to be sure. The copies recorded by Manzoni[1] as discovered by the bookseller Carlo Ramazzotti and in the Börsenverein catalogue[2] cannot now be identified. The other two – the Newberry Library copy and that in the collection of early writing books bound together in the eighteenth century, later bought by William Morris, and now in the possession of the Society of Antiquaries[3] – are markedly different. The first contains the *bellissimo Ragione di Abbacho* mentioned on the title page – the arithmetical tables compiled by Angelo da Modena, a property which Ugo da Carpi had acquired and engraved, and included in most of his writing books. The second does not, but has a very interesting variant

1. *Studii di Bibliografia Analitica*, p. 106 ff.
2. *Katalog der Bibliothek des Börsenvereins der Deutschen Buchhändler*, 2nd ed, Vol. II (1902), p. 696.
3. This remarkable volume contains four writing books; *La Operina* (1525), *Il modo, Lo presente* 1524 (2nd printing) and the *Thesauro de Scrittori* 1525.

page 21. In place of Arrighi's page beginning *Grave fatica*, there is a specimen of *antiqua tonda*, not filling the page and looking very out of place. There is a full specimen alphabet and a 7-line quotation from Isocrates (an unexpected source), and it is signed *Genesius de la Barrera Hispanus Carmonensis scrip.* Genesius de la Barrera, from Carmona near Seville, was a Spaniard working in Rome, like Ruano later. In 1519 he wrote 'a manuscript book in a script closely resembling that of Arrighi' which is now at Paris (Bibl. nat. lat. 244).[1] He was presumably employed to provide the 'copy' for the alterations required to the title and colophon of *La Operina*, and may have produced this page as his own contribution. He seems to have had no further share in Ugo da Carpi's operations, unless he was responsible for some of the material in the *Thesauro* which does not appear elsewhere. This, however, as will be seen, seems implausible.

The analysis of the *Thesauro de Scrittori* is more involved. A fair number of copies exist, variously dated, and these may be roughly divided into four main groups. The first of these is the original edition of 1525, of which two copies are known, again at Newberry and in the William Morris-Society of Antiquaries volume. Secondly, there are the two intermediate states represented by the Biblioteca Civica Berio copy at Genoa (1532) and the Cambridge University Library copy (the date has been trimmed off, but it is presumably before 1535). Finally, there is the group of copies all dated 1535, among which at least five different issues can be distinguished, differing in the setting of the type-set parts, in minor variations of order, and an occasional duplication, such as may be found in one of the two Douce copies at the Bodleian Library, Oxford (see table). Of this last group, some at least cannot have been printed before c. 1545, but the date on the title page appears to have remained unaltered from 1535 on. Omitted from this provisional arrange-

1. See A. Fairbank 'The Arrighi Style of Bookhand' in *The Journal of the Society for Italic Handwriting*, No. 35 (1963), p. 14, and subsequent articles by him and F. A. Thomson, ibid., nos. 63-5 (1970).

ment are a probable edition of 1530, recorded by Essling and in Maggs Brothers' Catalogue 509; the Newberry Library copy, cropped like the Cambridge copy, which A. F. Johnson doubtfully dated 1530, but may perhaps belong to the fourth group; and a series of editions mentioned by Essling in a footnote, all supposed to be printed by the Nicolini at Venice, whose existence may be considered doubtful.

The pattern which emerges from a comparison of the contents of the four groups is an interesting one. There is no significant difference between the two copies dated 1525. Allowing for the insertion of four pages in the middle of the first quire of the Newberry copy, that may well have been accidentally omitted in the other, the contents are more or less the same, apart from the third quire which seems to have been folded inside out (although the signatures appear in the right places), with the curious result that the two pages of *lettere a groppi* are separated. The main source at this stage is clearly a copy of the second 1524 edition of Tagliente: only in this edition were the adaptations of Fanti's constructions set out at length over 21 pages; the order, too, although irregular, conforms most closely to that of the second 1524 edition, and unlike subsequent editions of Tagliente, the 'group' pages (containing items 9-12 and 26-29 of the table) remained unaltered. But some of the material comes from other sources. One page of *mercantesca* and the specimen of *formata* type can only come from a 1525 edition of Tagliente; the text and the initial blocks in it, however, appear to be imitated from a lost 1525 edition or one still later, since they do not appear in any existing copy of Tagliente before 1530-1. The blocks of Ugo da Carpi's *La Operina* are used only once, page 13 *Te bisogna* re-appearing among the examples of Tagliente's *cancelleresca*. Two pages show a 'strapwork' gothic alphabet identical with pages 20-1 of Arrighi's *Il modo*, although here they are set against a *criblé* background.

There are four remaining pages of examples that cannot be traced to any known exemplar. Two of these, the title and the

Epistola ali lettori are self-explanatory. The latter is a masterpiece of generalised misinformation which contrives to imply that the contents are the product of an academy of scribes. The other two are a gothic lower case alphabet which is a reverse copy in white on black of that on page 24 of *Il modo*, and a page headed *lettera Cortigiana di Roma de Copiste per scrivere supplicatione minuto et altre materie*. This has all the appearance of being incomplete: there is a white space in the middle where it seems as if a sentence in the smaller of the two sizes of writing shown ought to be inserted under the lines of capitals, to counterbalance a similar pair of lines at the foot of the page. It seems possible, then, that the *lettera Cortigiana* page, as well as the three variant pages certainly derived from Arrighi, were based by Ugo da Carpi on specimen sheets left behind by Arrighi, not all in finished form. This possibility will become near certainty when the additional material in the later groups is considered; here the material is even more imperfect, and moreover bears Arrighi's name. In the meantime, it is clear that Ugo da Carpi may have drawn on sources other than a printed copy of *Il modo* for the strapwork alphabet, although it is also possible that the first state of the *Thesauro* (on the evidence of the text) appeared long enough after 1525 or the publication of *Il modo* to allow imitation of the printed version.

One other feature of the early *Thesauro* demands notice, namely the type in which the text is printed. This was noted briefly earlier à propos Blado's printing equipment. It is a curious type, badly fitting and irregular in set; it is used with two sets of capitals neither of which fits it, one being too large, the other too small. It appears in two other books printed by Blado in 1526, both pamphlets put out in the interest of Charles V: *Aboccamento della maesta cesarea, et del re d'Francia* and *Pace & capituli fatte infra la C.M & lo Christianissimo re di Francia.*[1] All three books also contain the initial set *ACH* closely connected

1. The dating of these two ephemera suggests that the *Thesauro* itself may not have appeared until the year after the date on the title page.

with Tagliente, and it is really no surprise to discover that the type is Tagliente's calligraphic italic, distorted almost beyond recognition by being cast with a vertical instead of a sloped alignment. It has one other curious feature: an inverted *p* is regularly used in place of *d*, a feature caused perhaps by ignorance in Rome of what had been intended in Venice. It is not surprising that the type had apparently little success; it does not seem to have been used again after 1526.

It is probable that at least one printing and possibly more took place between the two dated 1525 and the next to survive, dated 1532. This intermediate printing probably omitted the arithmetical tables of Angelo da Modena, since the words *con una ragione dabbaco* have been removed from the 1532 title, although the tables are included. As the 1532 printing is short (44 leaves against 46 in the longer of the two 1525 printings), it is possible that the intermediate printing was shorter still, perhaps only of 40 leaves. The 1532 order comes half way between the 1525 and 1535 arrangements. The text is now set in the Arrighi italic obtained by Blado between 1527 and 1530. The contents include the title page of Tagliente *Lo presente* for the first time, which is dated 1532 also. Both pages of type specimens are omitted as is the greek alphabet. Two more pages from *Il modo* are shown, the *littera per notari* and the gothic *a-y*, the reversed version of the latter being omitted. Perhaps by now Ugo da Carpi had access to a copy of *Il modo*, since many more blocks from it appear in the later printings. One more original piece of material is inserted, a half page block (again seemingly based on an incomplete original) headed *Lettera/ da Bolle/ Antiche* and 'signed' at the end *Lud. de Henricis Vicentinus*. This may well have been intended by Arrighi as a further page (following the two of the ordinary *lettera da bolle*) illustrating the other hands required in the papal chancery, like the *lettera cortigiana*. It seems, at any rate, to prove that Ugo da Carpi had retained, not Arrighi's blocks, but the copy for blocks unfinished or not yet begun when the quarrel took place.

The next printing, the third group, has been seen only in a copy badly cropped at the foot. The date is no longer visible; only the upper parts of MDXX are left, and these are common to all editions after 1525, when the V was cut away and alterations made in type much smaller in size than the woodcut numerals. The chaldean alphabet is omitted, but ten new pages from *Il modo* are added, and the reversed gothic a-y is restored. Among the new pages from *Il modo* is the second half only of the two page set of fine lombardic outline initials. This seems to have been added as a filler at the end, with the *criblé* background left unfinished; there is also a gash at the end of the tail of the bowl of *R*. It is possible that this is one of the rejected blocks for the original *Il modo*, although at this late stage it is more likely to have been copied from the printed version. The last fragment of Arrighi material appears in this printing (but not elsewhere) on page 70: it is a short specimen of *cancelleresca*, *Dñs adiutor/Lud. Vicentinus Rome* followed by two lines of alphabet. This printing is the longest to survive, consisting of 100 leaves imposed inset and signed A[1]-25; one curious feature is that it is extensively mis-signed, although it is bound in the correct order.

The various printings dated 1535 require no special comment. Although the type-set matter differs in all five of the copies seen, the order and number of the blocks remains constant, with only very minor variations. At some point, the decorative initials in the text, originally copied from Tagliente, were dropped in favour of others, presumably more modern in appearance, adapted from those used by Giolito in the 1540s; the Arrighi type is still used.[1] No additions to the plates were made, but the *Te bisogna* page from *La Operina* and the *Dñs adiutor* fragment are both omitted, and the text further condensed to make a convenient 'even working' of 96 pages. As the title-page date

---

1. One of the copies in the Bodleian Library, Oxford, (Douce C. 601) is a copy of such a late impression.

never changes, it is difficult to conjecture when the last printing took place.

It will be clear by now that the successive printings of the *Thesauro* throw some further light on the origins of the blocks in Arrighi's *Il modo*. Ten of them, it will be remembered, could not be attributed either to Ugo da Carpi or Celebrino. Four blocks appear in the *Thesauro* before the main borrowing from *Il modo* takes place: nos. 61 (which has already been identified as 'Roman'), 67 (the pair of strapwork alphabet blocks which has affinities with the definitely 'Roman' lombardic alphabet) and 69. It is interesting to note the appearance (if late) of what appears to be a rejected block for the lombardic set. It is possible also that the two pages of *Lettera da bolle* (nos. 62 and 63), of which the *Lettera da bolle antiche* appears to be a continuation, were also produced in Rome. In the remainder (nos. 65, 68, 70 and 74), Ugo da Carpi took only belated interest or none at all; the last in particular is connected with the separate decorative initials which Arrighi must have obtained in Venice.

Chapter 8

CONCLUSION

It is hard to gather together all these scattered and tangled threads into a concise and clearly defined pattern. One feature that stands out is the dominant influence of Arrighi; his works were copied by others, but he himself imitated others only in such minor matters as the arrangement of type. The most important task has been to try and establish the chronology of his career, and this may be briefly summarised. *La Operina* was not issued in 1522 but later, after Arrighi's quarrel with Ugo da Carpi – after September 1523, when it seems likely that Ugo was still at work on the blocks for *Il modo*, but before June 1524, when Arrighi had type as well as a printing press with which he might have made good its defects. Arrighi's journey to Venice is to be dated after 12 April 1525, not in 1523, when (again if the books in *Il modo* are to be believed) Arrighi was at work in Rome. If Dr. A. S. Osley is right,[1] and Trissino's mention of 'M. Lodovico nostro' in a letter from Vicenza, dated 17 July 1525, to Tommaso da Lonigo in Rome refers to Arrighi, it is possible to define the date of Arrighi's removal more accurately. Trissino's reference to money troubles and offer to advance 25 or 30 ducats might well imply that Arrighi's quarrel with Ugo da Carpi had involved him in financial difficulties. If this is so, it follows that Arrighi cannot have reached Venice until the end of the summer. *Il modo*, then, may have been printed as late as summer 1526, if the evidence of the *Pagareti* block is to be believed; if it is not, then not much earlier in 1525 than the later editions of Tagliente printed in that year and the two printings of Celebrino *Il modo* dated 1525 and 1526. While in Venice, Arrighi had the punches for a new type cut (his previous type having been left to Trissino) probably by the punch-cutter re-

1. 'The Origins of Italic Type' in *Calligraphy and Palaeography*, p. 112 and note 18.

sponsible for Tagliente's italic, who may have been Eustachio Celebrino. This type was tried out in *Il Modo*, but considerably modified before Arrighi returned to Rome, by 19 October 1526. Finally, there ensues the last period of Arrighi's printing, with its unexpectedly wide variety, before his presumed death in the Sack of Rome. Some of his equipment, including a casting of the new type and some decorative material passes to Valerio D'Orico; the punches and other decorative material seem to have gone to Antonio Blado, who continues to use the type for another forty years.

The account of Tagliente and Ugo da Carpi's books is vitiated by the lack of surviving copies during the critical period 1526-30. It may be assumed that Tagliente's manual was produced, whether influenced by *La Operina* or spontaneously, to preserve the author's hand before his skill left him. He was already old in 1524, perhaps twenty years older than Arrighi, and probably ceased to practise about 1530. Ugo da Carpi may have been projected into publishing writing books by his abortive partnership with Arrighi. Apart from the few lines which he seems to have commissioned from Genesius de la Barrera, he had no apparent access to original material apart from some unused sheets attributable to Arrighi. His attempts to claim originality for his work, by seeming to attribute it to Sigismondo Fanti or an 'academy' of scribes have created considerable confusion, but his method of work was hardly exceptional by the commercial standards of his time.

All in all, the five years from 1525 to 1530 are chiefly remarkable for the extraordinary flood of writing books which poured out. Sixteen separate printings (at least) of four books – it is clear that there was an eager market for printed specimens of writing. What is more, the style set by these books, amplified by Palatino and Amphiareo remained dominant for another thirty years, and, despite the revolution produced by the new models of Giovanfrancesco Cresci, did not die until the end of the sixteenth century. Moreover, their reputation was spread over all Europe and counterfeit editions were produced at Antwerp for the northern market. They were the principal instruments (along with papal diplomatic correspondence) of the spread of the Italian hand to the rest of Europe.

TABLE

The object of this table is to indicate the origin and position of the material shown in fifteen writing books published between 1524 and 1539. Section A lists the contents in the first Tagliente edition of 1524, B the additions in the second 1524 edition, C those in the British Museum 1525 edition, and D those in the landscape edition of 1525. E lists the contents of Arrighi *Il modo*, while F represents a conflation of the two surviving copies of *Thesauro de Scrittori* 1525, allowing for the two extra leaves in the first signature in the Plimpton copy and assuming the folding of the third signature in the Morris copy to be correct. G - L represent the additional matter added in Tagliente 1530-1, *Thesauro* 1530 and 1532, Tagliente 1532-3, Arrighi *Regola* 1532 and 1533 (the contents of the two are the same, except that the last item seems only to appear in the second), the Cambridge *Thesauro* of *c.* 1532-5, *Thesauro* 1535 (ignoring differences between copies due to misfolding and resetting type), Tagliente 1536, and Arrighi 1538 and 1539 (the two are alike save in the altered colophon date). These horizontal divisions correspond with the vertical division of the columns. Page numbers in italic indicate information derived from sources other than copies of the actual books; those in square brackets indicate the 'secondary' position of material described more fully in another section. Page numbers followed or preceded by a solidus indicate that only the upper or lower part (respectively) of the item indicated appears on the page.

TABLE

	Tag 1524[1]	Tag 1524[2]	Tag 1525[1]	Tag 1525[2]	Tag 1525[3]	Arr Il modo	Thes 1525	Tag 1530-1	Thes 1530	Thes 1532	Tag 1532-3	Arr 1532/3	Thes 1532-5	Thes 1535	Tag 1536	Arr 1538/9
A 1. Title: *Lo presente*	1	2	1	–	–	–	–	1	5	5	1	–	5	5	1	–
2. Cut of writer's tools	2	*1	*1	–	–	–	2	*1	2	2	*1	–	3	2	*1	–
3. Dedication (type)	3-4	3-5	2-4	–	3	–	–	2-4	–	–	2-4	–	–	–	2-4	–
4. *Io te notifico*	5	6	5	–	–	–	5	5	9	9	5	–	9	9	5	–
5. *Eglie manifesto*	6	7	6	–	6/8	–	6	6	6	6	6	–	6	6	6	–
6. *Aa . . . z. Spirti gentil . . . venite*	7	25	13	–	/19	–	17	13	14	17	13	–	14	14	13	–
7. *Le litere cancelleresche*	8	8	7	–	7/	–	7	7	7	7	7	–	7	7	7	–
8. *Qvesta altra* (interlaced)	9	13	12	–	–	–	16	12	13	16	12	–	13	13	12	–
9. *Se brami* white on cartouche	10	14	–	–	–	–	10	–	15	10	–	–	15	15	–	–
10. *Non sia duro*	10	14	18	–	–	–	10	18	15	10	18	–	15	15	18	–
11. *Se lhuomo*	10	14	18	–	–	–	10	18	15	10	18	–	15	15	18	–
12. *dove non* white on cartouche	10	14	–	–	–	–	10	–	15	10	–	–	15	15	–	–
13. *Lultima vostra*	11	15	17	–	13/18	–	20	17	27	20	17	–	27	27	17	–
14. *Li merchatant*	12	16	14	–	9/16	–	18	14	25	18	14	–	25	25	14	–
15. *Beat^mo*	13	9	9	–	–	–	13	9	10	13	9	–	10	10	9	–
16. *Questa altra canc. nodaresca*	14	10	10	–	4/	–	14	10	11	14	10	–	11	11	10	–
17. *Avenga che pendente in contrario*	15	11	11	–	5/14	–	15	11[5]	12	15	11	–	12	12	11	–
18. *Benche io te habia scritto*	16	12	8	–	–	–	8	8	8	8	8	–	8	8	8	–
19. *Orlanndino*	17	17	15	–	12/	–	19	15	26	19	15	–	26	26	15	–
20. *Chonsiderando*	18	18	18	–	15	–	22	18	29	22	18	–	29	29	18	–
21. *Eccho qui la virtu*	18	18	–	–	26	–	22	–	29	22	45	–	29	29	45	–
22. *Sapienti*	18	18	–	–	21	–	22	36	29	22	44	–	29	29	44	–
23. *Spirti gentil . . . molti bei fiori*	19	21	–	–	23/	–	–	–	–	–	–	–	–	–	–	–
24. *HIE* &c interlaced caps	20	28	28	28	–	–	32	28	42	32	29	–	42	42	28	–
25. Mercantesca caps: *Io sappia*	21	19	19	–	–	–	23	19	30	23	19	–	30	30	19	–
26. *Fidelium dominus* open moderna	22	20	33	–	20	–	11	36	16	11	44	–	16	16	44	–
27. *Che val*	22	20	–	–	15	–	11	38	16	11	44	–	16	16	44	–
28. *Chi cerca*	22	20	18	–	24	–	11	18	16	11	18	–	16	16	18	–
29. *Considerando* open canc	22	20	–	–	–	–	11	–	16	11	–	–	16	16	–	–
30. *Le lettere Francesche*	23	35	23	–	/23	–	27	35[5]	34	27	43	–	34	34	43	–
31. *La lettera antiqua tonda*	24	24	22	–	/17	–	26	22	4	4	22	–	4	4	22	–
32. *Questo alphabeto serve a persi*	25	34	–	–	–	–	69	23	45	61	23	–	49	45	23	–
33. *La lettera bollatica*	26	26	21	–	–	–	25	21	32	25	21	–	32	32	21	–
34. *La lettera Imperiale*	27	27	20	–	–	–	24	20	31	24	20	–	31	31	20	–
35. Hebrew alphabet, white on criblé	28-9	30-1	30-1	–	–	–	34-5	30-1	43-4	35-6	38-9	–	43-4	43-4	38-9	–
36. *Lettere a groppi*	30-1	36-7	24-5	–	–	–	28-9	24-5	35-6	28-9	24-5	–	35-6	35-6	24-5	–
37. *Questo . . . alphabeto . . . e caldeo*	32	33	–	–	–	–	70	–	–	6	–	–	–	–	–	–
B 38. *Lucidario* title	–	1	–	–	–	–	–	–	–	–	–	–	–	–	–	–
39. *Tutti color . . . cercare* (ital). *Lor vostra santissima . . .* (rom) *El tempo . . . bella Aurora* (ital).	–	22-3	–	–	–	–	71[2]	–	–	–	–	–	–	–	–	–
40. *Questo . . . alphabeto e greco*	–	29	–	–	–	–	4	–	–	–	–	–	–	–	–	–
41. *Questo . . . alphabeto e hebreo*	–	32	–	–	–	–	–	–	–	–	–	–	–	–	–	–
42. A-R on criblé rectangle	–	38	26	26	–	–	30	26	37	30	26	–	37	37	26	–
43. S-Z, A-Y on criblé shield	–	39	27	27	/22	–	31	27[5]	36	31	27	–	38	38	27	–
44. Geometrical constructions for 'gallica' and 'moderna' from Fanti *Theorica* 1514	–	40-61	–	–	–	–	38-59	–	47-67	38-59	30-6	–	45-8, 51-69	47-67	30-6	–
C 45. *P[er] questa prima*	–	–	16	16	10/11	–	21	16	28	21	16	–	28	28	16	–
46. 'Francesca' *a-z* white on black, decorated	–	–	29	31	–	–	29	–	–	37	–	–	–	37	–	–
47. *Venite* white on black cartouche	–	–	32	–	25	–	34	–	–	42	–	–	–	42	–	–
48. *Dove non* white on black cartouche	–	–	32	–	26	–	34	–	–	42	–	–	–	42	–	–
49. *E Brava* white on black cartouche	–	–	32	–	24	–	34	–	–	42	–	–	–	42	–	–
50. 'Formata' type specimens: collects *Concede nos* and *Actiones nostras*[3]	–	–	33	33	/20	[26]	60	36	–	–	44	–	–	–	44	–

	Tag 1524[1]	Tag 1524[2]	Tag 1525[1]	Tag 1525[2]	Tag 1525[3]	Arr Il modo	Thes 1525	Tag 1530-1	Thes 1530	Thes 1532	Tag 1532-3	Arr 1532/3	Thes 1532-5	Thes 1535	Tag 1536	Arr 1538/9
D 51. Title *Opera di Giovanniantonio*	–	–	–	–	1	–	–	–	–	–	–	–	–	–	–	–
52. Blacks from Celebrino *Il modo*	–	–	–	–	2	–	–	–	–	–	–	–	–	–	–	–
53. *Lettere Greche*	–	–	–	–	21	–	–	38	–	–	45	–	–	–	45	–
E 54. Title *Il modo*	–	–	–	–	–	1	–	–	–	–	–	33	–	–	–	34
55. Text, including blocks of knife & pens	–	–	–	–	–	2-8	–	–	–	–	–	34-40	–	–	–	33, 36
56. *Da Merchatanti: Li principij*	–	–	–	–	–	9	–	–	22	–	–	42[8]	22	22	–	37
57. *Pagareti*	–	–	–	–	–	10	–	–	23	–	–	41	23	23	–	38
58. *Nota Studioso*	–	–	–	–	–	11	–	–	19	–	–	43	19	19	–	39
59. *A-Z. Stolto chi ... senza Radice*	–	–	–	–	–	12	–	–	20	–	–	44	20	20	A-Z	40
60. *Littera per notari*	–	–	–	–	–	13	–	–	33	26	–	45	33	33	–	41
61. *Lr̄a da bolle*	–	–	–	–	–	14	–	–	18	–	–	46	18	18	–	42
62. *Quapropter ... Invia virtuti ... via*	–	–	–	–	–	15	–	/33[6]	68	–	/41[6]	47	72	68	/41[6]	43
63. *Littera da brevi*	–	–	–	–	–	16	–	–	24	–	–	48	24	24	–	44
64. *A-Z on cartouche, Giamai ... pellegrine*	–	–	–	–	–	17	–	–	21	–	–	49	21	21	–	45
65. 'Lombardic' caps, outline on criblé	–	–	–	–	–	18-19	–	32-3[6]	–	–	40-1[6]	50-1	92	88	40-1[6]	46-7
66. Strapwork 'gothic' *a-z*	–	–	–	–	–	20-1	36-7[4]	–	39-40[4]	33-4[4]	–	52-3	39-40[4]	39-40[4]	–	48-9
67. *A-Z* rom caps, white on black	–	–	–	–	–	22-3	–	–	–	–	–	54-5	–	–	–	50-1
68. *a-y* 'gothic'	–	–	–	–	–	24	–	–	41	37	–	56	41	41	–	52
69. *a-z, duce deo* open 'moderna'	–	–	–	–	–	25	–	–	–	–	–	57	–	–	–	53
70. 'Formata' type specimens: collects *Actiones nostras* and *Deus in nomine*[3]	–	–	[33]	–	[20]	26	–	–	–	–	–	–	–	–	–	–
71. Specimens of small rom and ital type	–	–	–	–	–	27	–	–	–	–	–	–	–	–	–	–
72. Specimens of larger rom, ital and formata	–	–	–	–	–	29	–	–	–	–	–	–	–	–	–	–
73. 'Lettere a groppi', white on black	–	–	–	–	–	28	–	–	–	–	–	58	–	–	–	54
74. Colophon *Stampata ... Intagliatore*	–	–	–	–	–	30	–	–	–	–	–	–	–	–	–	–
F 75. Title *Thesauro*	–	–	–	–	–	–	1	–	1	1	–	–	1	1	–	–
76. *Epistola al[l]i lettori*	–	–	–	–	–	–	3	–	3	3	–	–	2	3	–	–
77. *Lettera cortigiana*	–	–	–	–	–	–	9	–	17	12	–	–	17	17	–	–
78. *Te bisogna* from *La Operina*	–	–	–	–	–	–	12	–	–	60	–	–	71	–	–	–
79. *a-y* gothic, white on criblé	–	–	–	–	–	–	33	–	46	–	–	–	50	46	–	–
G 80. *Eccellentissimo M. Giovanni*[7]	–	–	–	–	–	–	37[7]	–	–	–	–	–	–	–	–	–
H 81. *Lettera da Bolle Antiche*	–	–	–	–	–	–	–	66	69	–	–	72	69[8]	–	–	–
I 82. *ihs* monogram, decorated black on white	–	–	–	–	–	–	–	–	–	–	29	–	–	–	29	–
J 83. Title *Regula da imparare*	–	–	–	–	–	–	–	–	–	–	1	–	–	–	–	–
84. *Recetta da far inchiostro*	–	–	–	–	–	–	–	–	–	–	–	59	–	–	–	–
K 85. *Dn̄s adiutor	Lud. Vicentinus*	–	–	–	–	–	–	–	–	–	–	–	–	70	–	–
L 86. *& accio che* from *La Operina* (1st state)	–	–	–	–	–	–	–	–	–	–	–	–	–	–	–	35
87. *D'Orico colophon*	–	–	–	–	–	–	–	–	–	–	–	–	–	–	–	55

NOTES

1. In these editions the block appears in various positions in the text.   2. The 1524 texts are much abbreviated here.   3. These two items, although substantially the same (see pp. 182, 184-6 above), are listed separately in order to present both the Tagliente and Arrighi material complete.   4. The initials are set against a crible, not white, background.   5. The cuts made in the blocks for the 1525 landscape edition are clearly visible on these pages.   6. Arrighi's letters are copied, but instead of his signature the conclusion of the second page of *Lettera da bolle* is inserted.   7. The full set of three dedication blocks may have appeared in an earlier edition, now lost.   8. The order is here transposed, and the original first block of *Mercantesca* (now second) appears without its heading, which, however, reappears in 1538 and 1539.

ACKNOWLEDGEMENTS

I had no right to expect the help I have received in preparing this draft, and yet it is perhaps impertinent to be surprised at the generosity of those who have spared time to help with the problems that have cropped up. First of all my thanks are due to Alfred Fairbank who generously answered questions about the William Morris volume of writing books then in his custody, and allowed me to waste his time talking about it. My work at the British Museum was made much easier by Howard Nixon, George Painter and Dennis Rhodes; at the Bodleian by Giles Barber; at Cambridge by John Oates and F. J. Norton; and at the Victoria and Albert Museum by Miss Irene Whalley. M. André Jammes told me of his work on Arrighi's share in the map blocks for Calvo's great paths of ancient Rome. James Mosley read and commented on part of the first draft, and, with Harry Carter, provided invaluable information about the technique of punch-cutting. Graham Pollard and Berthold Wolpe both gave me the benefit of their long acquaintance with the subject. Mr Roland Baughman, Head of Special Collections at Columbia University Library kindly provided a microfilm of the 1525 *Thesauro*. Mr F. A. Thomson allowed me to discuss the chronological problems with him. The director of the Archivio di Stato di Roma and the prefect of the Archivio Segreto del Vaticano responded generously to my inquiries. Among printed sources, I owe most to Mr A. F. Johnson's 'Catalogue', and to Dr. Casamassima's several articles and the recently published *Trattati*. Without these, my task would have been immeasurably harder; indeed, I doubt if it would have been practicable. Mr Fairbank's articles in the *Journal of the Society for Italic Handwriting*, and those by Lamberto Donati, Francesco Barberi and Luigi Servolini in *La Bibliofilia* and elsewhere have all provided useful links in the chronology, as have those by the late James Wardrop in *Signature*.

But it is on the *Studii di Bibliografia Analitica* of Giacomo Manzoni that I have most leaned for support. Manzoni's understanding and knowledge of bibliographical techniques, especially those applicable to writing books, was far ahead of his time. He was a remarkable man, not only as a bibliographer. He was born at Lugo on 24 October 1816, and died there on 30 December 1889. A life long supporter of the unification of Italy, his first public office was as president of the

205

Cassa di Risparmio at Lugo. When Pius IX became pope and began to make concessions to liberal opinions, Manzoni took the advantage of the opportunity and in 1848 became a member of the council of deputies at Rome. In the same year he fought with the troops under Durando in the Veneto. He returned to Rome to take part in the moves which followed the neutralist Allocution of Pius IX, and was elected a deputy in the constituent assembly called as a last resort before the pope took flight. In the famous sitting of 9 February 1849, he voted for the republic. The triumvirate under Mazzini, recognizing his abilities, made him Minister of Finance, and entrusted him with the vital financial mission to Paris and London to raise funds for the new republic. (While in London, he found time for book sales; he kept 11 catalogues, June-November 1847, at least one of which, that of Don Miguel del Riego, he annotated.) When Pius IX was restored Manzoni went into exile, and stayed a long time in Greece. In 1854 he returned to Italy and made his home in Piedmont, where he was secure from arrest. In 1859 he went back to his native Romagna where he spent the rest of his life, taking a large part in local politics and government.

His book collection absorbed a great deal of his time in his later years, and the sale catalogue (1892) makes impressive reading. As well as many incunabula and Aldines he had no fewer than eighteen early writing books, including copies of *La Operina* 1525 and the *Thesauro* 1525. Next to the latter in the catalogue is a work noted as 'Opera arteficiosa la quale con grandissima arte ... ecc', which is described as a 'contrefaçon de la précédente edition'. What this may have been is hard to say; but it is possible that it was a copy of the one or more intermediate editions of the *Thesauro* published between '1525' and 1532.

Last of all I must record my deepest debt to Stanley Morison, without whom I should never have embarked on this complex and still largely unsolved problem.

STANLEY MORISON'S SHORT BIOGRAPHY

Stanley Morison was born in 1889, on 6 May, the feast of St John *ante portam Latinam*, the patron saint of printers. Nothing else in his humble origins suggested that he would become, as he did, the dominant force in typography and the history of printing in the twentieth century. He was brought up in London (which he never willingly left), left school at 14 and became a clerk in the city of London. In his spare time, he went to the British Museum, saw the Rosetta Stone and 'began to wonder why the several branches of the human family wrote in the funny ways they did'; in 1908, bred an agnostic, he was received into the Roman Catholic Church. These two events, which were to colour his life, were succeeded by a third. On 10 September 1912, *The Times* produced a Printing Supplement which caught Morison's eye; he bought it, read it from cover to cover, and was instantly captivated, both by the articles on modern printing and the historical articles, both liberally illustrated. Led by an advertisement, he subscribed to the new journal of printing and the graphic arts, *The Imprint*. It too contained an advertisement, for an assistant on the journal. Morison applied for and got the job in 1913.

This sequence of events brought Morison to printing and publishing. *The Imprint* led to employment by the Catholic publishers, Burns & Oates, where he met Francis Meynell, later founder of the Nonesuch Press. The two young men shared strong socialist principles and conscientious objection to World War I; both spent some time in prison for their beliefs. They also formed the Pelican Press, where they put their belief in good typography to practical purpose. After the war, Morison joined the equally famous Cloister Press; gradually he became known in the world of printing. He met Oliver Simon, and together they founded *The Fleuron*, the famous periodical whose eight volumes (1923-1930) contained much of Morison's important early work, as well as being a show-case for his own and other fine typographic work. In 1923 he became typographical adviser to the Monotype Corporation, and in 1925 also to the Cambridge University Press. For Monotype, he produced a host of new type-designs, instantly popular, among them Baskerville, Fournier, Bembo and Ehrhardt; for Cambridge, he created a house-style of unsurpassed elegance and rationality. In addition, he produced two great folios, *Four Centuries of Fine Printing* (1924) and *Modern Fine Printing* (1925).

In 1930, after a decade of fertile and brilliant work, Morison's career was crowned by the commission to re-design *The Times*. He became closely involved with the newspaper; characteristically, he approached the matter historically – *The English Newspaper* (1932) was a by-product of his work. He devised a new type for the new design, 'The Times New Roman', an adaptation of classic status, now the most used (and abused) type design in the world. The inauguration of the new design in 1932 made Morison the most famous typographer in the world. From now on, although he never abandoned his commitment to good type design, he became progressively more interested in the history of lettering. At Monotype, he commissioned new designs from others, Perpetua and Gill Sans from Eric Gill, Spectrum and Romanée from Jan van Krimpen. At Cambridge, he continued to supervise the design of books, with his close friend the University Printer, Walter Lewis. At *The Times*, he became involved in the writing of *The History of The Times*, a vast task finally completed in 1952. Besides this, *The Art of Printing* (1938), in fact a more general survey of letter-design, heralded the study of script and print from the 5th century B. C. to the present day which was to occupy the rest of his life.

But too soon, all this, the manuscript of his collected works, and his library, were destroyed in the war-time bombing of London. To another man, this would have been a crushing blow; to Morison it was a summons to redouble his work. He continued to work for *The Times*, becoming editor of the

T. L. S., completing the *History*, and acting as *éminence grise* to editors and management. He went to Chicago to advise on the new edition of the *Encyclopaedia Britannica*. Above all, he worked on his two last great books, *John Fell: the University Press and the 'Fell' Types* (1967) and *Politics and Script* (1972). He just lived to see the publication of the first, dying on 11 October 1967.

To all who knew him, Morison was a person of unique authority, learning and power of attraction. He was often compared to Dr Johnson, with whom he shared all these qualities, as well as a memorable strength of utterance. His own sense of design, its power undiminished by his opposition to anything that intervened between reader and text, has set its mark on the typography of our time. The printing types that he introduced have been equally influential. His historical writings have put the history of lettering and printing on a firm foundation. In this, and every other aspect of his life and work, he was a great man.

TO THE READER

I had the pleasure of meeting Stanley Morison back in 1960 when I had the opportunity of acquiring an important collection of books on Calligraphy. Therefore I asked the advice of another great scholar, A. F. Johnson of the Library of the British Museum, who introduced me to Stanley.

I was very much impressed by this noble figure; very thin, tall and always dressed in black. He immediately welcomed me with extreme cordiality and we established a long-lasting friendship until his passing-away in 1967.

After he had inspected the material, he accepted to write the 'Introduction' to my Catalogue, providing I went to Rome and retraced the lost manuscript of Luca Horfei da Fano. This work, of fundamental importance to the history of Italian script, had been searched for at great length, but to no avail, in the Vatican Library.

It was a great victory and I was warmly welcomed when I returned to London and remet Mr. Morison with the photographs and data . . . and thereupon he wrote the "Introduction" to my Catalogue, which was published in 1962.

To carry out our research and the schedule of the Catalogue, he often came to Milan, and our friendship developed more and more during the long hours of research conducted at the great work table in my office.

Stanley Morison was an extraordinary individual, always with a gentlemanly bearing, keen in his work, with great dignity and refined humour, but at the same time he was extremely human. He showed towards others a great intransigence, mixed with considerable understanding. He was able to give and receive the same generosity in his relationships with friends, and I had the great honour to be one of them. He was very spirited and amusing. Stanley Morison's character, when really known, revealed a great richness in understanding and humanity. I spent long hours with him discussing the many problems of life and culture, and I learned a great deal from him, particularly generosity and kindness towards others. It is with great emotion that I remember him, as every one of us should, as the most generous of scholars with great human feeling.

A deep religious sentiment dominated him in life: it was not a question of mysticism, but almost that of a naturalistic feeling for the problems of life and of "human being", as he would state. Just as our friendship was increased through our work, so it continued to grow and strengthen in the course of the years, always more vivid in our lives.

I very often went to London to stay with him. During our meetings he frequently spoke of his Manuscript on the history of Italian script and his theories and research, which remained unpublished. Obviously, as time passed, I was ever more certain that such an important work should have been published; I spoke to him about it with great enthusiasm and he was very pleased at my interest in his work; he presented the manuscript to me hoping that one day I would have it published. I am certain that Stanley Morison would be very touched by the "homage" paid to him by his friends, Nicolas Barker, Martino Mardersteig and myself, who, without any personal gain, wish to offer this work in his memory.

Martino Mardersteig generously offered to realize this precious work in Morison's memory, Morison having been a great admirer of Martino's father, the great Master of the art of printing. To him my thanks, for his enthusiasm and competence, shown in the realization of such a difficult, intelligent work.

After so many years, an accurate revision of the manuscript was necessary, and Nicolas Barker, Stanley Morison's best pupil, graciously undertook the task. Many years were necessary for such a work, but we now have the honour of presenting the unpublished manuscript by Stanley Morison in its last draft in such an elegant edition as that of the Edizioni Valdonega of Verona.

CARLA MARZOLI

LIST OF ILLUSTRATIONS

INDEX OF NAMES

THE TEXT OF THIS FIRST EDITION WAS SET
ON MONOTYPE MACHINES AND PRINTED LETTERPRESS
THE ILLUSTRATIONS WERE REPRODUCED IN DUOTONE
OFFSET IN THE STAMPERIA VALDONEGA, VERONA,
ON ACID FREE PAPER.
1990